Access to Assisted Reproductive Technologies

Fertility, Reproduction and Sexuality

General Editors:

Soraya Tremayne, Founding Director, Fertility and Reproduction Studies Group and Research Associate, Institute of Social and Cultural Anthropology, University of Oxford.

Marcia C. Inhorn, William K. Lanman, Jr. Professor of Anthropology and International Affairs, Yale University.

Philip Kreager, Director, Fertility and Reproduction Studies Group, and Research Associate, Institute of Social and Cultural Anthropology and Institute of Human Sciences, University of Oxford

Understanding the complex and multifaceted issue of human reproduction has been, and remains, of great interest both to academics and practitioners. This series includes studies by specialists in the field of social, cultural, medical, and biological anthropology, medical demography, psychology, and development studies. Current debates and issues of global relevance on the changing dynamics of fertility, human reproduction and sexuality are addressed.

Recent volumes:

Volume 43
Access to Assisted Reproductive Technologies: The Case of France and Belgium
Edited by Jennifer Merchant

Volume 42
Making Bodies Kosher: The Politics of Reproduction among Haredi Jews in England
Ben Kasstan

Volume 41
Elite Malay Polygamy: Wives, Wealth and Woes in Malaysia
Miriam Koktvedgaard Zeitzen

Volume 40
Being a Sperm Donor: Masculinity, Sexuality, and Biosociality in Denmark
Sebastian Mohr

Volume 39
Global Fluids: The Cultural Politics of Reproductive Waste and Value
Charlotte Kroløkke

Volume 38
Reconceiving Muslim Men: Love and Marriage, Family and Care in Precarious Times
Edited by Marcia C. Inhorn and Nefissa Naguib

Volume 37
The Anthropology of the Fetus: Biology, Culture, and Society
Edited by Sallie Han, Tracy K. Betsinger, and Amy K. Scott

Volume 36
Fertility, Conjuncture, Difference: Anthropological Approaches to the Heterogeneity of Modern Fertility Declines
Edited by Philip Kreager and Astrid Bochow

Volume 35
The Online World of Surrogacy
Zsuzsa Berend

Volume 34
Conceptions: Infertility and Procreative Technologies in India
Aditya Bharadwaj

For a full volume listing, please see the series page on our website:
http://www.berghahnbooks.com/series/fertility-reproduction-and-sexuality

ACCESS TO ASSISTED REPRODUCTIVE TECHNOLOGIES

THE CASE OF FRANCE AND BELGIUM

Edited by Jennifer Merchant

berghahn
NEW YORK • OXFORD
www.berghahnbooks.com

First published in 2020 by

Berghahn Books

www.berghahnbooks.com

Library of Congress Cataloging-in-Publication Data

Names: Merchant, Jennifer, editor.
Title: Access to assisted reproductive technologies : the case of France and Belgium / edited by Jennifer Merchant.
Description: New York : Berghahn, 2020. | Series: Fertility, reproduction and sexuality ; volume 43 | Includes bibliographical references and index.
Identifiers: LCCN 2019037817 (print) | LCCN 2019037818 (ebook) | ISBN 9781789204315 (hardback) | ISBN 9781789204322 (ebook)
Subjects: LCSH: Human reproductive technology--France. | Human reproductive technology--Belgium. | Human reproductive technology--Moral and ethical aspects.
Classification: LCC RG133.5 .A27 2020 (print) | LCC RG133.5 (ebook) | DDC 618.1/7806--dc23
LC record available at https://lccn.loc.gov/2019037817
LC ebook record available at https://lccn.loc.gov/2019037818

British Library Cataloguing in Publication Data

A catalogue record for this book is available from the British Library

ISBN 978-1-78920-431-5 hardback
ISBN 978-1-78920-432-2 ebook

Contents

Illustrations

Figure

Tables

Acknowledgements

Chapters 1, 2, 3, 6, 7 and 9 of this collection have been translated from French by Elizabeth Hargrett.

Foreword

Recognizing Donor-Conceived Families

A Major Issue in Europe's Bioethics Debates

Irène Théry

Between the European countries of France and Belgium, there is very little distance – not only in the geographical sense, but the sociological and cultural sense as well. Legally, both follow the system of continental law, which is based on the Napoleonic Code of 1804, and is traditionally contrasted with common law. In recent decades, however, the two countries have drastically diverged when it comes to the field of assisted reproductive technologies (ART).

In France, attitudes have generally been more rigid and based on principle than pragmatic, a trend that is reflected by the singular nature of the 1996 'bioethics laws' which continue to govern all medical activities in this domain. These laws are highly restrictive: ART is reserved exclusively for heterosexual couples suffering from 'pathological infertility'; surrogacy is prohibited and severely sanctioned; the filiation of children born abroad via surrogacy is not legally recognized; young women do not have the right to choose to preserve their oocytes; and people born of a sperm or egg donation have no way of knowing or accessing the donors who helped to conceive them. Generally speaking, the French legislature has made a sole exception to the fundamental rule of its criminal law for the case of bioethics: all that is not expressly permitted is prohibited. As a result, there is almost no room for negotiation/improvisation, or for researchers and clinicians to innovate, especially in the wake of two official reforms of the laws, and even with the advent of international technological innovations such as oocyte vitrification.

In Belgium, on the other hand, the environment has always been much more liberal and open to innovation. ART is open to all women under the age of 47, even if they are single or in a homosexual couple; surrogacy is unregulated but not prohibited, and is practised in many hospitals; voluntary oocyte preservation is available to all women who wish to access the procedure; and prospective parents using a sperm or oocyte donation have the choice between an anonymous or a known donor. The Belgian approach to these techniques has always been much more pragmatic. Though a law laying down the legislative framework for ART was finally passed in 2007, for the past half-century, Belgium's policy has generally been to place its trust in multidisciplinary teams of professionals who, in their respective hospitals, have long had the freedom to innovate, accept or decline to offer a particular procedure or practice, and establish their own codes of ethics.

As France prepares a major reform of its bioethics laws (scheduled for 2020), one cannot help but wonder: for how long will the French and Belgian approaches continue to diverge?

On the one hand, an alignment between the two countries' policies seems inevitable. Indeed, year after year, an increasing number of French citizens have expressed their desire for French laws to move towards a more open policy in opinion polls. Furthermore, future parents facing France's prohibitive laws need only to go abroad to seek what their own country denies them. Thus, for the past twenty years, French lesbian couples who wish to access ART have travelled *en masse* to Belgium, and today their 'Thalys babies' (named after the high-speed train running between Paris and Brussels) are a reality that can no longer be ignored. In fact, the opening of adoption to same-sex couples by the 2013 law legalizing gay marriage has made it possible to regularize the situations of lesbian couples who have accessed ART in Belgium (or Spain) by allowing the birth mother's spouse to adopt her children. For many in France, this legal context has come to be viewed as hypocritical, a fact that renders the situation increasingly unstable. Various social and political figures have taken note: in his 2017 electoral programme, for example, the elected President of the French Republic, Emmanuel Macron, announced his commitment to open access to

ART to all women. In June 2017, the National Consultative Ethics Committee (CCNE) also delivered a long-awaited opinion that favoured such a measure.

On the other hand, however, many others have mobilized in opposition to any changes to the law. Large demonstrations decrying same-sex marriage were organized in 2012–13 by 'La Manif Pour Tous', an offshoot of the very active traditionalist Catholic communities in France, and put tremendous pressure on politicians. Today, it is possible – as in the case of the opening access to ART for all women – that these communities continue to impede any further developments to the law, as well as any and all challenges to the 'French bioethics model'.

It is nonetheless on the basis of reference models, and not merely individual opinions, that bioethical issues are the most important, as evidenced by the case of surrogacy – arguably the most controversial issue at hand. Here, the comparison between France and Belgium (and more broadly the questions that this comparison raises concerning *borders*) proves illuminating for English-speaking readers – not only for those who are particularly interested in the two countries, but also for all those concerned with the general evolution of bioethics, as the contrast between France and Belgium sheds light on a poorly understood question. Once one gets past the opposition between the more dogmatic and the more liberal positions, it quickly becomes clear that the biggest controversies focus on a specific practice: ART with a donor. Statistically, the practice is squarely in the minority: in France, it represents only 5% of births facilitated by ART. ART using a donation attracts the most controversy because it lies at the intersection of two major avenues for societal evolution. The first, of course, is technological innovation, which is generally associated with the field of bioethics: major changes in the possibilities of ART (and thus in the ethical and political questions surrounding the practice) have been introduced with the freezing of gametes, *in vitro* fertilization and preimplantation genetic diagnosis. The second has no direct relationship to biology or medicine, and instead comes from the history and social perception of filiation, and more generally that of kinship. In deciding to focus this book on all forms of ART using a donation – whether sperm, an oocyte, an embryo or gestation – the fact of introducing a transnational comparison between France and Belgium, and including a study of cross-border practices of intended parents, Jennifer Merchant has made a very relevant choice, making it clear that the challenge gamete donation presents to our cultural models of family and kinship can be observed from many different angles.

These questions are especially important because ART using a donation is not only a medical 'technique', but also (and most importantly) a new social practice for parents, donors and families in general. I have proposed to call this practice *l'engendrement avec tiers donneur*, a term that directly translates to 'conception with a third party' but is most commonly expressed in English by instead referring to its outcome: 'donor-conceived families'.

These new ways of conceiving, giving birth and building families challenge a number of borders, many of which can be found beyond the merely geographical boundaries between one country and another. They blur mental boundaries and categorical boundaries, and reveal the 'limits of kinship', as Mary Douglas called them in her remarkable book *Purity and Danger* (1967), which offered profound reflections on these issues of conceptual, mental and social margins, and internal and external borders.

What is a parent? Or, more precisely, who do we want to call a parent? The question has long been asked, and couples of intended parents in which one partner participates in the reproductive process and the other does not pushes us to the realization that this question is much more complex than the traditional opposition between 'biological parent' and 'social parent' would suggest (not least because the two overlap in this case). Today, it is clear that this question is, in fact, incomplete. The chapters collected in this book reveal that it cannot be asked without its corollary: what is a donor? Furthermore, how does one go about qualifying the links between children who come from the same donor? These are precisely the questions that French laws eschew, or at least attempt to eschew, showing how difficult it remains to consider the respective roles and complementary relationships between donors and parents. For the social sciences, however, taking this complementarity into consideration, and supporting above all a broader understanding of the experience of those involved, is a key issue. But how should we approach it? Beyond the different legislative decisions made on ART and surrogacy between one country and another, it seems that only a relational approach that recognizes the existence of all the actors involved (as well as their respective families), and which seeks to understand how their clear yet coexisting roles and responsibilities are gradually established, can allow us to truly understand the unique experiences of these new families, especially given the often complex stories behind the creation of their children.

The Particularity of the French Bioethics Model

When attempting to grasp the unique nature of the French bioethics model, it is useful to look to the past. In the early 1970s, the cryopreservation of semen was the great international innovation of the time. While it did not necessarily lead to the first insemination with donated sperm (as this had been practised in secret by some gynaecologists since the nineteenth century [Pulman 2010]), the development transformed an essential element in the process: from then on, it would be possible to separate the moment when the sperm donation was made from the moment of its use. Now, the moment of donation is followed by a period in which the sperm is stored in vials kept at minus 196°C in laboratories and sperm banks – a period which now substantially separates donors from recipients. In this paradigm marked by new human possibilities, as well as the technological ability to stop time, ART using a donation has flourished.

At first, the idea that everything needed to be organized in secret prevailed in most countries, as did the insistence that parents were not, under any circumstances, to talk about the procedure. At this point, sperm was the only available form of gamete donation, so paternal conflict between the husband and the donor was not far from people's minds, replacing the archetypal conflict between the husband and the lover. The importance of secrecy to the procedure, then, seemed self-evident. The role of each participant was guaranteed by the triptych 'secret, anonymous identity and the lie': anonymous donors were unlikely to find themselves the subject of a subsequent search for one's paternity, for instance, since the donor disappeared just as quickly as he appeared, and the child's intended father could pass for the birth parent without fear of eventually being challenged. The parents could thus forget about the sperm donation, along with the subterfuge in which they had participated: 'nothing' had happened. As for the child, they were not told about it. At the time, nobody could imagine that a child's interest in the matter might diverge from that of their parents.

We may never be able to measure all of the consequences involved, but we can highlight four major sociological factors that explain why the *Ni vu ni connu* ('don't ask, don't tell') model emerged. First, this new practice was, in fact, a continuation of an ancient one: couples have always known how to discreetly resort to the services of a lover when seeking offspring in the case of an infertile husband. Second, in the early years of ART, the only available gamete donations were masculine. As a result, paternal filiation, unlike maternal filiation, had always been 'voluntary', especially since the biological link between the father and the child could be proved. Third, legal mechanisms such as presumption and legal recognition of paternity were already in place, which bound the child to the man who was presumed to be the biological father, even if he was not. Fourth, since male sperm donation is a very simple procedure, it could be considered as being almost insignificant, as if to say, 'give us five minutes of your time and then you can disappear' – a markedly different situation than would later be observed in the case of oocyte donation and, *a fortiori*, gestational surrogacy.

From the *Ni vu ni connu* Model to One of *Responsibility*

Eventually, the *Ni vu ni connu* model began to crumble. With the development of ART, it became clear that what was at stake was not just an attempt to modernize an ancient system, but the creation of a completely new social practice, invented by an advanced, democratic society: donor conception. The primary vehicle for this transformation was the consideration of the needs, then the rights, of the child. Around the world, professionals gradually ceased to urge parents to keep the procedure a secret. Quite the opposite, they began to tell parents that it was necessary to tell the child how they were conceived. Many countries called the principle of the donor's definitive anonymity into question, invoking the right of the child to eventually access his or her biological origins.

The old *Ni vu ni connu* model was thus challenged, while a new regulatory principle, which we will call the Responsibility principle, began to emerge internationally. On an ethical level, what organizes the Responsibility principle is the increased value placed on the duty to 'answer for one's actions. Planning for the child's future, their developmental needs and their fundamental rights, lies at the centre of this principle. The social practise of maintaining appearances, previously so important that it was undertaken regardless of the high psychological and emotional costs incurred with regard to family intimacy, was replaced by the rising value of authenticity, and new attention paid to the quality of the relationships between the individuals participating in donor conception.

In this context, ART using a donation gradually ceased to be perceived as a strictly corporeal form of pseudo-procreation, and single women who wanted to become mothers – as well as an increasing number of lesbian couples – began to ask themselves, 'why not us'? In some countries, such as Belgium, Great Britain and the United States, legislation was not needed to allow these women to access ART, since doctors had never believed that it was their responsibility to decide which categories of people did or did not have the right to access their techniques, let alone decide what was or was not lawful when it came to general transformations in the traditional family model. Other countries have followed this example, changing their laws. So far, any and all evolution to these laws has been stifled in France.

French Barricades

Therein lies the double-edged peculiarity of the case in France. As the *Ni vu ni connu* model is being challenged, doctors who have difficulty letting go of the total control they exercise within this model (e.g. they choose the donor, pair it with accepted recipients, maintain the secrecy surrounding the donor's identity, and have exclusive access to said identity, etc.) developed a whole system to preserve this model. Thus, the concept that gamete donation was a 'therapy' intended to cure 'pathological' infertility emerged. It is not difficult to see that this approach is in fact pseudo-therapeutic; unlike in cases where medicine treats people and allows them to procreate, this is obviously not the case with gamete donation. Until now, French biomedicine has refused to recognize that donor conception is a 'social arrangement', a remarkable social innovation that requires medical knowledge and technique. One major result of this attitude has been the exclusion of single women and homosexual couples from access to ART.

Secondly, in 1994 French lawmakers engraved this pseudo-therapeutic approach into the country's 'bioethics laws'. In so doing, filiation came to be granted by biomedicine, and a new very specific form of filiation was created for parents of children born with the help of a gamete donation. Thus, in order to establish paternal filiation, the traditional system of establishing biological filiation is applied: 'presumption of paternity' if the child's parents are married, and 'legal recognition' if they are not. But the filiation established through this system is radically different from that applied to children conceived without the help of a donor. Since the first bioethics laws were passed in 1994, Article 311-20 of the French Civil Code is the only one that cannot be contested. Consequently, a highly specific kind of filiation was invented in 1994: *biological pseudo-filiation*. This distinct legal relationship prompted an immediate outcry from family law practitioners, but their criticism fell on deaf ears, as ART had already been relegated to the position of being governed by biomedical law.

Today, there are increased calls to modify this situation. For example, another way of establishing filiation in the case of procreation using a donation has been proposed, is very simple and could apply to both opposite-sex and same-sex couples: the institution of a 'joint declaration of future filiation/parentage', signed at the time of the intended parents' consent to ART.[1] Establishing filiation this way, however, calls for yet another significant shift in mentalities, requiring us to understand the highly specific nature of donor conception, and recognize it for what it is: a new way of bringing children into the world.

Towards the Recognition of Donor-Conceived Families

Conception is a significant human act, and cannot be reduced to the merely biological dimension of procreation. It is precisely because of the lack of distinction between *conception* and *procreation* that in cases of donor conception the reasoning is often the same as if the case were one of conflict over paternity, with two men competing for the same child. Thus, we commit to an 'either/or' rather than to an 'and' logic, the latter being the only possible way to imagine the respective roles of each of the members of the parental couple, as well as the complementary role of the donor.

With regard to the receiving couple, what is the role of the partner who does not participate in the procreative process? Take, for example, the case of a heterosexual couple in which the man is sterile. Obviously, this is not a case of procreation, but neither is it one of adoption. If the child is born, it is because the process leading to its conception, and then to its birth, has been undertaken not only by a fertile woman but by a sterile man as well. Though the man has not participated in procreation – and here lies the novelty of donor conception – he has, in fact, helped to conceive the child. Indeed, human conception does not just have a physical dimension (that of procreation), but psychic, mental, emotional, intentional and even institutional dimensions as well, all of which add to the act's value and meaning in our human world. The sterile man can participate in all the dimensions of conception except one: the strictly procreative one. Because he has taken on the responsibility of engaging in this conception by declaring himself the future father of the child, this intended parent, though sterile, is as much a co-parent of the child as the mother who engages in procreation.

What if both members of the recipient couple participate in conception, but only one participates in procreation – what role does the *donor* play? Clearly, the donor has participated in the procreation of the child, and is thus a biological parent. And because we are talking about humans, and not interchangeable materials used to aid the all-powerful monolith of biomedicine in artificially creating life, the number of children that can come from the same donor is strictly limited.[2] But the donor also understands that this act of procreation is meant to allow *others* to become parents. The status of the donor falls outside of all notions of filiation. The status of the donor and the status of the parent are both logically and legally incompatible. Thus, those who imagine that children who ask to know the identity of their donor are in fact looking for a 'father' are gravely mistaken, and have failed to grasp the complex/profound logic of donor conception.

The choice to conceive does not belong to the donor, who simply makes the act possible for others. Thus, although donors participate in a fundamental dimension of conception –procreation – they cannot be defined as a co-parent of the child. By lending his/her procreative capacity to the intended parents, he/she thereby renounces his/her role in the conception of the children he/she has helped bring into the world. What he/she offers, then, is a gift that is much more than a simple donation of an 'element of the human body': the gift of conception.

Thus, the gift of conception represents a break from many of the major presuppositions underlying the Euro-American kinship system. Indeed, it is the only case in which medical and legal institutions recognize that a person who has a biological (via procreation), genetic (via gamete and/or embryo donation) or gestational (via surrogacy) link with a child has never had any intention to become the child's parent, and rules that he or she cannot be made into a parent against their will. What, then, is the donor's relationship to the child? How can we understand this relationship not only in the negative sense (that is to say, by what it is not), but in the positive sense as well (by what it is)? The dimension of gender is crucial to this understanding, a fact that is confirmed by the contributions in this book. As long as only sperm donations were permitted, it was believed that the donor could be 'forgotten'. But women's donations, especially those which involve carrying and giving birth to someone else's child, are too rooted in the person and the body to allow for such an obliteration. Surrogacy requires one to consider the meaning and value of the particular donation of procreative capacity, which enables others to become parents. It also requires us to think about the relationship between the donor and recipient as not necessarily dangerous, which is commonly thought in France, but as a resource – perhaps even the most important resource in a process that requires each actor to give careful attention to the others involved. These issues are explored in the following chapters, and thus provide a new lens through its comparative approach: not only a comparative legal examination of France and Belgium which demonstrates the stark contrasts between these two countries, but also with sociological and anthropological analyses of the practices of parents who have embarked on cross-border ART or surrogacy.

Irène Théry is a specialist in the sociology of law, Research Director at the Centre national de recherché scientifique, and renowned French expert of the changing landscape of families. She introduced the now widely used term '*famille recomposée*' (blended families) and has published numerous books and articles on family law, gender and the family, and same-sex families. She has headed several French governmental advisory boards relative to changing family law in France and participated in many others.

Notes

1. This is one of the key proposals in the *Filiation, origines, parentalité* report, op. cit. ch. 7.
2. French law prohibits more than ten births from the same donor.

References

Pulman, B. 2010. *Mille et une façons de faire un enfant, la révolution des méthodes de procréation*. Paris: Calmann-Lévy.

Théry, I., and A.-M. Leroyer. 2014. *Filiation, origines, parentalité: Le droit face aux nouvelles valeurs de responsabilité générationnelle*. Paris: Odile Jacob.

INTRODUCTION

Jennifer Merchant

This book is the first of its kind to compare the institutions and practices in assisted reproductive technology (ART) between two neighbouring countries whose peoples share the same language (in Brussels and Wallonia) and basically the same modern culture. Yet, despite these two countries sharing and interacting constantly with similar culinary tastes, music, movies, pop culture, mass media and social networks, literature, dance and other art forms, despite the homogeneity in the way democracy is practised in these two countries, and despite similar democratic political and legal structures, access to ART is strikingly different. Discrimination written into French law acutely contrasts with non-discriminatory access to ART in Belgium.[1]

The contributors to this volume are social scientists from France, Belgium, England and the United States and represent different disciplines: law, political science, philosophy, sociology, anthropology. Each author has attempted, through the prism of their specialties, to demonstrate and analyse how and why this striking difference in access to ART exists. Together, these contributions also highlight how this disparity between these two countries accentuates cross-border practices (especially France to Belgium and/or other countries abroad), with all the legal and sometimes medical risks this may entail as well as the economic burden this has on middle-class and disadvantaged French couples/persons who want to have a child.

For several decades now, French and Belgian scholars have been studying and analysing the practice of ART in France and Belgium, and have essentially published in French. This is another reason why this book is unique. For the first time, anglophone readers will be introduced to French and Belgian fieldwork and analysis, unknown until now for want of many anglophones able to read French. Because of the language barrier, it has not been possible for anglophone scholars to see how their work sheds often highly surprising and disturbing light on ART practices that have thus far remained in the shadows of international academia. Most preconceptions of how ART is carried out in France are based on stereotypical views, for example that France is a progressive and liberal state and that ART is accessible to all. These misconceptions will have to be reviewed in light of the work presented here.

Though conceptual and methodological approaches differ according to the social science discipline each author represents, there is a strong narrative thread that unites these chapters. Each one exemplifies how ART practices cannot be confined within the social, political and economic regimes of individual nation-states. An additional robust thematic that establishes coherency despite the diversity of the book's chapters is the focus on same-sex families, the status of embryos and the place and role of third-party donors. The book is divided into four parts: Part I, 'Visible Borders: Law and Public Policy'; Part II, 'Invisible Borders, France, Belgium'; Part III, 'Same-Sex Families and Surrogacy'; and Part IV, 'Cross-Border Practices'. Part I essentially lays out the juridical framework of ART practices in France and Belgium: France presented by the French legal scholar Laurence Brunet, and Belgium presented by the Belgian lawyer and legal scholar Jehanne Sosson. This will allow readers to grasp the striking differences in the governing of ART practices, which will then enable them to better comprehend the ensuing chapters that focus on actual practices and perspectives of French and Belgian persons relative to ART and all the issues surrounding them: the status of the embryo, same-sex couples, single-women access, surrogacy, the question of donor anonymity, the important role that social media now plays, and the viewpoint of French and Belgian ART practitioners.

Part II focuses on three issues that remain relatively absent from the public debate and/or appear too controversial. Chapter 3 (a sociological survey by Séverine Mathieu) discusses how the embryo is represented by French couples. Chapter 4 illustrates via four interviews of two French and two Belgian ART practitioners the untenable situation that French OB-GYNs are placed in when solicited by persons who have no right in France to access ART and the difficult obstacles that French trans people have to face to access ART. The interviews of the two Belgian OB-GYNs show the other side of the coin – their willingness to treat French patients and even others from different countries. The last chapter touches on a very sensitive issue, that of donor anonymity, and how it plays out in the Belgian context.

Part III focuses on French same-sex families and surrogacy. Chapter 6 (a survey by Jérôme Courduriès, anthropologist) demonstrates how French gay men become parents via surrogacy abroad and the ties they maintain (or not) with the surrogate mother subsequent to the birth of the child. Chapter 7 (a survey of same-sex families by Martine Gross, sociologist) shows how French same-sex families have used their creativity to invent specific names for each person who is part of the engendering and parenting of a child. Chapter 8 (a survey by Michael Stambolis-Ruhstorfer, sociologist) clearly highlights the determinant role that social media plays today in assisting French same-sex couples to find ways to have the child they desire.

Part IV ends the book with three chapters that visibly demonstrate how strict limits and laws in France are easily side-tracked. Chapter 9 (a survey by Dominique Mehl, sociologist) focuses on French 'solo moms' and the difficult path that awaits them when they decide to become a mother. Chapter 10, written by the bioethicist Guido Pennings, provides substantial data relative to cross-border France-to-Belgium occurrences. Lastly, Chapter 11, written by the philosopher Marie Gaille, analyses the centrepiece of this book's objective, that is to say that relying on national policy to govern ART is at worst dangerous and at best illusory.

Jennifer Merchant is a professor of Anglo-American legal and political institutions at the Université de Paris II (Panthéon-Assas). She is a leading researcher in bioethical issues of comparative public policy with expertise in North American and European policy, and the politics and regulation of medical technologies involving human reproduction. She is also an expert in French law and politics on embryo research and assisted reproductive technology.

Note

1. The French case differs not only from Belgium, but from other EU countries as well. For a full panorama of access to ART in Europe, see https://www.touteleurope.eu/actualite/pma-quels-droits-en-europe.html (accessed 24 June 2019).

Part I

VISIBLE BORDERS
LAW AND PUBLIC POLICY

Chapter 1

ART AND FRENCH LAW

THE ADVANTAGES AND INCONVENIENCES OF THE THERAPEUTIC MODEL

Laurence Brunet

It is impossible to understand the singularity of French law concerning assisted reproductive technology (ART) – established for the first time in 1994 – without taking into account the legal bioethical framework that governs it. In 1994, the goal of the French legislature was not only to regulate assisted reproductive practices, but to identify common values in an effort to establish norms for all medical uses of the human body. From the start of the parliamentary proceedings in the 1980s, several camps clashed (Mehl 1999). Meanwhile, the civil society outside the circles of experts such as the National Consultative Ethics Committee largely remained silent (Mehl 1998).[1] The originality of the French approach, therefore, was its codification of general principles that express a minimum political consensus, one that lies somewhere between liberal openness to scientific progress and distrust of medical and scientific practices that could harm the human person. This led to the vote of two laws on 29 July 1994 that instituted a framework using a two-pronged approach:[2] first, major principles concerning the respect of the human body were introduced into the Civil Code (Chapter 8), and second, the Code of Public Health established the rules governing various biomedical practices, including ART.

This double approach is intricately interwoven. In the French Civil Code, alongside the principles that ensure 'the primacy of the individual' and prohibit 'any offense to the dignity of said individual' (art. 16-1 c. civ.), one finds rules regarding the non-ownership of the human body and the non-commercial removal or transfer of any part of the body (art. 16-5 and 16-6 c. civ.), rules that were intended to be applied specifically to the field of gamete and embryo donation. The principle of the anonymous donation of body parts or materials remains one of the founding determinants of French bioethics, and states that 'the donor cannot know the identity of the recipient, nor can the recipient know that of the donor' (art. 16-8 c. civ.). This principle is perfectly illustrated by the rule of anonymity that governs the donation of gametes and embryos. Adding to this approach, we should mention a principle that directly concerns ART: that which states that all surrogacy contracts are null and void (art. 16-7).

It is clear that the general principles iterated in the French Civil Code are mutually binding. The condemnation of surrogacy contracts, for example, strengthens the principle of non-ownership. Similarly, the principle of anonymity was designed as a corollary of the principles of non-ownership and free disposal of human body parts: by preventing the donor and recipient from knowing each other, the state legislature effectively prevented the existence of a market where human bodily material could be directly bought and sold 'over the counter' (Thouvenin 1995; Camby 2009). A general, uniform and mandatory regime was thus established in 1994 to oversee all uses of the human body, beginning with ART techniques. According to national legislation, this bioethics 'charter' was intended to be permanent and not to be considered for any type of modification in the two subsequent revisions of the second part, which expressly provided the legislature to adapt the biomedical framework to scientific progress. Hence, while the regulation of different practices listed in the Code of Public Health (CSP) was amended twice (on 6 August 2004 and 7 July 2011), the block of general principles has remained unchanged, protected in a specific chapter of the French Civil Code.[3]

It is important to analyse the two-pronged framework of the French bioethics law because it is both unique to France and a major obstacle to any development in practices and standards. This framework explains why the evolution of ART techniques has remained subject to full compliance with the principles of non-commercial practices and anonymity that continue to govern the circulation of bodily material. However, the originality of the French bioethics law is not limited to its fundamental principles, which guarantee respect for the human body and its elements. This originality is just as apparent when we focus on a particular field of bioethics, that of assisted reproductive technologies (ART).

The uniqueness of the normative framework of ART lies in its purpose, which has remained unchanged since 1994, and is linked to these new reproductive technologies. The latter are allowed only insofar as they can provide a medical solution to a physiological dysfunction. The therapeutic model underlying the framework governing ART has thus led to the establishment of strict access conditions. The first part of this chapter is devoted to the application of the different components of this therapeutic model. In the second part, we will examine the limits of this normative framework in light of the restructuring of family patterns and the rise of cross-border ART (Rozée 2011).

Many Borders Due to the French Therapeutic Model

The therapeutic model that serves as the starting point for the regulatory framework concerning ART is composed of three parts. It imposes strict limits on access (A), but implies generous support from the community (B), all the while providing specific rules regarding filiation in the case of gamete donation (C).

The Medical Aim of ART

This goal dictates strict conditions of access, and gives medical teams broad power in deciding who can and cannot access ART.

Limits to Access

ART is characterized as a 'medical response to a medical problem' (Assemblée Nationale [French National Assembly] 2010). The law states that it 'seeks to remedy the infertility of a couple, or prevent the transmission of a particularly serious illness from a member of the couple to the child' (art. L. 2141-2 of the CSP).

ART in France cannot be considered as 'comfort care' but as a means of 'repairing an essential function of the human species; reproduction' (Assemblée Nationale [French National Assembly] 2010). The wording of the law was amended in 2011 to leave no doubt on this point, and insists that 'the pathological nature of [the patient's] infertility' be 'medically diagnosed'. ART is explicitly described within a therapeutic framework, and cannot simply constitute an alternative means of procreation, left to the discretion of individuals. This point precludes the admission of infertility due to sexual orientation or privacy as a reason for recourse to ART. Undergoing ART for any other purpose entails severe punishment by the law (art. L. 2162-5 CSP: five years' imprisonment and a 75,000 euro fine).

Since ART in France serves to alleviate the inability to procreate naturally, it must necessarily be modelled on the pattern of natural procreation. Consequently, under the law, only a heterosexual couple may access ART. 'The man and woman in the couple must be living and of child-bearing age, and must first consent to embryo transfer or insemination' (art. L. 2141-2 al. 2).[4] Since the second revision of 7 July 2011, it is no longer necessary to be married, nor is it necessary for unmarried couples to provide evidence of a *vie commune* (i.e. proof of a 'conjugal life' such as a shared bank account, bills under both names, etc.). Proof of the stability and continuity of the couple is also no longer required, but the medical team must nevertheless ensure that a couple wishing to access ART at the very least live under the same roof. Therefore, the law continues to state that should the couple cease to live together, continuation of treatment will be denied.

By requiring both members of the couple to be alive, the law effectively prohibits all *post mortem* reproduction. This prohibition was expressly mentioned by the legislature in 2004, which stated that 'the death of one of the two members of the couple precludes insemination or embryo transfer'. This clarification was added in response to political and social controversies that followed several cases brought before the courts, in which widowed wives requested the restoration of gametes that were frozen before the deaths of their husbands, or the implantation of cryopreserved embryos in order to carry out their parental projects.[5]

The framework required by French law in order to access ART is supposed to ensure the child's best interest: a family unit built by his or her (two) parents is considered to be the most suitable structure within which to raise a child, as French law still finds that it is in the child's best interest to have 'a father and a mother, no more, no less' (Théry 2010: 5). It must be understood that such a framework, which mimics the traditional family model of a heterosexual couple, initially worked towards gaining social acceptance of medical reproductive techniques in France, which continue to be accused by certain movements of flouting the traditional means of procreation.[6]

The ban on double gamete donation can also be attributed to the therapeutic model, as well as the pressure to imitate 'natural laws' of procreation. French law contains an exhaustive list of techniques that ART centres are allowed to implement. The list of biological processes used in ART was established by the Ministry of Health after having consulted the Agency of Biomedicine (art. L. 2141-1 CSP).[7] The law requires that the embryo originates from at least half the gametes of one member of the couple (art. L. 2141-3 CSP). Instructions for the use of a third-party donor are also laid out in detail; one couple can host another couple's embryo only when no other solution is possible, whether due to double infertility, or because one member of the couple is infertile and the other risks passing down a genetic disease to the child (Lévy-Dutel 2015). Furthermore, embryo hosting is subject to a binding legal procedure both for the couple that gives away its surplus embryos and for the couple who will receive the embryos (art. L. 2141-6 CSP). It is clear that the legislature intended to ensure a genetic foundation for ART as often as possible, in response to the desire of infertile couples to have a child who will inherit half of their DNA. The existence of a biological link, however minimal, is believed to facilitate the integration of the child into his or her family.

The Terms of the Decision

It is precisely with the aim of protecting the child's best interest that the medical team plays a key role in access to ART. The law generally reserves discretion for the medical team prior to ART.

Prior to carrying out an ART procedure, the members of the centre's multidisciplinary medical team must meet with the couple for an interview. This interview serves to inform the couple on the legal and regulatory framework of ART, on the different technical methods that may be employed, each method's success and failure rate, and the risks and constraints associated with them. A guide supplementing this information must also be provided. One month after the final interview, the couple's request must be confirmed in writing in order to be considered valid. These discussions are an opportunity to 'verify the motivation of the couple' and to remind them that adoption is a possible alternative (art. L. 2141-10 CSP).

French law attributes to the doctor the responsibility of protecting the interests of the unborn child. The doctor can, after consulting with the multidisciplinary team, postpone the implementation of ART if he or she considers that extending the waiting period 'is in the interests of the unborn child'. Where the law makes a provision for a deferral, deontological rules allow the medical team to 'refuse support within the limits set by law and the code of ethics' (see the order of 3 August 2010 concerning 'Rules of Good Clinical and Laboratory Practice of Medically Assisted Procreation', II.2). The regulatory framework thus allows the medical team to express its possible doubts about the advisability of an ART technique. Sometimes, the team can be placed in a delicate position, caught between providing assistance to an infertile couple, evaluating alternative therapeutic procedures, and fulfilling their responsibilities to the future child. Nevertheless, the law stresses the need for a thorough and collective discussion of problematic cases within the multidisciplinary team before making any decisions.

Financial Coverage

Because ART is considered to be a medical response to a pathological dysfunction, the treatments, as well as the biological and clinical procedures associated with them, are financially provided for on a national scale. The restrictive framework of ART in France, which is defined as a medical procedure, receives generous funding. The French system offers egalitarian access to ART treatments for all couples affected by infertility, who pay next to nothing for the treatment. In this respect, France stands out among Western countries as one of the few where almost all the costs of ART are covered by the state. Hence, when the ART process is implemented in an institution authorized by the health authorities,[8] and includes the list of procedures and services, health insurance covers 100 per cent of the treatment, with the exception of certain biological procedures that fall under the responsibility of the couple.[9]

Some limits are nevertheless imposed on access to full coverage: the woman, for example, must not be more than forty-three years old. This requirement does not necessarily guarantee that the medical team will consent to the implementation of ART, however, as access can be denied to a couple if the woman is older than forty and thus has a limited oocyte reserve. For artificial insemination, coverage is limited to six donations (one per cycle), and for IVF the state covers up to four attempts (from oocyte collection to embryo transfer *in utero*). It should be noted that in the case of a successful pregnancy, even if it does not lead to the birth of a living child, a new attempt at ART can be covered financially if the woman is under forty-three years of age. This measure does not mean that women over forty-three cannot have recourse to ART, but in this case, the couple has to assume the cost of the treatment. It should also be noted that coverage by Social Security does not place an age limit on men.

A Special Regime of Filiation when Using Donated Gametes

When a couple has recourse to ART, the usual rules governing the establishment of filiation apply. However, special rules are applied in the case of gamete or embryo donation. The principle of anonymous gamete donation has led to the ban on establishing a legal relationship between the donor and the child born as a result of the donation, in the unlikely event that the former is identified.[10] Indeed, no legal charges can be brought against the donor (art. 311-19 c. civ.).

The recipient couple must provide their consent in a joint declaration before a notary. This solemn declaration is submitted under secure, anonymous conditions, and without the presence of a third party. This joint statement is an opportunity for the notary to inform the couple of the consequences of using donated gametes, and to explain that the family relationship between the child and the recipient couple's donor is protected by specific regulations (art. 311-20 c. civ.).

In the establishment of maternity, ordinary law applies: in the case where the woman who gives birth has benefited from an egg donor, she is legally the mother of the child so long as she is designated as such on the birth certificate (art. 311-25 c. civ.). The establishment of paternity, however, depends on whether or not the couple is married. If a couple is married, the husband of the mother is presumed to be the father of the child (art. 312 c. civ.); if a couple is unmarried, there is no legal presumption that the mother's partner is the father of the child. Furthermore, consent to use gamete donation approved of by the notary cannot be equated with an acknowledgement of paternity. The establishment of paternity requires that the man voluntarily recognizes the child as his own before the Civil Registry (art. 316 c. civ.). If he does not recognize the child as his own, the law can compel him to do so: first, because the man consented by writing to ART treatment with gamete donation, his liability can thus be incurred, and he may be required to pay damages to the mother; second, paternity can be recognized forcibly by a court if the man is sued for paternity (art. 311-20 c. civ.).

The notary must also inform both members of the couple that their consent to such a reproductive technique prohibits any challenge to the filiation of the unborn child, for reasons that it does not conform to biological reality. Legal action can only be pursued if the child was in fact not conceived using ART with a gamete donation, or if the consent of one member of the couple was not given prior to the ART procedure (art. 311-20 c. civ.).

The result of this general framework is a near-perfect and almost irrefutable imitation of birth by 'natural procreation'. The donors, placed out of the reach of any curious parties, are hidden in the process,[11] and the child's legal status bears no trace of their involvement in his or her creation. The efforts of medical teams to find a donor that shares physical similarities with the infertile couple (so as to avoid any obvious physical differences between the child and his or her parents) also reinforce this will to 'imitate' nature (Brunet 2011).

Attempts to challenge this obliteration of the donor have been numerous. The process has been compared to a 'nearly perfect crime' (Iacub 1997), or associated with the *Ni vu ni connu* (neither seen nor recognized) rule (Théry 2010). During the revision of the law in 2011, movements throughout the French civil society brought together researchers, renowned psychoanalysts and individuals born of gamete donation (Kermalvezen 2008, 2014) who were seeking the identity of their biological parent(s), and who called for abandoning the principle of donor anonymity.[12] Despite this mobilization, the principle was maintained. The legislature gave precedence to the supposed interests of the child in his or her family: the donor's cloak of anonymity would help infertile couples to invest in parenting by avoiding any feared rivalries between the intended father and the biological father. In particular, public authorities expressed the concern that lifting donor anonymity would lead to a decrease in the already low number of willing gamete donors, due to the fear of becoming an auxiliary father down the road.

The framework of ART, based on a medical model, may seem protective for those who are fortunate enough to have access to it. This restrictive framework, however, also excludes many people who, having no alternative means to become parents, must travel to other countries.

Crossing Borders for ART Access Abroad

Due to the lack of access to ART services in France, cross-border practices are numerous, but it is impossible to take full stock of them. This section will therefore be limited to those situations that have led the French judicial hierarchy to take a position and support the legislature.

Obstacles to the Recognition of Same-Sex Families Who Have Accessed Sperm Donations Abroad

While families formed by gay and lesbian couples are now legally recognized ('Same-Sex Marriage Law', 17 May 2013), this does not mean they benefit from the same rights and advantages as heterosexual couples. Here, the legislature has much unfinished business.

Following a long series of bitter and violent debates, the 17 May 2013 law is considered as a true 'reform of civilization' (Théry 2013) by permitting persons of the same sex to marry, and thus allowing them to have children through the process of adoption. Although the right to adoption for same-sex couples is not expressly provided for in this law, it results from the mechanical effect of the right of two persons of the same sex to marry. If they are married, two persons may apply to jointly adopt a child, or one of them may request the adoption of the child of their spouse. The opening of marriage to persons of the same sex thus implied the possibility for gay and lesbian couples to start a family through adoption (Leroyer 2013). On the other hand, access to ART (which would allow same-sex couples to carry out a parental project in which the child would be conceived using the gametes of one of the partners) still remains closed to these couples. Indeed, the legislature has found itself faced with persistent protests from various groups in the civil society who have organized large demonstrations in the streets of France's major cities in an effort to persuade public authorities to maintain their positions.[13] Hence, the French legislature has thus far refused to amend the framework of ART in order to allow lesbian couples to access sperm donation. Assisted reproductive technology remains reserved for heterosexual couples who suffer from medically diagnosed pathological infertility. In its decision of 17 May 2013,[14] the Constitutional Council confirmed the difference in the treatment of heterosexual couples and homosexual couples, barring the latter from access to ART 'due to their different situation regarding procreation'.

The opening of access to adoption, especially intra-family adoption for same-sex couples, has ultimately undermined the existing framework of limited access to ART. Where, indeed, would the child come from? There are very few adoptable children, both in France and abroad. In France, state wards offer approximately eight hundred adoptable children per year, and the number of foreign adoptable children has steadily declined each year (1,343 in 2013 compared to just over 3,500 in 2010) (Mignot 2015). In 2010, more than twenty-four thousand couples were registered and awaiting children. Adding to this, few foreign countries accept applications from same-sex couples, with many refusing to let a homosexual person adopt a child from their country. It is therefore not uncommon for some countries to ask unmarried candidates to produce a sworn statement attesting to their heterosexuality (Assemblée Nationale [French National Assembly] 2013). For a lesbian couple, the only way to start a family is through the use of a sperm donation from abroad. Thus, the legislature has managed to avoid opening access to ART for lesbian couples, while tacitly allowing the 'regularization' of same-sex families through artificial insemination practised abroad, and the adoption of the resulting child by the spouse of the mother. There has been little doubt on this point; in both the National Assembly and the Senate, amendments prohibiting the adoption of a spouse's child conceived using an ART technique contrary to the conditions established by French law have been proposed. All have been rejected (Assemblée Nationale [French National Assembly], 18 April 2013 session). It seems that for the legislature, the adoption of a spouse's child is permissible even if the child is the result of a procedure that circumvented French law – even though such circumvention is passively encouraged.

The large majority of the courts have considered that the adoption of a spouse's child is permissible provided the legal conditions are met, regardless of how the child was conceived. Nevertheless, some courts have refused to grant adoption under these circumstances, citing evasion of the law in the case of artificial insemination abroad via a donor. Recently, the Court of Cassation, the highest court in France, was called upon to make a final judgement in the matter. In its decision of 22 September 2014, the Court held that 'the use of medical assistance for procreation through artificial insemination with an unknown donor abroad poses no obstacle to the granting of an adoption'. First, none of the essential principles of French law are violated, and second, the same-sex marriage law of 18 May 2013 authorized the mother's spouse to adopt the child without 'mentioning any restrictions on the means of conception of the child'. The judges of the Court of Cassation thus legalized the recognition of families formed by lesbian couples, a job that the legislature has thus far avoided due to pressure from the aforementioned groups.

All that being said, the second mother (the one who has not given birth) still occupies a subordinate legal status, and is required to abide by a judicial procedure in order to establish her maternity. This is a source of cost and stress, especially if the judge, as he or she has the right, orders an investigation to ensure that the adoption is in the best interests of the child. These judicial barriers are compounded by the high cost accessing sperm donation abroad, as well as increased health risks associated with inadequate gynaecological monitoring experienced by pregnant women (Académie nationale de médecine 2014). As a result, several specialists in French family law (Théry and Leroyer 2014) and public institutions have taken positions in favour of extending access to ART to all women (Haut Conseil à l'Egalite Entre les Hommes et les Femmes [High Council on Gender Equality] 2015; Defenseur des Droits [Human Rights Defender] 2015; Conseil d'Etat [Council of State] 2018), including recently the French National Consultative Ethics Committee (CCNE 2017, 2018). It is also worth noting the recent initiative of doctors who have demanded, among other things, the lifting of the ban on sperm donations for women, regardless of their sexual orientation.[15]

Evolution in this direction, however, is not guaranteed due to persistent strong opposition, for example from a group of legal practitioners, Juristes pour l'enfance (Legal Practitioners for Children), an association 'centred around the defence of the best interests of children, whether born, not yet born, or expected, and for the protection of children in all forms'.[16] This association does not hesitate to intervene in and oppose applications for adoption initiated by the spouse of the mother, to the extent that the Court of Cassation has had to step in.[17] With regard to legislators, a committee of senators recently expressed itself in favour of the current status quo, and thus against the opening of access to ART to lesbian couples, as they feel this access could only lead to the 'equating of procreation with the aid of a donor to the "natural procreation" of the recipient couple', a situation that the commission deemed undesirable (Sénat [French Senate] 2016).

The Battle for the Recognition of Families Who Have Gone Abroad for Surrogacy

Both traditional and gestational surrogacy have been severely condemned in the French Civil Code since 1994.[18] Even before the legislature became involved, the Court of Cassation had had the opportunity to sanction the practice of surrogacy by refusing to establish a bond of adoptive filiation between the child and the intended mother, even if she were also the biological mother.[19] Since then, the Court of Cassation has maintained this position.[20] No proposals were made – with some exceptions (Sénat [French Senate] 2008) – to soften the national stance on the illegality of surrogacy during the two revisions of the bioethical legal framework. The Court's rigidity on the matter, however, has clearly not had its desired effect: far from dissuading couples who have no other means of having a child of their own from resorting to surrogacy, these couples are forced to seek alternatives abroad. Furthermore, cross-border surrogacy practices have expanded as a result of the legal recognition of same-sex couples and their involvement in parental projects (Gross 2012). Once the children are born, these parents bring them back to France and seek to have their foreign birth certificates entered into French birth registers, thus achieving legal recognition of their parentage.

The first obstacle in this process is the repatriation of the child or children. This step is especially difficult when French nationality is refused to the child because of uncertainty regarding the intended parents' legal relationship to the child, thus preventing them from obtaining a passport from the French consulate in the country in which the child was born. Nevertheless, administrative judges have ordered French authorities to issue provisional travel documents as soon as all of the information on the birth certificate is confirmed as true beyond a reasonable doubt.[21] Recently, border personnel were instructed to be more tolerant in the name of protecting the best interests of the child to not be separated from her/his intended mother.[22]

When it comes to the registration of foreign birth certificates, however, violent debates on the subject have extended far beyond the courtroom, and with the help of the media, invaded the French political scene.[23] For now, public debate focuses on the exploitation of female surrogates and the commodification of children (Fabre-Magnan 2013; Frison-Roche 2016: 85),[24] whereas the courts, on the other hand, must take a stance on the consequences of the ban on surrogacy for children born of this practice, and decide whether it is in the children's interest to register them. Until 2014, the Court of Cassation stood firm on the matter: it had always opposed the registration of foreign birth certificates, maintaining that such an act was contrary to French public order. According to the Court, a surrogacy agreement contradicted the essential principles of French law, in particular the 'unavailability of personal status'.[25] Over time, the Court of Cassation hardened their stance even further, invoking the notion of fraud, and not only refused to register foreign birth certificates, but in one case went so far as to revoke the recognition of the biological father in France.[26] In this case, the result was an uncertain status for the children born of surrogacy for whom French nationality was not guaranteed, a situation that can cause major problems with regard to the entry of children into French territory, despite a limited number of temporary solutions.[27] Likewise, as they had no access to a will and testament, these children had no family heritage. In this case, intended parents thus have no fundamental rights when it comes to exercising parental authority (Théry and Leroyer 2014: 221–22; Fulchiron and Bidaud-Garon 2014).

This case law was challenged by the European Court of Human Rights (ECHR) in two rulings rendered on 26 June 2014 (*Labassée* and *Mennesson*).[28] Although the European judges recognized the right of each country to prohibit recourse to surrogacy, they also considered that the refusal to register the birth certificates of children born of surrogacy undermined 'their identity within French society'. According to the ECHR, the legal consequences of non-recognition by French law of the relationship between the children and their intended parents 'significantly affected the right to respect for private life, which implies that everyone must be able to establish the substance of his or her identity, including the legal parent-child relationship'. Accordingly, a serious question arose as to the compatibility of that situation with the children's best interests, respect for which must guide any decision in the regard of the ECHR. The Court also pointed out that the analysis took on a special dimension when, as in the aforementioned cases, the biological father was deprived of any possibility of establishing his paternity of the children involved.

The decision drew the ire of those who opposed any recognition of surrogacy in France. Many denounced what they felt to be an unacceptable decline in the sovereign power of states in fundamental ethical issues. Legal experts, on the other hand, were divided on the interpretation of the decision, the wording of which left a good deal of uncertainty: did the ECHR require the recognition of the dual filiation of the children with respect to their biological parent as well as the intended parent, or was the state only required to legally recognize the biological parental link? All sides of the debate were in agreement on one point: the decisions of 26 June 2014 were binding in France, and the country's courts were now required to put an end to the contradictions between their internal legal order and international human rights law.[29] The appeal by the European Court to the French legislature and government to pass a law in conformity with their decision seemed clear, but both abstained from any intervention. France's judges thus found themselves alone in the search for new solutions that respected the identity of the children born abroad of surrogacy.

The administrative courts immediately acted on the European ruling, granting certificates of French nationality to children as soon as a parental link with a French citizen was established in a foreign birth certificate that the courts considered probative.[30] The judges of the Court of Cassation, on the other hand, only made a partial ruling on the matter in two decisions rendered on 3 July 2015, due to the highly specific nature of the cases referred to them.[31] Both cases concerned two male couples who had enlisted the aid of a female surrogate in Russia. The birth certificate included the names of one of the men and the surrogate. Therefore, the Court emphasized, they were not required to rule on the issue of the transcription of filiation with respect to the second intended father. After 'finding that the foreign birth certificates were neither unlawful nor forged, and that the facts declared therein correspond to reality', the Court held that 'the surrogacy agreement did not preclude the entry of the birth certificate into French civil status registers'. Although the presumption of fraud no longer bars the recognition of the filiation of these children, the reverse is only partial: the relationship with the intended parent (whether the intended mother in a heterosexual couple, or the second father in a male couple) remains precarious, especially since the Court tends to place a higher priority on the recognition of biological parental links, rather than on elements which attest to the legal reality presented by the foreign birth certificate.

Eventually, it is this biological interpretation of kinship that the Court of Cassation upheld in several rulings rendered on 5 July 2017: if the parents mentioned in the foreign birth certificate are the biological father and the intended parent (mother or second father), then the registration will only be partial, seeing that any mention of the intended mother or father will be annulled.[32] Nevertheless, the Court of Cassation provided a means for the intended parent to establish legal filiation: the adopting parent, husband or wife of the legal parent, can request the adoption of the child (intra-family adoption). Though this compromise guarantees a child born of surrogacy a legal link to his/her intended parents, the juridical procedure to arrive at such a result is dubious to say the least. Indeed, because the foreign birth certificate mentions both the biological parent and the intended parent, once back in France the latter's name must be 'purged' from the document before the intended parent can begin adoption proceedings. Hence, the intended parent must adopt the child who is already considered as hers/his in the foreign document delivered. The essential principles of the French bioethics law – the unavailability of personal status, the invalidity of surrogacy agreements – are safe and sound but at what price for the families concerned? The procedures they have to go through – request for a partial registration of the child in the birth register document followed by adoption procedures by the intended parent – are long and complicated, and attain the same result if a simple and direct recognition of the original foreign birth certificate were allowed.

It seems, therefore, that the battle has not been completely won for the families of children born of surrogacy, and for those who demand the French authorities' complete and direct recognition of filiation established abroad (Defenseur des Droits [Human Rights Defender] 2015; Théry and Leroyer 2014: 226).[33] That being said, it is unlikely that the intended parent will be relieved of the necessity to adopt his/her own child in light of vehement reaction on the part of groups against surrogacy following the decisions of the Court of Cassation that, for these groups, amounted to encouraging surrogacy. Their mobilization places an enormous amount of pressure on public authorities, both left-wing and right-wing political groups; the alliance of Catholic movements as well as some French feminist groups and even certain lesbian associations against surrogacy are manifold.[34] Many groups have acted without hesitation; Juristes pour l'enfance, for example, filed a complaint against American agencies who advertised surrogacy services in France and solicited interested couples (their litigation was not successful) (Chapleau 2015). Juristes pour l'enfance has also intervened in proceedings for applications for the registration of foreign birth certificates in a show of support of the decision of the Public Prosecutor's Office, which opposed the registration of the name of the intended mother. In this particular case, the Court de Cassation overruled.[35] Meanwhile, the French Parliament published a report by the Senate's legislative commission which called on the legislature to expressly prohibit the recognition of any form of filiation of an intended parent in the French Civil Code, and to reinforce existing criminal sanctions by raising the maximum number of penalties incurred (Sénat [French Senate] 2016: 77–85).[36] In addition, the latest reports of the French National Bioethics Committee (Comité consultatif national d'éthique) echoes these recommendations made by the Senatorial commission (CCNE 2017: 40–41; CCNE 2018: 122–24).[37]

This being said, it is highly unlikely that the legislature will intervene in this highly sensitive subject, thus continuing to drive desperate couples who are unable to access ART in France to go abroad and access expensive cross-border surrogacy conventions (Brunet 2018: 572) and/or engage in fraudulent practices and even the black-market sale of children (Lamoureux 2016). Surrogacy is a subject that is still acutely demonized and ideologized in France that it seems impossible to take it into serious consideration and to design a national legal framework.

Today, the French ART model is in crisis. This therapeutic and non-patrimonial model, which tightly controls access to these medical services in exchange for full financial coverage from the state, has proven ineffective, and those who are excluded are inexorably undermining its very foundations. The fight for the recognition of reproductive autonomy has gained substantial ground, particularly in the civil society and in some judicial circles.[38] The legitimacy of the state in restricting access to various forms of ART is gradually being called into question. However, if access to ART becomes more a matter of individual rather than collective responsibility, French people might face the risk of witnessing the end of state funding for these treatments (Fournier 2007). This perspective was discussed in one of the latest French Bioethics Committee reports: 'The use of ART techniques for non-medical reasons could eventually be financed by the persons requesting access'. The report went even further, stating that 'the state could establish a hierarchy of access that prioritizes access for medical reasons' (CCNE 2017: 24, 28, 44). This led some analysts to conclude that 'contrary to heterosexual couples, homosexual couples would access available gametes only after heterosexual couples' demands were fulfilled, and on the additional condition that homosexual couples pay for their medical treatment!' (Fournier, Brunet and Delaisi de Parseval 2017). No doubt, financial coverage will be a delicate topic when the bioethics bill is debated in parliament.[39]

Laurence Brunet is a legal scholar and research associate of the Institut des Sciences juridique et philosophique de la Sorbonne (UMR 8103). Her work focuses on French family law and its evolution, with special emphasis on new family configurations, children born of surrogacy, and the status of transgender individuals.

Notes

1. The National Consultative Ethics Committee was founded in 1983 to address the ethical concerns that have arisen from the evolution of research in health and life sciences. Its pre-eminent role in the field of bioethics was confirmed by the law of 6 August 2014. See Lazar 2003, and Didier Sicard's introduction therein (p. 2).
2. Law no. 94-653 amends the French Civil Code, and law no. 94-654 amends the Code of Public Health.
3. It should be noted that this bioethical 'charter' was reinforced by the passage of the ban on human cloning by the law of 6 August 2004 (art. 16-4 c. civ.).
4. However, on 15 June 2017, the French National Consultative Ethics Committee issued a report (avis 126) recommending access for lesbian couples and single women to ART (CCNE 2017). This now must be debated in parliament and voted on, and could be a long drawn-out process.
5. A request for a *post mortem* embryo transfer has gone all the way to the Court of Cassation: Civ. 1, 9 January 1996, *La Semaine juridique* 1996, II, 22666, note Claire Neirinck; *Dalloz* 1996.376, note Frédérique Dreifuss-Netter; *Revue trimestrielle de droit civil* 1996.359, obs. Jean Hauser. For more on the debate on *post mortem* embryo transfers, see Brunet 2000: 57.
6. In particular, the Lejeune Foundation, an organization whose power to act is reinforced by the weekly online press review *Généthique*, the only French-language bioethics review of its kind. See also critical discussion on the subject in the two collective works: de Vilaine, Gavarini and Le Coadic 1986, and Testart 1990.
7. Upon the first revision of the bioethical framework on 6 August 2004, the Agency of Biomedicine (ABM) was created. One of the missions of the agency is to monitor, evaluate and, if necessary, carry out checks on medical and biological activities in the fields of human reproduction and embryology.
8. Artificial insemination and ovarian stimulation nevertheless can be implemented by gynaecologists in their private practice.
9. See subchapter 9-2 of chapter 9 of book II of the *Common Classification of Medical Procedures*.
10. The principle of anonymity deprives the donor of any and all information on the actual use of his donation; they cannot know how many children they have helped to produce, or even if there are any at all. The donor only knows in advance that his gametes will not lead to the births of more than ten children (art. 1244-4 CSP).
11. Nevertheless, in the case of therapeutic necessity, non-identifying information on the donor can be provided to the parents and to the child by a doctor (art. L. 16-8 c. civ. and art. L. 1211-5 and L. 1131-1-2 CSP).

12. See the Procréation Médicalement Anonyme association (http://pmanonyme.asso.fr/).
13. These groups come under the umbrella association called 'La Manif Pour Tous' (http://www.lamanifpourtous.fr/). Accessed 24 June 2019.
14. Cons. const., decision no. 2013-669 DC, 13 May 2013, *Revue de droit sanitaire et social* 2013.908, note Laurence Brunet; *Dalloz* 2013.1643, chr. Frédéric Dieu; *Actualité Juridique Famille* 2013.332, obs. François Chénedé; *Constitutions* 2013.166, obs. A.-M. Le Pourhiet; *Revue trimestrielle de droit civil* 2013.579, obs. J. Hauser.
15. 'Nous, médecins, avons aidé des couples homosexuels à avoir un enfant même si la loi l'interdit', *Le Monde*, 16 March 2016 (http://abonnes.lemonde.fr/idees/article/2016/03/17/pour-la-creation-d-un-veritable-plan-contre-l-infertilite_4884871_3232.html). Accessed 24 June 2019.
16. See http://juristespourlenfance.com/. Accessed 24 June 2019.
17. Cass Civ. 1, 16 March 2016 (no. 239).
18. The civil penalties outlined in article 16-7 c. civ. (on the invalidity of surrogacy contracts) were accompanied by criminal penalties (art. L. 227-12 and 227-13 of the Penal Code) for any intermediaries involved, in addition to the intended parents and the woman who carried and gave birth to the child. So far, there have been very few convictions.
19. Cass., Ass. Plén., 31 May 1991, *La Semaine juridique* 1991, II, 21752, concl. Dontenwille, obs. F. Terré; *Dalloz* 1991.417, rapp. Y. Chartier, note D. Thouvenin; *Revue trimestrielle de droit civil* 1991.517, obs. D. Huet-Weiller.
20. Cass Civ. 1, 29 June 1994, *Dalloz* 1994.581, note Yves Chartier; Cass Civ. 1, 9 December 2003, *Dalloz* 2004.1988, note Elizabeth Poisson-Drocourt.
21. Council of State, 4 May 2011, *Dalloz* 2011.1995, obs. Adeline Goutenoire; *a contrario* see Council of State, 8 July 2011.
22. Council of State, réf., 3 August 2016, *Dr famille* 2016, no. 202, obs. Hugues Fulchiron; *Dalloz* 2016.1700, note Patrice Le Maigrat; *Dalloz* 2017.261, obs. Fabienne Jault-Seseke.
23. The registration of foreign certificates is managed by the central office of the civil status registers of the Ministry of Foreign Affairs, which is located in Nantes.
24. With regard to collectives, see Collectif CoRP (Collective for the Respect of the Human Person), http://collectif-corp.com. Accessed 24 June 2019.
25. Cass Civ. 1, 6 April 2011 (3 arrêt), *Dalloz* 2011.1522, note Denis Berthiau and Laurence Brunet; *Actualité juridique Famille* 2011.262, obs. François Chénedé.
26. Cass Civ. 1, 13 September 2013 (2 arrêts). See Fulchiron and Bidaud-Garon 2013: 2349. Cass Civ. 1, 19 March 2014 (2 arrêts). See Fulchiron and Bidaud-Garon 2014: 905.

27. Despite the correction of the 'Taubira' memorandum of 25 January 2013 and the granting of provisional travel documents (see note 26).
28. These cases involved matters that had already been the subject of the Court of Cassation's judgements of 6 April 2011: ECHR 26 June 2014, *Mennesson c/France* and *Labassée c/France, Dalloz* 2014.1773, chr. Hugues Fulchiron and Christine Bidaud-Garon; ibid. 1797, note François Chénedé; ibid. 1806, note Louis d'Avout; *Actualité Juridique Famille* 2014.396, obs. A. Dionisi-Peyrusse; *La Semaine juridique* 2014.877, note Adeline Gouttenoire; *Revue trimestrielle de droit civil* 2011.616, obs. Jean Hauser.
29. Nevertheless, see Fabre-Magnan (2015), who warns not to 'take the European Court of Human Rights' reasoning at face value'.
30. Council of State, 12 December 2014, *Dalloz* 2015.352, rapp. Xavier Domino; ibid. 357, Hugues Fulchiron and Christine Bidaud-Garon, 'the "Taubira memorandum" on the validation of certificates of French nationality'.
31. Cass., Ass. Plén., 3 July 2015 (2 arrêts), *Dalloz* 2015.1481, editorial Sylvain Bollée; ibid. 1819, note Hugues Fulchiron and Christine Bidaud-Garon; *La Semaine juridique* 2015.1614, note Adeline Gouttenoire.
32. Cass., 5 July 2017 (no. 824, 825, 826, 827), *Actualité Juridique Famille* 2017.375, obs. François Chénedé; ibid. 431, obs. Pascale Salvage-Gerest; *Dalloz* 2017.1737, note Hugues Fulchiron.
33. See also the CLARA Association (http://claradoc.gpa.free.fr/), the Association of Gay and Lesbian Parents (APGL, https://www.apgl.fr/), the Association of Homoparental Families (ADFH, https://adfh.net/); and the petition signed by 170 citizens in the newspaper *Libération* (http://www.liberation.fr/societe/2014/12/16/gestation-pour-autrui-2-000-enfants-sans-etat-civil-reconnu_1164970). All accessed 24 June 2019.
34. See the charter for the universal abolition of surrogacy: http://abolition-gpa.org/charte/. Accessed 24 June 2019.
35. Cass Civ. 1, 5 July 2017, no. 825.
36. See also the proposed law no. 227, 14 October 2014, which aimed to block efforts made by French men and women to find a surrogate, submitted by Jean Leonetti: it was rejected without debate.
37. Conseil d'Etat (Council of State, Section des rapports et des études, aforementioned) 2018: 74–87.
38. One must first mention the legal victory for the right to start a family, won in the European Court of Human Rights. See notably ECHR, Gd ch., 3 November 2011, *Affaire S. H C/ Autriche, Revue trimestrielle de droit civil* 2012.284, obs. Jean-Pierre Marguénaud.
39. In favour of full state funding, see Conseil d'Etat (Council of State) 2018: 63–65; CNCDH (National Consultative Commission on Human Rights) 2018: 11.

References

Académie nationale de médecine. 2014 (27 May). Jouannet Pierre (reporter), 'Information, Ouverture de l'assistance médicale la procréation avec sperme de donneur à des indications non médicales', *Bulletin de l'Académie Nationale de Médecine* 198 (4–5): 951–71.

Assemblée Nationale (French National Assembly). 2010. Alain Claeys (president) and Jean Leonetti (reporter), *Information Report of the Taskforce on the Revision of the Bioethics Laws*, doc. no. 2235.

Assemblée Nationale (French National Assembly). 2013 (17 January). Legislative Committee, Erwann Binet (reporter), *Report on Same-Sex Marriage*, doc. no. 628.

Assemblée Nationale (French National Assembly). 18 April 2013 session. 14th legislature, regular session of 2012–2013, verbatim record. http://www.assemblee-nationale.fr/14/cri/2012-2013/20130222.asp#P4703_0264. Accessed 24 June 2019.

Brunet, Laurence. 2000. 'De la distinction entre "personne" et "chose" en droit civil: à propos du transfert *post mortem* d'embryon', in 'La recherche sur l'embryon: qualifications et enjeux', *Revue générale de droit médical* (special issue, 1): 57–60. https://www.decitre.fr/revues/revue-generale-de-droit-medical-n-special-la-recherche-sur-l-embryon-qualifications-et-enjeux-5552912359011.html. Accessed 24 June 2019.

Brunet, Laurence. 2011. 'Procréations médicalement assistées et catégories "ethno-raciales": l'enjeu de la ressemblance', in G. Canselier and S. Desmoulins (eds), *Les catégories ethno-raciales* à *l'ère des biotechnologies*. Paris: Société de législation compare, pp. 135–54.

Brunet, Laurence. 2016. 'Le principe de l'anonymat du don de gamètes en France: un pilier au socle d'argile?', in Pierre Jouannet (ed.), *Procréation, médecine et don*. Paris: Lavoisier pp. 99–117.

Brunet, Laurence. 2018. 'Le recul de l'ordre public face aux pratiques transfrontières de gestation pour autrui: trop…ou pas assez?', *Actualité juridique famille* 11: 572.

Camby, Carine. 2009. 'Anonymat et fondement des lois de bioéthique', in Catherine Paley-Vincent and Pierre Jouannet (eds), *L'embryon, le fœtus, l'enfant: Assistance médicale* à *la procréation et lois de bioéthique*. Paris: Eska, pp. 274–75.

CCNE (National Consultative Ethics Committee). 2017. Avis 126. 'Avis sur les demandes sociétales de recours à l'assistance médicale à la procréation'. http://www.ccne-ethique.fr/fr/publications/avis-du-ccne-du-15-juin-2017-sur-les-demandes-societales-de-recours-lassistance#.WZFmz4ppzq1. Accessed 24 June 2019.

CCNE (National Consultative Ethics Committee). 2018. Avis 129. 'Contribution du Comité consultatif national d'éthique à la révision de la loi de bioéthique 2018–2019'. https://www.ccne-ethique.fr/sites/default/files/avis_129_vf.pdf. Accessed 24 June 2019.

Chapleau, Béatrice. 2015. 'Le délit d'entremise en vue de la maternité pour autrui', *Dalloz* no. 17: 1775.

CNCDH (National Consultative Commission on Human Rights). 2018 (20 November). 'Avis relatif à l'assistance médicale à la procréation', 8–10. https://www.cncdh.fr/sites/default/files/181120_avis_relatif_a_lassistance_medicale_a_la_procreation_pour_envoi_mail_.pdf. Accessed 24 June 2019.

Conseil d'Etat (Council of State), section des rapports et des études. 2018. 'Etude à la demande du Premier ministre, La révision de la loi de bioéthique: quelles options pour demain?', 47–63. https://www.conseil-etat.fr/ressources/etudes-publications/rapports-etudes/etudes/revision-de-la-loi-de-bioethique-quelles-options-pour-demain. Accessed 24 June 2019.

Défenseur des Droits (Human Rights Defender). 2015 (3 July). Notice no. 15–18. http://www.defenseurdesdroits.fr/sites/default/files/atoms/files/ddd_avis_20150703_15-18.pdf. Accessed 24 June 2019.

Delaisi de Parseval, Geneviève. 2008. *Famille* à *tout prix*. Paris: Seuil.

de Vilaine, Anne-Marie, Laurence Gavarini and Michèle Le Coadic (eds). 1986. *Maternité en mouvement: Les femmes, la re/production et les Hommes de science*. Presses universitaires de Grenoble and Editions Saint-Martin de Montréal.

Fabre-Magnan, Muriel. 2013. *La gestation pour autrui: Fictions et réalité*. Paris: Fayard.

Fabre-Magnan, Muriel. 2015. 'Les trois niveaux d'appréciation de l'intérêt de l'enfant', *Dalloz* no. 4, 7629: 224.

Fournier, Véronique. 2007. 'Un enfant… mais pas à tout prix', *Le Monde*, 26 May, interviews by S. Blanchard. http://abonnes.lemonde.fr/societe/article/2007/05/26/un-enfant-mais-pas-a-tout-prix_915349_3224.html. Accessed 24 June 2019.

Fournier, Véronique, Laurence Brunet and Geneviève Delaisi de Parseval. 2017. 'Beaucoup de bruit pour rien', *Libération*, 4 July. http://www.liberation.fr/debats/2017/07/04/procreation-beaucoup-de-bruit-pour-rien_1581544. Accessed 24 June 2019.

Frison-Roche, Marie-Anne. 2016. 'Sophistique juridique et GPA', *Dalloz* no. 2, 7671: 85.

Fulchiron, Hugues, and Christine Bidaud-Garon. 2014. 'L'enfant de la fraude', *Dalloz* no. 15, 7596: 905.

Fulchiron, Hugues, and Christine Bidaud-Garon. 2015. 'Gestation pour autrui internationale: changement de cap à la Cour de cassation', *Dalloz* no. 31, 7656: 1819.

Gross, Martine. 2012. *Choisir la paternité gay*. Toulouse: Eres.

Haut Conseil à l'Egalite Entre les Hommes et les Femmes (High Council on Gender Equality). 2015 (26 May). 'Contribution to the debate on access to ART', notice no. 2015-07-01-SAN. http://haut-conseil-egalite.gouv.fr/IMG/pdf/hce_avis_no2015-07-01-san-17.pdf. Accessed 24 June 2019.

Iacub, Marcela. 1997. 'La construction juridique de la nature dans la reproduction hors-nature: les fécondations artificielles dans les lois bioéthiques', in Francis Ronsin, Hervé Le Bras and Elizabeth Zucker-Rouvillois (eds), *Démographie et politique*. Dijon: Éditions universitaires, pp. 161–73.

Kermalvezen, Arthur. 2008. In collaboration with Blandine de Dinechin. *Né de spermatozoïde inconnu…* Paris: Presses de la Renaissance.

Kermalvezen, Audrey. 2014. *Mes origines: une affaire d'Etat*. Paris: Max Milo.

Lamoureux, Marine. 2016. 'Une mère porteuse condamnée à un an de sursis à Blois', *La Croix*, 22 March. http://www.la-croix.com/France/Justice/Une-mere-porteuse-condamnee-avec-sursis-Blois-2016-03-22-1200748265. Accessed 24 June 2019.

Lazar, Philippe. 2003. 'Jusqu'où l'éthique peut-elle être institutionnalisée?' in *A Study by the National Consultative Ethics Committee, 20th Anniversary*. Paris: Presses universitaires de France – Quadrige, pp. 957–61.

Leroyer, Anne-Marie. 2013. 'La loi n° 2013-404 du 17 mai 2013 ouvrant le mariage aux couples de même sexe. Au passé, présent, futur', *Actualité Dalloz*: 1687. https://www.dalloz-actualite.fr/edition/2013-07-12 . Accessed 24 June 2019.

Lévy-Dutel, Laurence (ed.). 2015. *Le grand livre de la Fertilité*. Paris: Eyrolles.

Mehl, Dominique. 1998. 'Bioéthique – Revue de presse', in René Frydman, Muriel Flis-Treves and Béatrice Koeppel (eds), *Les procréations médicalement assistées: vingt ans après*, colloque Gypsy III. Paris, O. Jacob, pp. 151–74.

Mehl, Dominique. 1999. *Naître? La controverse bioéthique*. Paris: Bayard.

Mehl, Dominique. 2008. *Enfants du don – Procréation médicalement assistée: parents et enfants témoignent*. Paris: Laffont.

Mignot, Jean-François. 2015. 'L'adoption internationale dans le monde: les raisons du déclin', *Populations et sociétés*, Monthly Bulletin from l'Institut national d'études démographiques (National Institute for Demographic Studies), no. 519, February.

Rozée, Virginie. 2011. 'L'AMP sans frontière', *Bulletin* épidémiologique *hebdomadaire* 23–24: 269–73.

Sénat (French Senate). 2008. Michèle Andre (president), Alain Milon and Henri de Richemont (reporters), *Information Report from the Taskforce on Maternal Surrogacy*, no. 421. http://www.senat.fr/rap/r07-421/r07-421.html. Accessed 24 June 2019.

Sénat (French Senate). 2016. Legislative Committee, Yves Détraigne and Catherine Tasca (reporters), *Information Report on Medically Assisted Procreation and Surrogacy*, no. 409. https://www.senat.fr/notice-rapport/2015/r15-409-notice.html. Accessed 24 June 2019.

Testart, Jacques (ed.). 1990. *Le magasin des enfants*. Paris: François Bourin.

Théry, Irène. 2010. *Des humains comme les autres: Bioéthique, anonymat et genre du don*. Paris: ed. de l'EHESS.

Théry, Irène. 2013. 'Mariage de même sexe et filiation: rupture anthropologique ou réforme de civilisation?', *Dr. famille*, Study no. 17.

Théry, Irène, and Anne-Marie Leroyer. 2014. *Filiation, origines, parentalités: Le droit face aux nouvelles valeurs de responsabilité générationnelle*. Report submitted to the Delegate Minister for the Family. Paris: O. Jacob.

Thouvenin, Dominique. 1995. 'Les lois du 1er juillet 1994 et du 29 juillet 1994, ou comment construire un droit de la bioéthique', *Actualité législative Dalloz*: 149–216. https://www.dalloz-actualite.fr/search/node/thouvenin. Accessed 24 June 2019.

Chapter 2

ART and Surrogacy in Belgium

No Borders for Access – Few Borders for Kinship

Jehanne Sosson

When it comes to Assisted Reproductive Technology (ART) and surrogacy in Europe, Belgium is considered an 'open state'. Many non-Belgians, namely the French, cross their borders in order to come to Belgium, where access to both ART and secure parenthood is not only legal, but widely available.

Although the law[1] has defined general conditions of access to ART[2] techniques as well as the destination of supranumerary embryos and gametes since 2007, it does not address surrogacy. While this technique is not prohibited by law, and is thus currently unregulated in Belgium, discussions about putting such regulations into place were underway in the country's previous legislature.[3]

No Borders for Access

ART

The Law of 6 July 2007 opened access to ART to the general public. The legislature that put the law into place did not establish criteria regarding the profile of the applicant(s) – therefore, anyone (or almost anyone) can access ART. The law defines the founder(s) of a parental project as 'any person who has made the decision to become a parent through an assisted reproductive procedure, regardless of whether the technique is performed with his or her own gametes or embryos'.[4]

This open access is linked to the legislative and societal context of the time: the Belgian legislature, having allowed same-sex couples to marry in 2003,[5] then decided to allow them to adopt children in 2006.[6] Adoption had also long been open to heterosexual married and unmarried couples, as well as to single men and women. It was not, at the time, part of the political agenda to seek restrictive conditions for access to ART, and the question of access to these techniques was rarely addressed during the discussions leading up to the passing of the law, which was mainly designed to endorse and accredit *de facto* practices (which, up until that point, had been implemented by approved fertilization clinics)[7] without actually restricting them.

The starting point in Belgium was thus fundamentally different from that in France: no bioethics laws were in place that might have prohibited or restricted access to certain ART techniques. The law reflected and supported already existing and accepted practices, which varied depending on the particular ethical, religious or philosophical sensitivities of the clinic in question, or the guidelines established by the clinic's ethics committee (Derèse and Willems 2008).

Any person, whether single, married, or unmarried and living with a partner, can therefore have access to ART in Belgium. A couple seeking reproductive assistance, for example, are not required to provide proof of the relationship's stability. Furthermore, one's sexual orientation has no impact on his or her access to ART, and the availability of ART for single women remains unrestricted. Similarly, nothing in the law requires Belgian nationality or residency in order to access ART in the country, an important detail that has resulted in many applications for ART procedures from abroad, notably from France.

The only limits on access to ART put into place by the Belgian legislature concern the age of the women who undergo the procedure: they must be forty-eight years of age or under at the time of implantation, though egg retrieval[8] and requests for embryo implantation or gametes for insemination are only open to adult women aged forty-six or under. There is no age requirement, however, for sperm retrieval, nor is there an age requirement for a man who wishes to be involved in a parental project. It should also be mentioned that insemination or embryo implantation can occur *post mortem*, provided the procedure was expressly provided for in the original contract, and takes place between six months and two years after the death in question.[9]

Since the general eligibility requirements established by the law are so broad, in practice it is the fertility clinics that decide whether or not to accept an application for ART. These clinics must, 'when appropriate', verify that the causes of infertility or subfertility in the woman or couple applying for treatment have been determined and processed according to data acquired using scientific methods and for the express use of the profession.[10] Some applications may be accepted in one centre and rejected in another. The centres are expected to provide utmost transparency about their options regarding access to treatment, and can express a conscience clause in response to any request they receive. In any case, however, they must notify the applicant or applicants of their refusal to comply with the request in writing, either specifying the medical reasons for the refusal, or invoking the conscience clause. If the applicant wishes, the clinic must also provide them with the contact information of another clinic where they can seek treatment.[11]

These provisions clearly reflect the Belgian legislature's efforts to refrain from dogmatism and uphold ethical pluralism regarding access to ART. The principles of freedom and transparency that govern the matter are thus twofold: the wants and needs of individuals must be heard, but no professional can be forced to carry out a legal act that goes against their perceptions of what is or is not ethically acceptable (Derèse and Willems 2008). If the application is accepted, accurate information and counselling is then provided to the interested parties, and a contract laying out the terms of the procedure, as well as the destination of spare embryos or gametes, is established.[12]

Access to ART is also facilitated by the fact that under certain conditions, a Social Security beneficiary in Belgium may be reimbursed through this health insurance policy for any pharmaceutical products administered during treatment for *in vitro* fertilization. Those benefiting from Social Security can also be reimbursed for the costs of the procedure, so long as it takes place in a hospital with a care programme that is accredited for these techniques ('Reproductive Medicine B') and provided the woman concerned is younger than forty-two years of age, with a maximum of six cycles per woman. The law governing the number of embryos that can be implanted varies depending on the age of the woman being treated.[13]

Surrogacy

No specific law currently regulates surrogacy in Belgium; as a result, any contract concerning surrogacy is generally considered void.[14] Nevertheless, the procedure is practised in reality, whether administered by hospitals that practise reproductive medicine, or 'naturally' achieved by couples outside of hospitals via a 'simple' artificial insemination.

Currently, no conditions are required as such to access surrogacy (Derèse 2013). While the conditions for access to ART techniques that serve as one of the steps in the process as defined by the Law of 6 April 2007 must be met (described above), the hospitals that practise the technique can establish their own conditions of access, such as that of the civil status of the intended parents (one woman, one man, heterosexual couples, or homosexual couples) or surrogates, the obligation (or lack thereof) to provide all or some of the genetic material, the relationship with the surrogate (some centres in Belgium, for example, prefer that the surrogate be a relative or friend of the intended parents), the requirement (or lack thereof) that the surrogate has already been pregnant, and the residency or nationality of the parties involved (Autin 2013). Commercial surrogacy is prohibited in Belgium as per the general principles of civil and criminal law that prohibit human commercialization. Surrogacy practised outside of a hospital, on the other hand, avoids being subject to any conditions of access.

This particular phenomenon is what motivated the Belgian Parliament to commission a report on the potential creation of a 'powerful legal framework' for surrogacy in Belgium.[15] After conducting numerous hearings, the Belgian Senate published a substantial synthesis report in December 2015 in which each Belgian political party represented in the legislature gave its views as to whether legislation regulating surrogacy, notably the establishment of conditions of access, was needed.[16] The majority of the parties positioned themselves in favour of a legislative framework as well as a ban on surrogacy for commercial purposes.[17] With regard to access to the procedure, opinions are divided. There seems to be a general consensus, however, on the idea that if a law were to be established, at least one of the intended parents would be required to provide his or her genetic material, and the surrogate mother would not be allowed to be genetically related to the child. Conversely, when defining who exactly can resort to surrogacy as part of a parental project, while the majority of the political parties advocating a legislative framework are willing to provide access to both singles and couples (both homosexual and heterosexual), some strongly advocate limiting cross-border ART by adopting rules requiring intended parents to have Belgian citizenship or residency for a certain period of time (e.g. two years). Some also recommend requiring that the surrogate mother be a legal resident in Belgium.[18]

This report should be the basis for a discussion on law proposals in the House of Representatives.[19] But it is currently impossible to determine if and when a discussion will be held, leaving the possibility of adoption of a law governing surrogacy in Belgium as an open question. It is possible, however, that access to surrogacy in Belgium will be limited by the aforementioned legal guidelines in the future.

Few Borders for Kinship

The 'open' access to ART and surrogacy, legally established or accepted under the ethical pluralism umbrella, has also constituted an open door for the Belgian legislature to enable and even guarantee to children born via ART techniques access to legal parenthood that corresponds to the parental project that triggered the use of these techniques. The Belgian government has not only provided wide access to ART, but has gone so far as to take steps to ensure, through its jurisprudence, that the child's legal filiation is established with his or her intended parents.

ART

Although the Law of 6 July 2007 regulates assisted reproductive processes, it does not regulate the establishment of legal filiation. Articles 27 and 56 of the law clearly state that with regard to gamete insemination or an embryo donation, 'the rules of filiation as established by the Belgian Civil Code weigh in favour of the author(s) of the parental project'. Furthermore, no claim concerning legal filiation or its financial consequences is open to donors. At the same time, however, no claim can be brought against the donor(s).

It is therefore certain that the sperm or egg donor, whether anonymous or known,[20] will never be legally recognized as the father or mother of the child. He or she will never be authorized to dispute the parentage of the child or legally concerned by a claim from the child should they seek to establish legal filiation with them.

In the case of ART for a heterosexual couple, the intended parents become the legal parents of the child according to the general rules governing legal parentage. The woman who gives birth to the child after receiving an egg donation will be the legal mother, in accordance with the general rule that the child's mother is the woman who gives birth.[21] In the case of sperm donation, the husband will become the father of the child by applying the presumption of paternity.[22] If the intended parents are not married, the intended father can legally recognize the child with the consent of the mother.[23] In both cases, it is therefore unnecessary to go through the process of adoption in order to legally 'attach' the child to their intended parent(s).

As regards same-sex couples, in 2006, Belgium opened access to adoption to them.[24] It is therefore possible for two men or two women to become the parents of a child. For lesbian couples who use artificial insemination or *in vitro* fertilization, this involved becoming the legal parents of a child through adoption.

Nevertheless, in 2014 the Belgian legislature decided that it was inappropriate for the second mother to have to establish her legal relationship with the child via adoption (which is only possible up to two months after the child's birth), and subsequently created a unique and innovative family model that would allow the child to have from its birth onwards two legal mothers (or, more precisely, a mother and a 'co-mother'). It was ruled that the establishment of dual filiation for the second woman had to be founded on the parental project.[25] Applying the adoption process was not retained as a possible satisfactory solution. Instead, the decision was made to transpose the set of rules that permit the establishment of filiation for heterosexual couples, thus providing female couples with a parental project as well.

This decision resulted in the law of 5 May 2014, which entered into force on 1 January 2015.[26] Thus, when a woman who is married to another woman gives birth to a child, her wife is now automatically given the legal filiation of the child by presumption: Article 325/2 of the Belgian Civil Code provides that any child born during the marriage, or within three hundred days of its dissolution or annulment, will have his or her mother's spouse as a co-parent.

If the woman who gives birth to the child is not married, but has planned for the child as part of a parental project with another woman, the latter may legally recognize the child as her own with the consent of the birth mother, either before or after the birth.[27]

Through this process, the birth mother's partner becomes a co-parent. If the mother who gave birth refuses to provide her consent to this recognition, the co-mother is entitled to obtain from the Family Court a decision that authorizes her, if it is not against the best interests of the child, to recognize the child without the consent of the birth mother. This decision could be based on the common parental project proven by the medically assisted procreation consent and the best interest of the child.

Finally, co-maternity may even be granted by a judgement in favour of a woman who, along with another woman, has consented to medically assisted procreation. If co-maternity is not established by presumption or recognition, it can be established by a court decision if the mother or child seeks legal action to this end.[28] The ART consent that provides the grounds for a common parental project can be considered as sufficient evidence to legally establish co-maternal filiation. If the birth mother disagrees with the establishment of legal filiation, the Court must verify that it does not jeopardize the child's best interests.

Consequently, the joint parental project of two women, grounded in their consent to ART in the contract signed with the fertilization centre, becomes the basis of their dual parenthood. The consent given by the two women who founded the parental project in the ART contract has the same legal effect as a blood relationship. This consent is at the heart of the provisions of the Act of 5 May 2014, and has become the basis for the establishment of legal filiation, despite the fact that this contract was not originally intended for this purpose, as it was initially drafted in order to lay out and define the conditions of going through the ART process. As noted above,[29] not only is access to medically assisted procreation widely open (that is to say, without specific requirements as to the duration or stability of the couples who can access it), but it is placed under the sole responsibility of medical teams that are required to provide the interested parties with 'accurate information' as well as 'psychological support before and during the process'.[30] As a result, in reality the duty to obtain informed consent from female couples, as well as the duty to alert them to said consent's irreversible consequences regarding legal parentage, is simply placed in the hands of health professionals.

Legal filiation that may automatically (by presumption of co-maternity in female married couples) or possibly (by recognition or judgement in unmarried couples) result from this consent to ART, notwithstanding the absence of any biological link, is undisputable:

it is not possible to challenge it. Firstly, legal action contesting such co-maternity[31] cannot succeed if it is proven that the wife or woman who has legally recognized the child consented to the conception of the child by way of artificial insemination or any other procedure with the aim of procreation prior to said conception.[32] Secondly, no parental link can be established between the child and the donor.[33] The contract between these women and the fertility centre therefore has significant legal consequences, meaning that a central role is given to a consent document that may be poorly or inadequately informed due to insufficient information on all the legal consequences involved in legal filiation.

It is worth pointing out that the Act of 5 May 2014 limited the number of parents to two: a child can only have two legal parents, even if, as part of their parental project, a female couple enlists the help of a known male donor in conceiving their child. Indeed, in the case of ART carried out in an approved fertility centre with the help of a known donor,[34] the establishment of the paternity of the donor is excluded by the Law of 6 July 2007.[35] However, if the couple informally enlists the help of a 'friend donor' outside the framework of an approved fertility centre, the women's rights to joint parenthood will not be protected, as the biological father could challenge the couple's co-maternity in order to establish his own legal paternity.[36]

All of these provisions apply only to female couples. Male couples are excluded since the parental project of two men requires the support of a woman and, by extension, surrogacy to carry the child. In 2014, the Belgian legislature decided to limit the granting of same-sex parentage at birth only to female couples, thus creating a gender bias among same-sex couples (Sosson 2014; Pluym 2015).

Surrogacy

Domestic Surrogacy

There is no law that currently regulates surrogacy: neither the conditions of access to the procedure,[37] nor the establishment of filiation with the intended parents. The common law of filiation is thus applied accordingly.

When surrogacy is carried out in Belgium and the woman carrying the child gives birth in Belgium, she is automatically legally recognized as the mother of the child. According to Belgian law, the name of the birth mother must appear on the birth certificate, which automatically establishes legal parentage with the woman named in the document.[38] The surrogate, whether she is the gestational mother or the genetic mother as well, is thus designated as the legal mother of the child.

As with any father, the intended father can legally recognize the child, with the consent of the mother (in this case the surrogate mother), so long as the child is still a minor.[39] The intended mother (or both parents, if the intended father does not legally recognize the child) may adopt the child. However, this process also requires the consent of the surrogate mother. When a male couple resorts to surrogacy, the second intended father can adopt the child.

Belgian courts have a long history of allowing the adoption of children from a surrogate.[40] Contrary to French law, no legal provision explicitly prohibits the use of a surrogate, and even if the contract with the surrogate is considered void,[41] Belgian courts have long considered that the child should not be 'penalized' and that it is in his or her best interests to be 'linked' to his or her intended parents. Therefore, Belgian courts generally allow full adoptions after surrogacy, and consider that this kind of adoption fulfils the legal requirements for adoption, namely 'fair motives' on the part of the parents[42] and respect for the best interests of the child. Case law shows that, after being more restrictive (notably in a case where the surrogate was the genetic mother of the child),[43] most Belgian Courts now consider that adoption can be granted in domestic cases of *non-profit* surrogacy.[44]

However, if the surrogate, who is also the legal mother, refuses to consent to either recognition by the father or the adoption of the child, the intended parents can find themselves faced with serious obstacles. If the surrogate refuses to relinquish the child, the contract is void, and she cannot be forced to do so.

In the discussions that took place in the Belgian Senate during the drafting of the preliminary report with the aim of building a possible legislative framework for surrogacy,[45] a reform of Belgian law that would allow the establishment of 'an automatic parental link between the intended parent(s)' and the child was proposed. Most Belgian political parties consider that the law relating to legal filiation should be adapted so that the intended parent(s) may automatically become the child's legal parent(s) without having to go through the adoption process, and without the surrogate first being named the legal mother of the child.[46] Even before this report, law proposals to this effect had already been submitted, notably proposing the establishment of legal filiation through a surrogacy contract that would be signed and sent to a civil registrar.[47] This rather radical idea, which would authorize the establishment of legal filiation by contract (currently prohibited by Belgian law) is no longer envisaged in the report. Instead, the report foresees the requirement to obtain a judicial decision before the surrogacy process. This judicial decision would allow the intended parents to be recognized as the legal parents from the moment of birth of the child.

International Surrogacy

Belgians also resort to surrogacy abroad, either because their applications in Belgium have been rejected, or because they are not able to meet the requirements of Belgian hospitals and fertility clinics with regard to medical indications, status (as with single men or male couples, whose applications may be less likely to be accepted) or failure to find a surrogate who is a family member or friend. Therefore, many travel to other countries that offer or have offered surrogacy with broader conditions of access, or even commercial surrogacy.

One of the first difficulties encountered is the *issuance of documents* (whether a passport or other travel authorization) allowing the child to return to Belgium when the child does not acquire the nationality of the country where he or she is born. Belgian courts have, at times, ordered the Belgian state to issue such documents *de facto*.[48] In a decision rendered on 8 July 2014,[49] the European Court of Human Rights rejected an appeal lodged against a court decision that, in a lower court, had at first refused to order state authorities to deliver travelling papers for the child; in the meantime, Belgian authorities had issued an authorization allowing the child born in Ukraine to return to Belgium. The European Court thus took the opportunity to clarify that the denial of travel documents to the child would amount to a violation of the child's right to a family life, a right protected by Article 8 of the European Convention on Human Rights. The Court also noted, however, that 'the Convention could not oblige the States to authorize the entry of children born to a surrogate mother into their territory without the national authorities having a prior opportunity to conduct certain relevant legal checks'. The Court went on to note that the Belgian authorities had initially refused to authorize the child's entry into the national territory because of the need to verify whether both Belgian and Ukrainian law had been complied with. The interference was therefore justified by the objective of preventing a criminal offence, notably human trafficking.

The second step in the process is Belgium's *recognition of the parenthood* established abroad with the intended parents. The basic principle is that any authority should recognize an authentic legal document from abroad, without recourse to any legal action, if its validity is established in accordance with Belgian law.[50] In the case of a refusal to recognize an act on the part of the administrative authorities (such as the state registrar), it is possible to lodge a complaint before the court. If the applicant is Belgian, the court will then examine whether the act could have been carried out under Belgian law, so long as the act is not contrary to international public policy in Belgium, and that there has been no legal fraud.

More often than not, Belgian courts rule that it is not contrary to public policy to recognize a birth certificate that was established abroad, or at least an authentic and legally valid certificate that recognizes the paternity of the child born from a surrogate mother. This being said, most Belgian courts do not consider a birth certificate as a means of establishing the legal maternity of the intended mother (if her name is stated on the document), nor do they always consider valid a double paternity with regard to the intended father's spouse in homosexual couples.[51] If the birth certificate is recognized as establishing only one legal paternal link, the mother and/or second father can adopt the child so that he/she will have both of his or her intended parents as legal parents.

With regards to the *nationality* of the child, the former is derived from the establishment of legal filiation, first with the intended father, and secondly with both parents after adoption if necessary. When filiation is established in a court ruling, such as with pre-birth orders in America, the conditions for recognition are less strict: the recognition of the judgement is affected *ipso jure* provided that it is not contrary to public policy, and that there has been no legal fraud.[52] The Court of Liège thus considered that it was not contrary to public policy to recognize a Californian judgement which stated that the filiation of children born through a surrogacy contract would not be established with the woman who gave birth, but with the intended parents, namely two gay men who were married. The Court of Liège thus ordered that the American birth certificates of the children drawn up following this court decision (which stated that the legal parents were both men) be accepted and integrated into the Belgian civil registry.[53]

This author's assessment is that there has been a shift towards facilitating and simplifying parental recognition via surrogacy carried out abroad, despite often laborious and complex analyses in private international law. This shift reflects Belgian pragmatism, which ultimately recognizes the interest of a child born from surrogacy to be legally attached to both the intended parents with whom he or she lives and forms a family.

One may fear, however, that this 'openness' demonstrated by the Belgian courts could be narrowed in the near future. Indeed, during discussions that took place in the Senate on the drafting of a preliminary report in view of creating a legal framework for surrogacy,[54] several political parties expressed their wish to toughen Belgium's stance on international surrogacy when the procedure is organized at the national level. The idea is to deter Belgians from resorting to surrogacy abroad if the legal standards for the procedure set in Belgium are not met (as with commercial surrogacy, for example). Some parties have even suggested prosecuting Belgians who turn to commercial surrogacy abroad.[55] It is not totally impossible that the establishment of a national legislative framework for surrogacy could eventually involve a hardening of Belgium's stance on recognizing international surrogacy, if Belgian legislators finally decide to pass a law.

Conclusion

Access to ART is broad in Belgium; firstly, because the law does not set specific criteria for access to ART, and secondly, because the country currently has no legal framework to regulate surrogacy. As a result, however, each fertility centre has the opportunity and responsibility to define its own criteria for access to ART. While ethical pluralism remains a fundamental principle, these centres share one common belief, namely that any commercial initiative (including possible existence or interference of intermediary agencies) must be prohibited.

Moreover, once a surrogacy or assisted reproductive technique is carried out, the Belgian legislature[56] and judicial bodies ensure, often at the cost of seemingly complex legal detours (especially regarding the recognition of filiation when surrogacy is carried out abroad), that the child's filiation is in line with the parental project that exists prior to the birth of the child. The recognition of parental ties with the intended parents is ultimately possible, whether established under the conditions of the general legal filiation principles that are common to ART access for heterosexual couples, legally facilitated (ART for female couples with legal co-maternity), or guaranteed by other, almost always feasible means (recognition or adoption following surrogacy). When a child is created via the intervention of a donor or surrogate, the original parental project is fully recognized as the basis for filiation, as a substitute in lieu of the blood ties that come with 'natural' procreation.

This 'Belgian model' (if we can call it that), characterized by open access to ART and a lack of criteria concerning access to surrogacy (apart from barring ART or surrogacy for commercial purposes), ensures and enables access to legal filiation. This model therefore differs radically from the 'French model', wherein the law limits access to ART and prohibits surrogacy, or the American-style model, which leaves open considerable possibilities (depending on the US state) for the commercialization of ART and surrogacy. It is still possible, however, that this model will be modified in the future, though it is difficult to tell when, especially if the Belgian legislature decides to restrict access to surrogacy and establishes stricter criteria than those currently in place (though this seems unlikely), or otherwise positions itself in opposition to surrogacy carried out abroad, or adopts a stricter position towards surrogacy carried out abroad under more lenient conditions than the ones that may be introduced in a potential future Belgian law with the aim of ensuring 'ethically acceptable' surrogacy procedures.

Jehanne Sosson is a family law expert. She is a professor at the UCLouvain (Université catholique de Louvain) and at the Université Saint-Louis Bruxelles. She is director of the Family Law Centre of UCLouvain. She is the author or editor of numerous publications in family law and comparative family law, with special interest in parenthood and family relationships. She has often been appointed as an expert in Belgium and abroad in these fields. She is also a practising lawyer at the Brussels Bar.

Notes

1. The Law of 6 July 2007, which concerns medically-assisted procreation and the use of supranumerary embryos and gametes, *Moniteur belge*, 17 July 2007, p. 38.575. Available (as are all the other legal texts

cited in this chapter) at http://www.ejustice.just.fgov.be/loi/loi.htm. Accessed 29 June 2019.

2. Defined by the law as 'all terms and conditions of the application of new medical technologies that aid reproduction in which one of the following are performed: 1. artificial insemination, or 2. an *in-vitro* fertilization technique, that is to say a technique in which, at some point during the procedure, access is given to the egg and/or the embryo'.
3. Cf. infra note 15.
4. Article 2.f of the Law of 6 July 2007.
5. Article 143 of the Belgian Civil Code, as amended by the Law of 13 February 2003.
6. Articles 343 et seq. of the Belgian Civil Code, as amended by the Law of 30 June 2006.
7. The organization and funding of these centres was, until 2007, regulated primarily by the establishment of the conditions that reproductive medical centres must meet in order to receive state approval. See notably the Royal Decree of 15 February 1999, which established the standards that healthcare programmes administering reproductive medicine must meet in order to be approved. *Moniteur belge*, 25 March 1999, p. 9556.
8. Donating gametes or an embryo is not paid for. It is generally supposed to be anonymous, but a non-anonymous gamete donation (though not an embryo donation) is possible in the case of an agreement between the donor and the recipient(s). Articles 22 and 57 of the Law of 6 July 2007. For more details concerning the question of anonymity in Belgian law, see notably Mathieu 2014; Schamps and Derèse 2008.
9. Articles 15, 16, 44 and 45 of the Law of 6 July 2007.
10. Article 6 of the Law of 6 July 2007.
11. Article 5 of the Law of 6 July 2007.
12. Cf. the Law of 6 July 2007, notably Articles 6 et seq.
13. Article 14.g of the Royal Decree establishing the nomenclature of health services with regard to compulsory healthcare insurance and benefits of 14 September 1984.
14. Which implies that if a surrogate mother (who is also the legal mother) decides to keep the child, it is impossible to 'force' her to give the child to the intended parents. Cf. notably Gallus 2013. On the contrary, some authors believe that the contract is valid (Genicot 2013).
15. Proposal for the preparation of an information report exploring the possibility of establishing a statutory scheme regarding joint parenthood, document 6-98/1, session 2014–2015, 3 December 2014, available at http://www.senate.be. Accessed 29 June 2019.
16. Information report exploring the possibility of establishing a statutory scheme regarding joint parenthood, document 6-98/2, session 2014–2015, 3 December 2014, available at http://www.senate.be.

17. The only party that considered that surrogacy should not be legally regulated was the CDH (Centre démocrate humaniste, or Humanist Democratic Centre) party, which cited the precautionary principle and called for the prohibition of any further surrogacies in Belgium (cf. notably the quoted information report [note 16], p. 339).
18. See the above-mentioned report [note 16], pp. 260–68.
19. For a summary of all the bills that have been formally introduced, cf. the above-mentioned report [note 16], p. 291 et seq.
20. See above, note 8.
21. Article 312 of the Belgian Civil Code.
22. Article 315 of the Belgian Civil Code.
23. Article 329 et seq. of the Belgian Civil Code.
24. See above, notes 1 and 6.
25. See notably the proposed law on the establishment of filiation with the co-parent, reported on behalf of the Justice Committee by M. Anclaux, Parliamentary Documents, Senate, regular session 2013–2014, 5-2445/3, p. 3 et seq. (available at http://www.senate.be, accessed 29 June 2019).
26. The Law of 5 May 2014 on the establishment of filiation with the co-parent, *Moniteur belge*, 7 December 2014 (amended and completed by the Law of 18 December 2014, *Moniteur belge*, 23 December 2014).
27. Article 325-4 of the Belgian Civil Code.
28. Article 325-8 of the Belgian Civil Code.
29. See above, notes 2–4.
30. Article 6 of the Law of 6 July 2007.
31. For more details on this issue, cf. notably Demaret and Langenaken 2015; Beernaert and Massager 2015; Pluym 2015; Seghers and Swennen 2014.
32. Cf. Articles 325-3, § 3 and 325-7 of the Belgian Civil Code.
33. See above, note 9.
34. Which is possible in Belgium, see supra note 9.
35. Articles 27 and 56 of the Law of 6 July 2007.
36. For more details on this legally complex situation, which go beyond this study on access to medically assisted procreation and surrogacy, see notably Beernaert and Massager 2015.
37. See above, note 6.
38. Articles 44 and 312 of the Belgian Civil Code. Another possibility consists of the surrogate mother giving birth anonymously in France (as anonymous childbirth is illegal in Belgium). In this case, the child has no maternal parenthood, and can be legally recognized by the intended father. This possibility has been activated when French couples come to Belgium for surrogacy with a French surrogate mother. In this case, they use the possibility offered by French law to give birth

anonymously, which is not possible in Belgium, while having benefited from a medical technique that is possible in Belgium but not in France.

39. Article 329bis of the Belgian Civil Code. And if the surrogate mother is unmarried. If she is married, her husband is presumed to be the father of the child (Article 315 of the Belgian Civil Code), and legal action is necessary in order to reverse this legal presumption of paternity, or to directly substitute it with that of the intended father (see notably Civ. Dinant, 6 February 2014, *Revue trimestrielle de droit familial*, 2014/3, p. 626, note J. Sosson, 'Mère porteuses mariées: danger?').
40. The first ruling was published in 1996: Brussels Youth Court, 4 June 1996, *Jurisprudence de Liège, Mons et Bruxelles*, 1996, p. 1182.
41. See above, notes 6 and 16.
42. 'Justes motifs', cf. Article 344.1. of the Belgian Civil Code.
43. Ghent Court of Appeals (15th chamber), 16 January 1989, *Tijdschrift voor Gentse Rechtspraak*, 1989, p. 52.
44. See notably, in chronological order: Brussels Youth Court, 4 June 1996, *Jurisprudence de Mons, Liège et Bruxelles*, 1996, p. 1182; Turnhouet Youth Court, 4 October 2000, *Rechtkundige Weekblad*, 2001–2002, p. 206, note F. Swennen; Antwerp Court of Appeals, 14 January 2008 (reforming Antwerp Youth Court, 11 October 2007), *Rechtkundige Weekblad*, 2007–2008, p. 1774, note F. Swennen; Brussels Youth Court, 6 May 2009, *Jurisprudence de Mons, Liège et Bruxelles*, 2009, p. 1083 et *Revue trimestrielle de droit familial*, 2011, p. 172, note J. Sosson; Huy Youth Court, 22 December 2011, *Revue trimestrielle de droit familial*, 2012, p. 403. See also Verschelden and Pluym 2013. On the contrary, in 2012, the Ghent Court of Appeals refused to grant the full adoption requested because it appeared that the adoption dissimulated the buying and selling of a child (the surrogate had received 1,600 euros per month during the pregnancy, which exceeds, according to the Court, the normal costs of a surrogacy) and considered that for-profit surrogacy is contrary to human dignity. As a result, the Court ruled that the adoption was not based on 'fair motives', and that the *de facto* relationship established between the child and the adoption candidate did not thwart this analysis (Ghent Youth Court, 13 June 2012, *Tijdschrift Jeugd- en Kinderrechten*, 2012/3, p. 261, note L. Pluym, 'Weigering volle adoptie na commercieel laagtchnologish draagmoederschap', quoted also by Henricot 2013).
45. See above, note 16.
46. Cf. the information report exploring the possibility of establishing a statutory scheme regarding joint parenthood, document 6-98/2, session 2014–2015, 3 December 2014, notably p. 364 onwards. (available at http://www.senate.be).
47. See notably the bill regarding surrogate mothers, submitted by Ch. Defraigne, Parliamentary Documents, Senate, extraordinary session

2010, no. 5-160; bill on the organization of surrogacy centres, submitted by M. Temmerman and G. Swennen, Parliamentary Documents, Senate, ordinary session 2010–2011, no. 5-929. For an analysis of these proposals, cf. Sosson and Mathieu 2013.

48. Brussels Court of Appeals, 31 July 2013, *Revue trimestrielle de droit familial*, 2014/3, p. 530, note J. Sosson and J. Mary, 'Gestation pour autrui pratiquée à l'étranger: l'intérêt de l'enfant, sésame d'une reconnaissance en Belgique?'; Brussels Civil Court (emergency interim proceedings), 6 April 2010, *Revue trimestrielle de droit familial*, 2010/4, p. 1164.
49. C.E.D.H. (2nd sect.), 8 July 2014, D. and others v. Belgium (req. no. 29173/13).
50. Article 27 of the Belgian Code of Private International Law.
51. See notably Ghent (15th chamber), 16 January 1989, T.G.R., 1989, p. 52; Turnhout Youth Court, 4 October 2000, *Rechtskundige Weekblad*, 2001–2002, p. 206, note F. Swennen; Antwerp Court of Appeals, 22 April 2010, *Tijdschrift voor Familierecht*, 2012, p. 43, note L. Pluym; Brussels Civil Court, 15 February 2011, p. 77 (http://www.ipr.be/, accessed 29 June 2019); Liège Court of Appeals, 6 September 2010, *Revue trimestrielle de droit familial*, 2011, p. 695, note C. Henricot, S. Saroléa and J. Sosson; *Journal des Tribunaux*, 2010, p. 634; *Jurisprudence Liège, Mons et Bruxelles*, 2011, p. 52, note P. Wautelet; Brussels Civil Court (12th chamber), 18 December 2012, *Revue trimestrielle de droit familial*, 2014/3, p. 544, note J. Sosson and J. Mary, 'Gestation pour autrui pratiquée à l'étranger: l'intérêt de l'enfant, sésame d'une reconnaissance en Belgique?'. Court of Appeal Gent, 20 April 2017, *Revue@dipr.be* 2017, liv. 3, p. 87; Court of Appeal Brussels, 10 August 2018, *Revue@dipr.be* 2018, liv. 8, p. 15, note P. WAUTELET, 'De l'intérêt supérieur de l'enfant comme facteur de neutralisation de la fraude à la loi'.
52. See Article 22 of the Belgian Code of Private International Law.
53. Liège Civil Court (3rd chamber), 15 March 2013, *Revue trimestrielle de droit familial*, 2013/3, p. 714, note C. Henricot, 'Gestation pour autrui transfrontière. Reconnaissance d'un double lien de filiation monosexuée: une première en Belgique?'.
54. See above, note 7.
55. See above, note 16.
56. See the law on co-maternity (note 26 above).

References

Autin, Candice. 2013. 'Gestation pour autrui: expérience d'un centre belge de procréation médicalement assistée', in Geneviève Schamps and Jehanne Sosson (eds), *La gestation pour autrui: vers un encadrement?* Brussels: Bruylant, pp. 9–21.

Beernaert, Jean-Emmanuel, and Nathalie Massager. 2015. 'La loi du 15 mai instaurant le régime de la comaternité: Trois femmes, un homme et un couffin', *Actualités du Droit de la famille* 4: 74–84.
Demaret, Marie, and Evelyne Langenaken. 2015. 'La loi portant établissement de la filiation de la coparente: bien dire et laisser faire', *Revue trimestrielle de droit familial* 3: 456–95.
Derèse, Marie-Noëlle. 2013. 'L'accès à la gestation pour autrui', in Geneviève Schamps and Jehanne Sosson (eds), *La gestation pour autrui: vers un encadrement?* Brussels: Bruylant, pp. 293–323.
Derèse, Marie-Noëlle, and Geoffrey Willems. 2008. 'La loi du 6 juillet relative à la procréation médicalement assistée et à la destination des embryons surnuméraires et des gamètes', *Revue trimestrielle de droit familial* 2: 279–359.
Fiorentino, Karen, and Allison Fiorentino (eds). 2018. *Mater semper certa est?: passé, présent, avenir d'un adage*. Brussels: Bruylant.
Gallus, Nicole. 2013. 'La validité de la convention de gestation pour autrui en droit belge actuel', in Geneviève Schamps and Jehanne Sosson (eds), *La gestation pour autrui: vers un encadrement?* Brussels: Bruylant, pp. 181–93.
Genicot, Gilles. 2013. 'Gestation pour autrui, autonomie personnelle et maîtrise corporelle: Plaidoyer pour un droit neutre et libéré', in Geneviève Schamps and Jehanne Sosson (eds), *La gestation pour autrui: vers un encadrement?* Brussels: Bruylant, pp. 155–79.
Henricot, Caroline. 2013. 'Gestation pour autrui transfrontière: Reconnaissance d'un double lien de filiation monosexuée: une première en Belgique?', *Revue trimestrielle de droit familial* 3: 721–29.
Herbrand, Cathy. 2012. 'La filiation à l'épreuve de la présomption de "paternité" pour les couples de même sexe: questionnements et perspectives à partir du cas belge', *Droit et société,* December (82): 689–712.
Massager, Nathalie, and Nicole Gallus (eds). 2017. *Procréation médicalement assistée et gestation pour autrui.* Limal: Anthémis.
Mathieu, Géraldine. 2014. *Le secret des origines en droit de la filiation.* Waterloo: Kluwer.
Pluym, Liesbet. 2014. *Draagmoederschap*. Gent: Uitgeverij Larcier.
Pluym, Liesbet. 2015. 'Juridisch statuut voor meemoeders – Commentaar bij de wet van 5 mei 2014', *Tijdschrift voor Familierecht* 5: 7–11.
Schamps, Geneviève, and Marie-Noëlle Derèse. 2008. 'L'anonymat et la procréation médicalement assistée en droit belge: Des pratiques à la loi du 6 juillet 2007', in B. Feuillet (ed.), *Procréation assistée et anonymat – Panorama international.* Brussels: Bruylant, pp. 125–52.
Schamps, Geneviève, and Jehanne Sosson (eds). 2013. *La gestation pour autrui: vers un encadrement?* Brussels: Bruylant.
Seghers, Gwenn, and Frederik Swennen. 2014. 'Meemoederschap zonder adoptie – de wet van 5 mei 2014 tot vastelling van de afstamming van

de meemoeder', *Tijdschrift voor Belgish Burgelijk Recht/Revue générale de droit civil* 10: 480–86.

Sosson, Jehanne. 2014. 'Filiation, origines, parentalités', in *Filiation et parentalité*. Brussels: Bruylant, pp. 5–33.

Sosson, Jehanne, and Julie Mary. 2014. 'Gestation pour autrui pratiquée à l'étranger: l'intérêt de l'enfant, sésame d'une reconnaissance en Belgique?' *Revue trimestrielle de droit familial* 3: 552–70.

Sosson, Jehanne, and Géraldine Mathieu. 2013. 'L'enfant né d'une gestation pour autrui: quelle filiation? Quels liens avec la mère porteuse?', in Geneviève Schamps and Jehanne Sosson (eds), *La gestation pour autrui: vers un encadrement?* Brussels: Bruylant, pp. 375–409.

Sosson, Jehanne, Geoffrey Willems and Gwendoline Motte (eds). 2019. *Adults and Children in Postmodern Societies: A Comparative Law and Multidisciplinary Handbook.* Cambridge: Intersentia.

Verschelden, Gert, and Liesbet Pluym. 2013. 'Chronique de jurisprudence belge concernant la gestation pour autrui (droit interne)', in Geneviève Schamps and Jehanne Sosson (eds), *La gestation pour autrui: vers un encadrement?* Brussels: Bruylant, pp. 195–212.

Part II

Invisible Borders, France, Belgium

Chapter 3

Does the Embryo Make the Family?

Access to Embryo Donation in France

Séverine Mathieu

'Anyone who wants to have children should be able to start a family', says a man who, along with his wife, has just finished donating an embryo. In an effort to prevent the destruction of surplus embryos during the *in vitro* fertilization (IVF) process, the French legislature authorized embryo hosting with the Law of 29 July 1994. This practice, the conditions of which are specified in the Law of 6 August 2004 and the implementation decree of 22 December 2006, is rare. Access is restricted to heterosexual couples for whom all other attempts at assisted reproductive technologies (ART) have failed. In 2004, the first child created from a living embryo donation was born. Since 2010, ten French regions hosting sixteen centres have performed this procedure. In 2012, the chance of becoming pregnant after an embryo transfer was around 30 per cent.

In 2015, fifteen French centres performed embryo donation; 148 couples donated their supplementary embryos, 145 transfers were performed for 128 couples, and twenty-seven children were born. This very low level of activity is set against the number of embryos eligible for a host that were stored in 103 ART centres (12,646 at the end of December 2015) and the number of couples who wanted to give their surplus embryos to another couple (4,025).

Pursuing a previous study on medically assisted procreation (Mathieu 2013), a new ethnographic survey was conducted in two embryo hosting centres. The results are based on observations of consultations and in-depth interviews with couples. In the first centre, four consultations with donor couples were observed. In the second centre, twenty-five consultations were observed (twelve donations and thirteen receptions, which represents almost the total annual activity of this centre with regard to embryo hosting). Following these consultations, nineteen interviews were conducted with ten donor couples and nine recipient couples. In addition to these meetings, I also conducted interviews with the physicians, biologists and psychologists of the centres observed in the study.

First, let us recall where these embryos come from. Every year, French ART centres send a letter to the couples having undergone *in vitro* fertilization that year to ask them if they wish to keep or destroy their frozen embryos. If they wish to destroy the embryos, they must confirm their decision within a period of three months by sending a certified letter. If five years pass without a response from the couple, the centres are allowed to destroy the embryos. Those who choose not to destroy the embryos can keep them for themselves, donate them to research or give them to another couple. This final process is called 'embryo hosting', a term that covers both types of couples involved in this practice: the donors and the recipients. How has access to this practice been regulated in France? What can it teach us about French representations of kinship?

Access: Reflection on the Ambiguous Status of the Embryo

Initial discussions on the possibility of embryo donation via ART were divided. The National Consultative Ethics Committee, whose decisions are not legally binding, was a key player in defining the status of the embryo, and was also divided on the subject, according to its Notice No. 18 of 15 December 1989 (CCNE 1989). While some members wondered whether they should see in the practice of embryo donation 'a reduction of the embryo to the status of genetic material used in therapeutic procedures for infertility, while considering their destruction as a lesser evil', others – reflecting the Notice No. 1 of 22 May 1984 on 'Embryo Tissue Samples and Dead Human Fetuses used for Therapeutic, Diagnostic and Scientific Purposes' (CCNE 1984), which considers the embryo to be a 'potential human being' – felt the need to 'prioritize the respect for the lives of these embryos, and attempt to ensure their survival and development by giving them to infertile couples under very carefully considered conditions'.

The latter are found in the law that establishes access to medically assisted procreation. It should be noted that in France, this access has expanded over time. Initially, in 2004, the Law in the Code of Public Health only granted access to embryo donation in exceptional cases: 'In exceptional cases, both members of the couple may sign a written agreement allowing the stored embryos to be hosted by another couple' (Art. L 2141-5, *Journal officiel* of 7 August 2004). Only couples 'for whom medically assisted procreation without recourse to a third-party donor is possible' could host an embryo (Art. L 2141-6, *Journal officiel* of 7 August 2004). Applications from couples in which one member is sterile and the other suffers from a hereditary genetic disease were also admissible according to the law. During the revision of the French bioethics laws in 2011, however, this article was changed. Now, 'a couple … can host an embryo only when medically assisted procreation techniques have been unsuccessful for the couple, or when the couple … renounces using ART' (Art. L 2141-6, as amended by Law No. 2011-814 of 7 July 2011, Art. 35). One must remember that in France it is forbidden to use both an egg and sperm donation (double donation). If both members of the couple are sterile, embryo donation is the only ART technique available to them.

Despite its revision, and the amendment that introduced the possibility for a couple to renounce intraconjugal ART and supposedly expanded access, the law also establishes a hierarchy that demonstrates the 'Recommendations for a Code of Practice for Embryos' issued by the French Agency of Biomedicine (ABM) in 2010. These recommendations stipulate that embryo hosting should only be a last resort, after the failure of all other attempts (ART within a married couple and ART with a third-party donor). The procedures governing access to embryo hosting are strictly codified, as evidenced by the two booklets written by the ABM (one for donor couples and one for recipient couples), which are distributed during the procedure and explain the terms and conditions of embryo hosting.

Any couple who has chosen to keep their embryos for a future parental project can later consider donating their embryos if they are no longer needed (in the case of IVF resulting in the birth of a child or children, for example, or because the couple has separated). Embryos destined for hosts must have been produced by couples composed of a woman under the age of thirty-eight and a man under the age of forty-five. The applications are examined by both a doctor and a biologist. If a couple chooses to donate their embryos, they must first sign a consent form. After three months of deliberation, the decision is made. In order to be considered valid, final consent must be recorded by the President of the High Court (Tribunal de grande instance, or TGI). In exceptional cases, the magistrate may ask to meet with the couple before confirming consent. The child born as a result of the embryo donation will be the child of the recipient couple; there is no possible familial link between the child and the couple who donated embryos. The donation, by law, is voluntary, anonymous and uncompensated.

Who can benefit from embryo donation? If both spouses suffer from infertility, are at risk of transmitting a genetic disease to their offspring, are unable to resort to other ART techniques for medical reasons or have already made unsuccessful attempts at these techniques, the medical team at an ART centre may propose embryo hosting to the couple. In order to engage in an ART technique with a third-party donor and establish filiation with the child or children born of the donation, they must first provide their signed consent to the President of the High Court (TGI), if they have not already done so. Next, the couple must obtain the authorization to host an embryo, signed by the President of the TGI and issued by the TGI.

It should be noted that doctors also have a great deal of leeway when it comes to ensuring access to embryo donation. This primarily affects the donors, as doctors are the ones who select prospective donors for couples who are candidates for embryo hosting. Doctors also note that it is extremely difficult to tell a couple that they cannot use their embryos. Two of the consultations that I observed in our study testify to this. In the first case, the couple disqualified themselves from the procedure before the doctors could issue a refusal, having alerted them to problematic genetic predispositions in the family. Relieved, the doctors could therefore say no without hesitation. In the second case, the two doctors preferred to postpone the refusal. Another couple whom I met tacitly understood that their embryos would not be accepted. 'I understand', the woman said to me, 'I don't think they're going to take them, but it's really hard – I almost feel like I'm killing my children'. The couple met with the doctors once more, as it was important for them to make sure that the doctors involved understood that this refusal was difficult for them. For those hoping to receive an embryo, it is also the doctors who ultimately decide whether or not to grant access to embryo hosting. Each applicant's file is reviewed during a team meeting. After taking into account medical criteria that are not only biological, but also social and psychological, the team decides to which couples they will offer access to embryo hosting. In the centre where I attended consultations, none of the requests for embryo hosting that were reviewed were made by recipient couples; in each case, the offer came from the doctors, who were in a position to evaluate how the couples renounce using intraconjugal ART as addressed by the law.

Finally, regarding access to this practice, it should also be noted that although an interview with a psychologist is only mandatory for recipient couples, this type of interview, which was observed in both centres, was also prescribed for donor couples. This decision, according to caregivers, is motivated by the very special nature of these kinds of donations. According to one doctor in the study, donor couples are, in a way, 'abandoning' their embryos, and embryo donation is a kind of 'prenatal adoption' (a term used elsewhere in systematic consultations to explain the reception of embryos to recipient couples). What is adopted in this case, however, is not a child: 'Look, I'm not saying that the embryo is a person', said one doctor, 'what I mean is that donating your embryos is like giving them up for adoption, so that's why I call it prenatal adoption'.

Doctors encountered in the study often showed a similar ambivalence towards the status of the embryo, and many questioned the decisions of the donor couples, reflecting a deep discomfort as well as the opinion that sometimes donors are not entirely aware of the implications of their decision. One gynaecologist believed that:

> Donors usually give up their embryos in the end, and it's clear that it's not always due to pure altruism .... Donors give because they're really disturbed by the idea of their surplus embryos being preserved in liquid nitrogen, but they're only clusters of cells. This debate in France has corrupted many patients' reasoning: it has created problems where there were none before. I personally feel that yes, people should have to approve the destruction or *ad vitam* conservation of their embryos, or for their donation to research, why not .... I usually understand where the recipients are coming from, but I cannot believe some donors.

It is in light of this ambiguity that we should consider access to and the use of embryo donation in France.

Thinking about the Embryo Makes It Real

How do the couples concerned, whether donors or recipients, understand access to embryo donation? First, one must consider the different representations these men and women have of the embryo, which may or may not inform each couple's approach to the procedure.[1] It should be noted that among the interviewees, many of them specified that prior to IVF they had never wondered what exactly constitutes an embryo. The temporality of the ART procedure, however, raises certain questions. Madeleine, a laboratory technician, said: 'For me, an embryo is a potential human being. Before, however, I never asked myself what exactly an embryo was. Before I had trouble conceiving, before being inseminated, before using IVF, I never questioned what an embryo was, even though I'm a scientist'.

Recipients often feel that as long as the child is not yet there, the embryo is simply reproductive material, and is not a child.[2] Temporality is fundamental here, but so is the moment in the ART procedure. Many recipients evoke a cellular representation of the embryo. Berthe, for example, explains: 'For me, an embryo is an embryo, period. I consider this embryo from a biological point of view. I do not even consider it a successful child. For me, it is a cluster of cells. So hosting an embryo is not so different from IVF. Our doctor calls it a "transplant"'. Conversely, among the donor couples I met, most were likely to represent the embryo as a kind of potential life which in no way belonged to them, but could eventually become a child. It is on this point that recipient couples see the difference: 'The goal', one man tells me, 'is to give people the chance to become parents. For me, it's also because this embryo is the beginning of a life – but the embryo is not a child in itself'.

During the study, my interviewees sometimes claimed to have been raised in the Catholic Church – of these men and women, few were still practising Catholics. Their representations of the embryo were not influenced by Catholic dogma, which would have led them to perceive of the embryo as a 'person'. It is with this mindset that Christian clinics such as 'Snowflakes', the centre studied by Chantal Collard and Shireen Kashmeri (Collard and Kashmeri 2011), implement embryo adoption programmes. If these people link the procedure to their Catholic values, it is rather within the context of the act of donating. Madeleine explains: 'I never considered the question of embryo donation as a Catholic. I don't know what the Church says about it. [*I explain that according to Catholic dogma, the embryo is a person*]. No, I didn't know that – that's not why I did it, nor why my husband did it, I believe .... On the other hand, if my values influenced my decision at all, it was in the act of giving, of reaching out to others to help'.

Generally, when I asked the couples who had decided to donate their embryos what those embryos meant to them, they often said that they were 'cells', 'cells that can create a child' and 'cells of the beginning of life', reflecting at least a rudimentary biological understanding. Some considered that the embryos were cells with a 'little something extra', or 'life', sometimes including the potential for a child or family that the embryo carried. Julie said: 'These embryos are cells that have multiplied for two days. I don't see that as a child .... Eventually, I would say that these embryos represent future or possible happiness ... but they are not children'. Being a parent changes the way the embryo is represented. When people who already have a child decide to donate their embryos rather than destroy them, it is often because they are now parents. Their status as parents changes the representations they previously had of the embryo. Pierre, with his child in his arms, says:

> Initially, when we started the whole process, when we started IVF, I considered these embryos simply as cells .... Since the birth of the twins, however, I can't just see them as cells .... Now that I've seen what an embryo can become, I can't imagine destroying the remaining embryos now. The embryo, even if it's not yet a child, is an embryo that can become a child. Destroying it would be like throwing it in the trash. It suddenly became clear to me: we had to give these embryos to another couple, and offer them the possibility of having a child like we did.

We must consider, then, another representation: the embryo as potential.

Finally, we must clarify that French conditions of access to embryo donation help to motivate donor couples. According to these couples, their donation is only possible in the French legal framework, which is very strict. By donating within this framework, these donors adhere to the cultural system in which they are also participants.[3]

Highly Regulated Access

As we have already mentioned, embryo donation is voluntary, free and anonymous in France. Couples who donate their embryos will not even know if the thawing has been successful, and will never be able to contact the couples who receive their embryos. The only information regarding donor couples that is communicated to recipient couples is the age of the woman (the word 'mother' is never mentioned) at the time of the embryo's conception. On the subject of anonymity, the men and women in our study tended to differ. The former seemed more attached to their anonymity, fearing that this embryo, if it were to become a child, might one day come 'knocking at the door and asking why we did this'. They feared being burdened down the line with a paternity that they did not want. 'Without anonymity, it's simple: I wouldn't have been able to do it', says Romain. In these cases, fatherhood is represented as something fragile, and independent of a deliberate act; something that can be imposed on them against their will. Women, reflecting society's dominant representations of gender,[4] take a more empathetic approach, focusing their discourse not on maternity, but precisely the person this embryo could become. Louise explains: 'I am attached to my anonymity, but I can understand that at a certain point, once a child has become an adult, he or she might want to know where they came from. I think it's a legitimate desire – I would understand. Although I must admit, I'd be mortified if that happened to me'.

Central to this issue of anonymity is of course the fear of a possible encounter between the child born of their donation and his/her siblings. This fear of incest, an unshakable taboo and phenomenon, points to the hypotheses proposed by Collard and Kashmeri (2011) relative to the Snowflakes programme, in which they note that there are many parents who insist that there are familial bonds between all of the children conceived in the same petri dish. Their study shows how new family ties are forged, and that genetic links are never perceived or experienced indifferently once they are known. In my study, these reservations were confirmed. Among the couples I met, this was the only reservation they carried with regard to anonymity. Josephine recounted that her sixteen-year-old daughter, to whom she had explained that she planned to donate her embryos, did not understand: 'She said she will have a brother or sister out there, and that they might cross paths later on. She said, "Imagine if my brother were to fall in love with his sister"'. Recipient couples find themselves confronted with these same questions. Sabine, for example, wonders: 'When it comes to anonymity, I'm kind of irrational. I think, what if one day he meets his siblings, and he doesn't know that they're his siblings? You never know. It would bother me if he wanted to marry someone one day, and had no way of knowing whether it was his brother or sister'.

With regard to this fear of incest, the power of certain stereotypes is apparent. Gérard, for example, said: 'Actually, there are several possible scenarios. We have a daughter, so by the time this works, there will be at least a seven-year difference between her and the boy that could come from our donation. I'm reassured by this, because a girl older than her husband is very rare, so there is little chance that my daughter will fall in love with a boy who turns out to be her brother'.

Donations are made and received in the same region, a fact that sometimes worries donors. One extreme case is that of Bernadette, who explained why anonymity scares her, and still makes her hesitate to donate her embryos:

> For me, the question of anonymity is very complicated. Actually, this is because of my particular family history. My grandmother had a child, my father. Up until he was twenty years old, my father was convinced that the man who lived with him was his father, his biological father. And then someone told him that the man who lived with him was not his biological father. From what he told me, the story ended there ... Later, I was born. I grew up and went to high school. And during my third or fourth year, I can't remember which, I met a boy. We spent a lot of time together .... My grandmother ended up finding out. I don't know why, but she had a kind of hunch, and asked my mother what his name was .... Finally, one day she explained that the grandfather of my friend was actually the father of my father. Suddenly, the boy and I had the same grandfather. It's an incredible story! So, when someone tells me that there is no chance that my children will meet their siblings conceived from our embryos, I take it with a grain of salt – I know that there is still a small chance.

Indeed, many elements, including temporality and personal history, need to be considered in order to understand what motivates or discourages donors.

In general, however, the donors I met in the study explained that these embryos were not a part of them; on the contrary, they existed as external entities. When justifying their donation, they often repeated that the relationship is not biological. Clarisse was one of the donors who felt this way: 'Parenthood is raising one's children. It's not genetic. I have friends who have adopted; they are as much parents as we are, because they encounter the same problems with their child as we do every day, and they receive and give as much love as we do'. Her husband Romain joined in: 'Being a parent means being present for my daughter, raising her, and teaching her things. It's more of an education. I am not the parent of the embryos. Ultimately, parenthood is not biological or genetic'.

Another interesting point to note: as was observed in Collard and Kashmeri's study, couples also brought up the issue of the interchangeability of cryopreserved embryos. They wondered about the coincidences of choice and luck that presided over the birth of their children: for example, one embryo could have been taken instead of another during the transfer. The one who was born, on the other hand, could have very well remained frozen and met another fate (Collard and Kashmeri 2011: 315). The idea is very unsettling, and can explain the very real discomfort of parents who still have surplus embryos. Fabrice told me that anonymity is a good thing, because 'if one day this child from our embryo comes to me and asks me why him, and not our child, I would be very uncomfortable'. Xavier seems to feel the same way: 'I would prefer not to know who receives the embryo. Otherwise, imagine: every time you see the child, you'll remember it was your embryo, and you'll look for similarities. Then you'll remember that the embryo was yours, but you didn't want it. You'll look at them and say "hey, he looks like his brother", but this one, we didn't want him. No, it's too weird!' How, then, are filiation and kinship understood? How does one gain the status of a parent?

Debiologized Kinship?

Donor couples often explain that kinship is not biological; what makes one a parent is the act of raising a child. Madeleine confirmed this point of view: 'The decision to raise a child outweighs the biological aspects of parenthood'. Bernadette, who still hesitates to donate, feels the same way: 'For me, the relationship is not biological. Being a parent is raising a child, being with him every day, and helping him grow'.

The fear of a sort of irrevocable biologization explains why these donor couples are so attached to their anonymity, otherwise they would not be able to participate in the process – but their biological link to the child could come back to haunt them without the protection of anonymity. One woman expressed her belief that 'anonymity is also important. It's a cliché, but I wouldn't want the child to come knocking on my door one day, saying they're my son or daughter. It's cliché, but hey, it's true – I'd be horrified. I'd say, who, me? It's not blood and genes that make a family, it's relationships'. Often, knowing what they would say to this child if he or she were to show up later on is problematic, even though it is not even they who would choose which embryo was to be transferred, but biologists and doctors.

If parenthood is therefore not biological, what distinguishes embryo donation, where there is no genetic link with the child's parents, from adoption? For those who receive embryos, the difference is significant, even if their doctor uses the term 'prenatal adoption' when describing embryo hosting. Recipient couples, and above all women recipients, explain that pregnancy makes parenthood 'natural' and, by extension, makes them mothers 'like the others'. This incorporation reintroduces biology and somewhat renaturalizes procreation. Berthe considers: 'With adoption, there is a veil of secrecy. With embryo donation, there's the fact of having carried the child for nine months: even if he or she does not have our genes, even if he or she got nothing from us, that's still something. It's less mysterious than adoption. As for pregnancy, it's something I share with the child, as well as with my spouse'. Thus, reproduction becomes a 'natural' activity again. Access to parenthood through gestation is visible to the public (pregnancy is in full view of everyone, though it doesn't indicate the method of conception) and makes these parents potentially 'normal' parents. Pregnancy is thus part of a strategy that normalizes the creation of a child conceived by ART (Becker 2000; Mathieu 2013). Interestingly, the man is also associated with the pregnancy in this case (Becker 2000).

This is what Alain points out: 'We had thought about adopting, but in the end we wanted the child to look a little more like us, like the both of us. Even if this embryo didn't come from us, there is the pregnancy – the child will grow in Alice's body, and I'll be there during the pregnancy'. Alice, his wife, agreed: 'Carrying the child allows me to think of the child as my own. I'm more certain of my maternity. When one adopts, it's adoption. Since I'm carrying the child, I have pictures of me when I'm pregnant .... There's a link that's created when the pregnancy is certain and out in the open. And as a woman, I want to experience pregnancy. Without this pregnancy, I wouldn't quite be a mother'. Barthélémy said: 'For me, with embryo hosting there's a pregnancy, my wife carries the child – it's totally biological'. Kamel felt the same way: 'It doesn't matter that the embryo comes from another couple; it doesn't bother me because it will be in my wife .... She'll be pregnant and that's what's important. For me, pregnancy will make her a real mother'. Zora, his wife, immediately corrected him: 'I don't like it when you say "real mother". You should say "mom", period. I'm his mom'. Pregnancy therefore provides access to parenthood, which becomes normalized. And though he reveals certain shortcomings with regard to his understanding of biology, Fabrice is overjoyed by the pregnancy: 'You're carrying him. He'll look like you'. By proclaiming this, he reveals the sparse knowledge he has of genetics, because the fact of carrying a child does not mean that said child is carrying your genes and thus will look like you.

With regard to the hesitation to adopt, testimonies in our study also shed light on the difficult experiences the process entails, as well as the fact that it is extremely strict and expensive in France. 'We can't afford to adopt', said Sandrine. Many will only turn to adoption once every other option has failed. It is also the difficulty in accessing adoption that often informs the request for access to embryo donation. This upsets one doctor: 'I believe that embryo donation has become a kind of ART technique, because we no longer have the motivation to improve adoption in France'. Many request access to embryo hosting because they are unable to access adoption through the French system.

All of the interviewees in our study, however, insisted that they consider parenthood as inherently biological, and in a sense they are right. Laurence and Luc agree on this point. For Luc, 'part of being a family is having a home and a roof, and belonging to a family circle that is both nuclear and extended .... The family is a space that helps you grow'. And for Laurence: 'The family is not necessarily made up of brothers, sisters, and blood relatives. It's not always biological'. According to Sabine: 'At first, I considered parenthood as genetic. But I soon realized that I wouldn't be able to live without children – so, I'd like to think there's a kind of parenthood that isn't genetic'. The passage of time and the failure of these men and women to have children through biological means changes their representations of kinship, and expands the range of options available to them.

For Berthe: 'The experience of being a parent must be lived. Being a parent is being there for every moment of every day in the child's life. It's passing on a little bit of us to the child, even if the embryo didn't come from us. Our psychiatrist told us that there is nothing of us in the embryo. For me, this is not an issue, it's not a problem .... What matters to me is that we'll share things with him, see him grow, learn things from him, and be with him'. If we were to remove the biological aspect of parenthood, and instead consider it through the lens of education and the transmission of values, then it is possible to accommodate an embryo. But carrying an embryo (and, therefore, gestation in general) 'renaturalizes' parenthood. This can help to explain the ambivalence of both recipient couples and donor couples.

In France, access is limited to heterosexual couples who have failed to conceive using ART and couples who suffer from a genetic predisposition that could cause problems for the mother or the child. In this context, access to embryo hosting is motivated largely by empathy. What, then, motivated the people I met in the study, in their opinions about whether or not access to embryo hosting should be extended to single women or homosexuals?

Acceptance of Contemporary Family Models

Reflecting the findings of a previous study (Mathieu 2013), the majority of the people I interviewed were open to new family models.[5] Interestingly, most of the donors (with one exception) said that they would not be opposed to donating their embryos to homosexual women. For Lucien, a prospective donor, 'It's a question of life, and if it's alive, it can bring joy to another couple, so why wouldn't you donate? And I would be fine with donating to single women or lesbian couples – I have no problem with that. The bottom line is that this living being helps another living being become a parent'. Julie, his wife, added: 'Not to flatter myself, but I think that once we decided to donate, it showed that we were tolerant people. Donors in general seem to be open-minded .... Everyone is entitled to happiness. And if that happiness means having children, it doesn't bother me if the person is homosexual. To donate your embryos, you have to be open-minded'. Gerard said: 'If the embryos are already there, why not donate them to single women or homosexuals? They can be good parents just like anyone else ...'. Romain said: 'I wouldn't have a problem with donating our embryos to single or homosexual women. I assume that if someone has reached the stage where they're willing to accept embryos that aren't their own, they have a desire to have children, and a capacity for love – and that's what makes one a parent'.

Most of those waiting for a donated embryo are also in favour of this kind of access, but on the condition that certain hierarchies be imposed. Berthe, for whom IVF has failed several times, would 'support access to embryo hosting for single and homosexual women, but after having gone through this whole process, I admit that I've become a little selfish and have my reservations. Single and homosexual women should have access, but only after all the straight couples have had their turn'. Myriam, whose husband suffers from a genetic disease, echoed Berthe's sentiment: 'Why not, but I want to have my child before they do. If gays want access to ART, they'll have to wait until after my husband and I do. I know, that's a bit selfish .... They could be good parents, but that's not the issue'. The scarcity of embryos available for donation has motivated them to establish hierarchies with regard to access.

When people oppose access to embryo hosting for single women and homosexual couples, they often refer to representations of the traditional family. Yvette, who had just donated her embryos, believes that: 'It would bother me a bit if these embryos were given to a single woman or a lesbian couple. I admit that I would be especially uncomfortable if they were given to a lesbian couple. For me, a family is made up of a father, a mother, and children'. Emeline is even more decided on the issue: 'I'm not for opening ART to homosexuals .... I'm not really into the idea of homosexual parents. If we give gay women access to ART, what's stopping us from opening access to gay men too? ... From a moral standpoint, I can't support it'. To these people, embryo donation must be accessed within a framework that respects 'natural' representations of parenthood.

We can therefore conclude that access to embryo hosting in France is selective, but nevertheless allows for the renewal of the traditional avenues for building a family, despite the ambiguous status of surplus embryos. In France, both embryo donors and recipients are in the process of reimagining the family. Extending access to embryo hosting is not inconceivable to them, even if it is clear that national cultures influence their representations of kinship.

Séverine Mathieu is Full Professor at École pratique des hautes études (EPHE, PSL), and Chair of Sociology of Religions in the Contemporary World. Over the past several years, her research has focused on the ethical issues of reproductive biotechnologies. She is now working on religious mobilizations underway during the debate in France of the revision of its bioethics laws, as well as on the representations of embryos in assisted reproductive practices.

Notes

1. In the future, I plan to study couples who decide to have their embryos destroyed, or donate them for research purposes.
2. On this subject, see also Mathieu 2013 and Giraud 2014 and 2015.
3. For more on the influence of culture on approaches to ART, see Becker 2000: 218–35.
4. Regarding gender and gamete donation, see Almeling 2011.
5. About these models, see Porqueres i Gené 2009.

References

Agence de la biomédecine (ABM). 2015. *Le rapport médical et scientifique de l'assistance médicale à la procréation et de la génétique humaines en France.* https://www.agence-biomedecine.fr/annexes/bilan2015/donnees/procreation/01-amp/synthese.htm. Accessed 29 June 2019.

Almeling, Rene. 2011. *Sex Cells: The Medical Market for Eggs and Sperm.* Berkeley: University of California Press.

Bateman, Simone, and Tania Salem. 1998. 'Embedding the Embryo', in John Harris and Soren Holm (eds), *The Future of Human Reproduction: Ethics, Choice and Regulation*. Oxford: Oxford University Press, pp. 101–26.

Becker, Gay. 2000. *The Elusive Embryo: How Women and Men Approach New Reproductive Technologies*. Berkeley: University of California Press.

Boltanski, Luc. 2004. *La condition fœtale: Une sociologie de l'engendrement et de l'avortement.* Paris: Gallimard.

Bruno, Catherine, Charlotte Dudkiewicz-Sibony, Isabelle Berthaut et al. 2016. 'Survey of 243 ART Patients Having Made a Final Disposition Decision about Their Surplus Cryopreserved Embryos: The Crucial Role of Symbolic Embryo Representation', *Human Reproduction* 31 (7): 1508–14.

CCNE. 1984. Avis no. 1. 'Avis sur les prélèvements de tissus d'embryons et de foetus humains morts, à des fins thérapeutiques, diagnostiques et scientifiques. Rapport'. https://www.ccne-ethique.fr/sites/default/files/publications/avis001.pdf. Accessed 29 June 2019.

CCNE. 1989. Avis no. 18. 'Etat des études conduites par le Comité concernant les dons de gamètes et d'embryons'. https://www.ccne-ethique.fr/sites/default/files/publications/avis018.pdf. Accessed 29 June 2019.

Collard, Chantal, and Shireen Kashmeri. 2011. 'Embryo Adoption: Emergent Forms of Siblingship among Snowflakes Families', *American Ethnologist* 38 (2): 307–22.

Giraud, Anne-Sophie. 2014. 'L'embryon humain en AMP, éléments pour une approche relationnelle', *Enfances, Familles, Générations* 21: 48–69.

Giraud, Anne-Sophie. 2015. 'Les statuts de l'être anténatal: un processus d'humanisation "relationnel": Assistance médicale à la procréation et

mort périnatale', Thèse d'anthropologie sous la direction de Dominique Memmi et Irène Théry, EHES.
Mathieu, Séverine. 2013. *L'enfant des possibles: AMP, éthique religion et filiation*. Paris: Editions de l'Atelier.
Mathieu, Séverine. 2017. 'Donner et recevoir des embryons en France', *Ethnologie Française*, 'Le corps reproductif' 167(3): 499–508.
Porqueres i Gené, Enric (ed.). 2009. Défis contemporains de la parenté. Paris: Éditions de l'EHESS.
Porqueres i Gené, Enric. 2016. 'Parenté et biotechnologies', *Journal des Anthropologues*, 'Parentés contemporaines', Séverine Mathieu, Mélanie Gourarier (eds), 144–45: 29–52.
Thompson, Charis. 2005. *Making Parents: The Ontological Choreography of Reproductive Technologies*. Cambridge, MA: MIT Press.

Chapter 4

ACCESS TO ART IN FRANCE AND BELGIUM

THE STANDPOINT OF FOUR ART PRACTITIONERS

Jennifer Merchant

This chapter will highlight the stark differences in ART practices and access in two countries that share the same border, the same language and the same demand for access to infertility treatment. Based on four in-depth interviews, the chapter summarizes and proceeds with a contextualized analysis of each one. All four practitioners were asked the same questions: where and when did you begin your studies in medicine; when and why did you become more particularly interested and specialized in assisted reproductive technologies; please provide a description of your typical work day; what are the socio-economic profiles of your patients; what is your point of view concerning the legislation in your country and in France/Belgium governing access to ART and how do you work with/around it?

Belgium: Dr Autin and Dr de Sutter

Candice Autin, OB-GYN, Director of the Saint-Pierre Hospital Infertility Clinic, Brussels

Personal Background

Candice Autin completed the equivalent of a French Bac S in Belgium, but was also extremely active in sports, notably athletics at a competitive level, and was often injured. After each injury, her sports doctor seemed to make everything right, and Candice began thinking to herself, 'this is really amazing, understanding how the human body works and fixing it'. She exchanged a lot on the matter with her sports doctor, and finally announced to her family that she wanted to go to medical school. At first, her family was reluctant, telling her 'the studies last many years, you're a woman…', and her professors were disappointed because they had always seen her embarking upon studies in a prestigious Polytechnical Institute of Higher Education. However, for Candice, once she decided she wanted to be a doctor, nothing would stop her.

During her medical studies, she automatically thought that she would eventually specialize as a sports physician; she changed her mind after her internship in an OB-GYN service, part of a series of compulsory internships in all hospital services before obtaining one's diploma. Before this particular experience in OB-GYN, she had said to herself, 'either I'll hate it or I'll love it', and she loved it. It combined all the aspects of medical care she appreciated: doctor–patient contact, surgical acts and the magic of helping a woman bring a child into the world. The fact that she was in a small maternity ward and not a huge hospital structure meant that as an intern she was able to deliver babies under the supervision of obstetricians. In her last year of medical school, she opted to do another internship in an OB-GYN service, and made her final decision to go into that field.

Her first three years of specialization took place in a Belgian public hospital, and she completed her medical internship after an additional two years at the Saint-Pierre University research hospital. She discovered how infertility treatment was being launched in the pioneer ward of that Belgian hospital. Once her specialization was completed, the director of the Saint-Pierre infertility ward offered to take Dr Autin on for three half-days a week, and she obtained partial leave to do so from her permanent hospital employer. The two hospitals had already established a collaborative network in neonatology, and Candice's part-time presence at Saint-Pierre would serve to enlarge and enrich this collaboration, in proximity both geographically and philosophically.

Early Practice/Beginning of Her Career

Saint-Pierre counts approximately three thousand births per year, and is aiming at five thousand in the future. Dr Autin focused her consultations and treatment on patients with infertility problems under the auspices of Annick Delvigne. Her work was accompanied by the already-existing psycho-social ward that was established in 1993, also by Annick Delvigne (along with the psychiatrist Marie-Laure Gustin), called 'Listening with Four Ears' , the name of the technique used by this ward and whose objective was to assist infertile patients. The initial and ongoing objective of this psycho-social ward is that every single request for infertility treatment must be 'heard by four ears': those of a psychologist and those of a specialist in somatic behaviour. For the OB-GYNs, it is a means to confront their limits *in situ*, in other words to make the choice not to have arbitrary limits based on, say, religious principles, but rather at each session to truly hear the patient's request, reflect upon it, and then decide in a collegial manner whether to go ahead with the treatment.

From a personal standpoint, Dr Autin felt ambivalence *a priori* in proceeding with access to ART for homosexual couples or single persons. However, after participating in numerous sessions, she was struck by the sheer humanity and wealth of exchanges between the psychologists, patients and OB-GYNs, so much so that her ambivalence was quickly replaced by the certainty that only in encountering patients and hearing their stories and requests could one make the right decision. In 2007, Annick Delvigne left the centre, asking Candice to replace her, which she did. It was quite a leap for her – she was only thirty-three years old and had recently given birth to her second child in 2006. But the entire team was behind her, including the other OB-GYN and the pioneer nurses of the first IVF babies who had been there since 1983.

Today, Dr Autin oversees the same group of staff minus one nurse who retired. All available techniques are employed in the centre, including Intra-Cytoplasmic Sperm Injection (ICSI, launched in 2003). This practice, controversial from the start due to lack of public and political debate on the matter, is also of concern to Dr Autin's ward. They practise what is called 'half-ICSI', that is to say if the man's sperm is sufficient in quantity (approximately 100,000 spermatozoids are needed to fertilize one oocyte), or does not have the best motility figures, they consider that the infertility problem might lay elsewhere, and so they proceed with ICSI on half of the retrieved oocytes and attempt 'normal' fertilization with the other half.

How Is a Typical Consultation Carried Out?

Situated in Brussels, in the heart of Europe and home to so many nationalities, immigrant or otherwise, Dr Autin's ward receives patients from all walks of life and of all ethnic origins. This largely motivated her choice to work at Saint-Pierre. Her patients include people in high-level positions at the European Commission as well as poorly educated Guinean immigrants, and all bring to the ward a wealth of experiences and encounters. Indeed, present in the Saint-Pierre ethical charter is the endeavour not to demonstrate medical authoritarianism, and this is why all decisions to begin infertility treatment are made by the whole staff. Also among them are patients who have tried for two years to become pregnant and have never had an infertility evaluation, and those sent by their personal OB-GYN who had already proceeded with this type of evaluation. The average maximum wait to obtain an appointment is approximately one month, but during certain periods delays can reach two to three months. After the necessary battery of tests are performed, a treatment plan is proposed to the patients; it can vary from simply monitoring a woman's ovulation over a period of time to see whether the problem originates there, to IVF and ICSI when none of the intermediary techniques have worked. Dr Autin always tells her patients at each step of the way that it is their decision, not hers.

Belgian law does not impose required meetings with a psychologist, but each infertility centre is required to propose such an encounter to all patients who are soon to undergo ART and provide for it if the patients request it. That being said, for treatment that involves gamete donation, surrogacy or any situation that makes the practitioner feel uncomfortable – for example advanced maternal age, a diagnosed psychiatric disorder, a particular married situation such as polygamy – a psychologist is automatically asked to speak with the patient(s) and participate in staff discussion as to whether or not to go ahead with the treatment.

This of course means that some patients are denied access to treatment, though this is rare. This decision is made after a series of role-playing sessions with the psychologist and the patient(s), which is presented as a means of assisting the patient(s) and not a means of evaluating or passing judgement on their future capacity as parents. The staff simply explain to the patient(s) that they are engaging upon a very particular request for medical treatment and as such the staff want to accompany them towards making the right decision. The psychologist plays the role of the child-to-be and asks questions of the future parents about how they see their role as parents. Patients are often destabilized, especially single patients. Following these exercises, if the staff are uneasy with the request, they meet with the patient(s) and justify their refusal to take them on.

For same-sex couples, the staff are not inspired by traditional psychological analyses that call for a male and female couple; they are quite aware of longstanding international sociological and psychological studies that refute this 'necessity' for the well-being of the child. These studies, considered by many practitioners in France to be 'activist' literature, are not received in this way at all because, according to Dr Autin, the staff see patients in reality and base their decisions on who their patients are. That being said, the staff do discuss the importance of a 'third party' with same-sex couples, a person who will enable the child to get past fusion with her/his mother(s). Indeed, there are as many heterosexual couples who argue, separate and divorce as same-sex couples, so the question of sexual orientation is irrelevant.

All in all, the majority of patients tell the staff that encounters with the psychological team are beneficial and helped them to find and use the appropriate words when explaining the situation to their respective families.

How Is This Financed?

In Belgium, the system differs slightly from France. Six IVF attempts are covered, but not 100 per cent. Each patient/couple has six IVF attempts financed over their procreative lifetime, not just per child. That being said, Belgium is of course less strict than France regarding selection criteria. A heterosexual couple with a poor prognosis of becoming pregnant, lesbian couples and single persons all have a greater chance of accessing IVF in Belgium than in France. This probably explains the high rate of French patients receiving treatment at Saint-Pierre. They are generally sent to Saint-Pierre by their own French OB-GYNs. Indeed, approximately 60 per cent of patients on Dr Autin's ward are French, bearing in mind that these only concern requests for sperm donation. For more 'classical' treatment such as IUI (Intra-Uterine Insemination) and IVF (In-Vitro Fertilization) the percentage of French patients is much smaller.

As for other techniques, Dr Autin refers to the practice of surrogacy, which is not prohibited in Belgium but tolerated. In her ward, she follows approximately five surrogacy family configurations per year, in other words very few. She is always astonished at the French obsession with a technique that is not widely practised. Meanwhile, another technique in France that was approved with hardly any debate at all – uterus transplants – is far from being realized in Belgium. On the other hand, Dr Autin's ward is receiving increasing demands from transgender persons M-F who want to freeze their sperm in Belgium before undergoing their transition.

The Future

Ideally, Dr Autin would like to see an end to cross-border practices that favour only the wealthy living in more prohibitive countries who come to Belgium. Not only does this context reveal levels of tolerance that are discriminatory, but from a public health and juridical standpoint, it is dangerous for both the couple and the ensuing child. Dr Autin would like to see the European Commission grab this issue by the horns and pass a European Directive that would govern all access to ART in the twenty-eight countries, one that extracts these practices from the market and creates a robust juridical framework for access to ART for all, no matter their gender, religious, ethnic, national and/or sexual orientation, as long as the role of medical intervention to help these patients is justified (hence including single women who prefer turning to a medical ward for artificial insemination rather than 'do-it-yourself-kits' or 'ART-With-Friends').

Petra de Sutter, OB-GYN, Professor of Gynaecology at Ghent University, Head of the Department of Reproductive Medicine at Ghent University Hospital

Personal Background

Dr de Sutter became involved in ART 'by accident', as she says. She studied medicine at Ghent University and then went for specialized training in gynaecology and obstetrics. As a medical undergraduate student, she worked in two laboratories, firstly as a voluntary researcher in a lab of physiology and histology, and secondly in a lab of rheumatology. There she learned how to process tissues and culture cells and work with *in vitro* culture systems. Her first years in gynaecology training coincided with the start of the Ghent University IVF laboratory (1986–88). Because of her lab experience working on cells and tissues *in vitro*, she was very quickly asked to run the IVF laboratory.

Dr de Sutter hesitated because what she really felt she wanted to do was deliveries; she had just performed her first hysterectomy and felt that gynaecology and obstetrics were her calling. At the same time, Dr de Sutter was passionate about scientific research and her experience working in the laboratories was enriching and challenging. She therefore went on to study infertility treatment in the US, completed two new medical PhDs in the field and produced six publications in the following year. Her research focused on determining factors for fertilization of human oocytes looking at unfertilized oocytes and their chromosomes, the genetics of oocytes in mice and in humans, preimplantation genetic diagnosis and polar body biopsies. After completing her second PhD in 1994, she agreed to head the infertility clinic at Ghent University Hospital, starting off with a very small unit – four members of staff altogether – and began her infertility consultations. For the past twenty-one years, she has been both an OB-GYN and a researcher in reproductive medicine.

Practice, Development and Patient Profiles

During her first ten years, Dr de Sutter focused on pre-natal consultations, obstetrics and surgery, but became more and more involved in fundamental research as well. This eventually led her to abandon surgery due to lack of time, and she now essentially focuses on reproductive medicine.

When Dr de Sutter began intensifying her work in reproductive medicine, most of her patients came from Ghent and the surrounding areas; they were heterosexual couples who had stopped using contraception for a while and still could not get pregnant. Dr de Sutter would carry out the normal protocol for diagnosis and then prescribe either hormone stimulation, artificial insemination or, finally, IVF. As the years went by, her ward began receiving more problematic cases involving heterosexual couples, but also requests from same-sex couples and single people. Today, 50 per cent of her centre's patients are from abroad. Waiting times are rather long because her centre has come to be known as highly qualified in treating complicated cases of infertility. That being said, Dr de Sutter and her colleagues were not satisfied with the fact that their University Hospital, a public health institution, was no longer catering to the patient population around Ghent, who were subjected to the same waiting times as foreign patients. They therefore set up two waiting lists, one for local Belgian and 'uncomplicated' infertility cases and one for patients from abroad with more complex infertility issues. Hence, Belgian patients have shorter waiting times.

Most of the centre's international group of patients come from the Netherlands, even though there are excellent infertility treatment centres in that country. However, it has always been slightly behind other countries in implementing new technology, for example oocyte freezing or TESE, which is a testicular biopsy using ICSI. Indeed, the case of ICSI is salient. The use of this technique was developed in Belgium (the injection of the sperm into the oocyte), and the Ghent Hospital was experiencing its first ICSI pregnancies in 1993, while in the Netherlands, the technique only started to be used from 1995. Long waiting lists and difficult access to ICSI encouraged many Dutch people to visit the Ghent centre, closer to them than centres in Brussels. In addition, Dutch patients only benefit from three infertility treatment reimbursements and are refused by centres even if they want to continue at their own expense. Dutch patients also express dissatisfaction with the medical community in their country, claiming they do not take the time to explain the details of the treatment and other options.

From a socio-economic standpoint, Dr de Sutter's patients, especially if they come from the Netherlands, are highly educated, professionally successful and financially well-off. It is rare that she treats persons from immigrant groups, who usually go to public assistance hospitals; those living in Ghent go to Comer (OCMW/ Openbaar Centrum voor Maatschappelijk Welzijn [social services]). Hence, the majority of her patients are from relatively upper middle classes, and this is mostly due to the influx of patients from abroad.

Dr de Sutter also receives patients from Germany, though most of them go to the east of Belgium, to Henkel, Ghent or Lowen. The ward also receives patients from France, from Lille or Paris, mostly on referral by their French doctors, because her centre is well known for its expertise and success; however, most French patients go to Brussels. That being said, Dr de Sutter works in collaboration with centres in Brussels, particularly in the realm of non-anonymous egg donation, which is not allowed in France, and of course with lesbian couples who request access to artificial insemination. Indeed, most of the French patients whom Dr de Sutter sees come to Belgium for legal reasons and not necessarily complex infertility issues.

Her ward also receives patients from the UK, notably because she has developed a technique called artificial oocyte activation. This is carried out in the event of using ICSI with sperm that lacks an activating protein (phosphazesizeta), which in turn does not activate the oocyte. Because the sperm is not able to activate the oocyte, it requires a certain form of chemical reaction. Her research centre developed a variety of diagnostic tests in this area and subsequently designed a protocol to overcome this deficiency in activation. The Ghent centre worked in collaboration on this technique with British researchers in Oxford, but the British are not allowed to carry out this form of artificial oocyte activation, so UK patients come to Belgium.

The Financial Cost

Dr de Sutter could carry out consultations outside of her hospital and charge several hundred euros, and could likely attract patients from abroad. However, Belgium has fixed prices for all infertility treatment. Patients get six reimbursed IVF cycles, and doctors are not allowed to ask for one cent more than the amount that has been fixed in the reimbursement. This is a national policy, whether in a Catholic hospital, a public hospital or a university hospital (like Ghent University Hospital). Private infertility clinics in Belgium usually charge ten times more than the costs incurred in a public hospital for treatment, and cater to the wealthiest of clients, both Belgian and foreign, because people often think that if it is more expensive, it is more successful, which statistics clearly refute.

The Evolution in Infertility Treatment over the Past Thirty Years

Dr de Sutter's assessment is based on both medical and sociological observations. Thirty years ago, fertility treatment was there for infertility problems in heterosexual couples with blocked fallopian tubes or poor sperm. Today, it is technology that is broadly available for so many other indications that are more sociologically based than before, for example availability in Belgium for single women, lesbian couples or gay couples. This is a positive evolution according to Dr de Sutter. In addition, whether you are a lesbian or single or heterosexual woman, we now observe that women tend to be older when they come for treatment, and when they have their first child. This is also a new sociological factor to take into account. Women study and start careers today, and it takes more time for them to find the right partner. Women struggle with this in our societies, and many in the medical community stigmatize them because they didn't start earlier to try to have children. This is not Dr de Sutter's position; she believes that our modern societies should do their utmost to allow women to have both a career and children, and to be able to raise them, which she feels is not currently the case.

Oocyte vitrification came on the scene as a partial solution to this general societal problem. When it started five years ago in Belgium, Dr de Sutter was rather excited about it. Now she harbours second thoughts about access and social inequality, as it is a very expensive procedure. Not all thirty-year-old women can pay several thousand euros to have it done. In addition, it is often presented as a guarantee for having a child later, a sort of insurance policy, which it definitely is not. Indeed, because of low success rates, it should not serve as an incentive for women to postpone childbirth.

Dr de Sutter also has issues with companies like Apple, Facebook and Google who pay for their employees' egg freezing while these women are in their most productive years. These women work hard for their companies, thinking that egg freezing is going to work. This raises serious moral and ethical questions. These companies would be better off building day care centres inside company walls rather than spending their money on egg freezing.

Like her colleague Dr Autin, Dr de Sutter would like to see a European law governing ART practices and access, but as a member of the European Parliament, she does not believe that this will ever happen. Europe would first need to find a common political and social ideal to follow, and this is far from being the case. This of course means that we will never be able to prevent cross-border practices and the discriminatory situations they engender. On the contrary, she sees a conservative backlash against some of the more scandalous cross-border practices we witness in some Eastern and Southern European countries, the idea that if we prohibit or abolish on a European level, it would work better than trying to frame a pragmatic and protective governance architecture for Europeans in the realm of ART. One only needs to look at the backlash relative to LGBT rights to see that we are leaning more towards prohibition than framing of ART policies. Pro-active anti-migrant and anti-LGBT parties are spreading, and their influence in the EU is growing.

France: Dr Jouannet and Dr Neuraz

Pierre Jouannet, Honorary Professor of Medicine, Specialist of Reproductive Biology

Pierre Jouannet was a medical student in Paris in the 1960s, a time of political upheaval not only in Paris but around the world. He participated with other medical students and physicians in the creation of the first family planning centre for students, providing information on contraception and abortion, an audacious thing to do knowing that both were illegal at the time. He continued on to teach Histology and Embryology at the Université Paris-Sud

(UFR Kremlin-Bicêtre, 1969–94), where he became Full Professor in 1986. He participated in 1973 in the creation of the first CECOS (Centre d'étude et de conservation des oeufs et du sperme/Centre for the Conservation of Gametes) with Dr Georges David. Meanwhile, his research activities focused on the fundamental, clinical and ethical aspects of assisted reproductive technologies. In 1994, he moved on with his team to head the Laboratory of Embryology Histology and Reproductive Biology at the Cochin-Saint Vincent de Paul Hospital (1994–2010) and also headed their sperm bank. He and his team were among the first French researchers to look more closely at the decline in sperm quality, and they were the first French physicians to treat transgender persons requesting ART. This was the topic of our exchange.

The first time a couple (one member having transitioned from female to male, F-M) came to see Dr Jouannet was in the early 1990s. They were requesting access to artificial insemination via donor sperm (AID). The couple consisted of a man and a woman, and the man was the person who had undergone transition from F-M, hence he could not have children; he could not produce sperm since he had no testis (having been sterilized prior to the transition). The couple were married and the civil status of the man had been legally recognized and enacted (change of name, etc.). Being exposed for the first time to this kind of situation, Dr Jouannet felt uncomfortable about proceeding. After lengthy discussions with his staff, they decided to take on the case. From a legal standpoint, they were not violating any law as the latter states that a medical team can provide ART to a 'heterosexual couple living together and suffering from infertility', which was precisely the case. Hence, for Dr Jouannet and his team, the questions they asked themselves during their discussions were not of a legal nature, but focused on other issues: how to inscribe this project of having a child in this man's life course? Was this a parental project of this man or of the time when he was a woman? And how did the wife feel about having a child with a person who had changed sex? What did it mean to her? What was the history of this couple? The team also asked itself questions about other people in their lives, family and friends. How did they feel about this situation? And last but not least, most importantly of all for the team was the issue of the well-being of the future child. What would be the consequences for this child if s/he found out that her/his father had previously been a woman? All these questions were put on the table and in the end they decided to go ahead with the couple's request.

Soon after, a second and then a third couple came to consult Dr Jouannet: the same configuration, a heterosexual couple wherein the man had previously been a woman and had transitioned and now needed a sperm donor for his partner. At around the same time, a few of France's public and university hospitals had created ethics committees to assist practitioners with any issues they might meet. Dr Jouannet got in touch with the Espace éthique de l'Assistance publique-Hôpitaux de Paris (http://www.espace-ethique.org) and took part in a sub-group on transgender issues. It was important for Dr Jouannet to discuss the issue in a pluridisciplinary group that in the end included fertility practitioners, other medical physicians, legal scholars, psychologists/psychiatrists and philosophers. In light of a slightly growing demand, a study protocol was proposed and approved by the sub-group (Jouannet 2014; Chiland et al. 2013).

The protocol put in place was almost the same as that for 'traditional' heterosexual couples requesting access to ART. First, the couple consulted with Dr Jouannet, then encountered and discussed their project with a psychologist working in the CECOS. During these two encounters, all the questions that were asked in regard to a 'traditional' heterosexual couple's request for sperm donation – their story and their parental project – were the same for a transgender couple. The latter, however, then had a second interview with a psychiatrist who had clinical experience in consultations with transgender persons in areas other than infertility/fertility issues. Following these three encounters, the team then discussed the case with the other members of staff. Dr Jouannet established the principle that if one member of the team who had encountered the couple had a valid argument to refuse treatment, and that this argument was persuasive to the rest of the team, the decision would be to refuse treatment. None of the arguments to refuse treatment were based on the transgender parameter of the couple, and all couples accepted the team's motivated decision either for or against treatment. Last but not least, before beginning treatment – and this is another difference with 'traditional' heterosexual couples – Dr Jouannet proposed to the couple that they and the ensuing child have follow-ups on a regular basis after birth and over a period of several years. There was no obligation to comply, and if the couple refused, this had no impact on whether they would receive treatment or not.

The acceptance of transgender couples and the establishment of Dr Jouannet's protocol met with great resistance and even strong criticism from the majority of other CECOS across France. There were approximately twenty-two centres around the country that were used to working with various reproductive medical teams, and many of them refused to transfer the transsexual persons requesting AID to Dr Jouannet's ward. A certain number of psychologists and psychiatrists publicly expressed their vehement opposition to this practice. Some of the CECOS refused to even receive these couples in consultation; the few who saw no objection would send them to Dr Jouannet's ward in order to include them in the protocol.

Today, things have evolved considerably and several CECOS now agree to work with reproductive medical centres for F-M couple configurations in accordance with the protocol Dr Jouannet put in place. Demand has never been very high, however; in 2007, when Dr Jouannet retired from practice, the Cochin Hospital CECOS had taken on eighty-six cases. Among them, sixteen couples (18.6 per cent) had abandoned treatment for a variety of reasons, and five requests had been refused (one because the man had not completed his civil status legal documentation, three others because the wife was too old, and one because the man demonstrated severe psychopathological disorders). Among the sixty-five couples who were treated, eight were taken on by their local CECOS. For the remaining fifty-seven, they followed up at the Cochin Hospital CECOS establishment. Thirty-two couples had become parents through AID in 2010; twenty among them had one child, eleven had two children, and one couple had four children.

In his experience, Dr Jouannet never treated M-F couple configurations. In the French context, this would be legally impossible. The M-F living with a man needs to have recourse to both egg donation and surrogacy, and the latter is prohibited in France; the M-F living with a woman (hence a lesbian couple) needs recourse to sperm donation, which is also prohibited in France because only heterosexual couples have access to ART.

Concerning access to ART for M-F couple configurations wherein the man previously froze his sperm before transition (doing so either in Belgium or the United States, as it is prohibited in France for reasons other than to preserve a man's fertility before medical treatment), the debate is still ongoing. Beyond the fact that access to ART would be legally impossible for this type of couple configuration, Dr Jouannet as well as many CECOS physicians remains dubious about the psychological motivation and impact on the future child of such a context. More specifically, Dr Jouannet described the request of a M-F living with his wife with whom he already had two children before his transition, who wanted to freeze his sperm before transition to possibly use it after transition if now-her companion wanted to have another. Most CECOS did not agree to comply with this request, so a number of transgender associations petitioned the French *Défenseur des droits* (Defender of Rights) in 2013 demanding the right for a M-F person to freeze their gametes before transition and use them post-transition. Several public consultative organizations were consulted on this matter: the Ordre des médecins (somewhat equivalent to the American Medical Association), the Agence de la Biomédecine (somewhat equivalent to the UK Human Fertilisation and Embryology Authority [HFEA]) and the Comité consultatif national d'éthique (the national bioethics committee) among others. The general consensus was that there was no medical justification for freezing sperm or oocytes before transition.

The Académie national de médecine, of which Dr Jouannet is a member, had a slightly different analysis: their report stated that if men transitioning to women were given appropriate hormonal treatment, they would not necessarily have to be surgically sterilized and they could recover normal testing and genital apparatus functions when stopping the hormonal treatment. At that time, this also echoed requests by transgender associations and other groups such as the Commission des droits de l'homme (Human Rights Commission) or the Council of Europe, who also argued that sterilization was not mandatory in transitional processes.

The debate continues on cryopreserving sperm prior to M-F transitions, but until the French government changes the law and allows access to ART for same-sex couples, even if there were an institutional and social consensus, in 2017 it remains illegal for lesbian couples to access ART treatment, and for both heterosexual and gay couples to have recourse to surrogacy. Therefore, even if gametes were frozen prior to transition, it would be impossible to use them legally in France through ART procedures, except in the unique case of a M-F who cryopreserved his sperm prior to transition, and whose partner is an infertile man. Even then, this couple would either need a surrogate uterus or a uterus transplant performed on the M-F person. There are uterus transplant programmes being carried out in France, but none so far on a M-F person.

Annick Neuraz, Medical Gynaecologist, Hôpitaux Lariboisière et Bichat, Paris

Dr Annick Neuraz completed her general medical studies in Paris and was from the start interested in specializing in gynaecology. She attended several training sessions at one of Paris's largest maternity wards at the Port Royal Hospital, and it is there that she was introduced to IVF techniques in 1983.

Very quickly, Dr Neuraz became aware of the importance that ART would take on; the year she graduated and became a practising gynaecologist, there were only two or three from her class who were interested in ART. As a gynaecologist, she knew that by specializing in fertility treatment she would be able to partake in a medical practice that would (1) concern patients from both an individual perspective and the perspective of a couple's dynamic and history, something that was rare if not non-existent in medical practice in general; (2) define the 'couple as patient' and interact with the couple's education, belief systems and surrounding friends and relatives; and (3) involve not only treating patients but also partaking in a societal adventure and change in family paradigms.

In addition, new technological and scientific innovations excited the specialists involved; they felt they were on the cutting edge. Dr Neuraz went through each and every innovation: coelioscopic egg retrievals (laparotomies) under general anaesthesia, transurethral ultrasound-guided egg retrieval, the emergence of a whole new group of medications, endo-vaginal ultrasounds, transvaginal sonographically-controlled ovarian puncture for oocytes, and so on.

From Port Royal Hospital, Dr Neuraz pursued a career as a fertility gynaecologist at the Bichat Hospital in Paris, where she stayed for approximately fifteen years. She then went to the Pierre Rouquès Hospital to work in its well-known progressive maternity ward, called Les Bluets (a well-known French maternity ward that respects pregnant women's pre-birth and birthing choices), then on to the Trousseau Hospital. She now has a private and public practice, based at the Lariboisière and Bichat Hospital in the ART units. All of the technical acts (egg retrieval, embryo cultures, embryo transfers) are carried out at Bichat. Consultations and simpler acts such as ovarian stimulations and inseminations are carried out at Lariboisière.

When asked about certain feminist critiques of ART and their arguments that these new techniques consisted in men gaining further control over women's bodies, Dr Neuraz disagreed. From the start, she always considered her practice as helping a couple, both the woman and the man. For Dr Neuraz, it sufficed to have a couple in distress coming for medical assistance to have a long-desired baby to understand this, and that it didn't only concern women's bodies. In fact, over time and with increased scientific knowledge about men's infertility problems, research expanded and developed new and useful male infertility measurements, which indeed took the focus away from infertility as a problem only of women's bodies. As the technology for male infertility improved, Dr Neuraz saw an increasing number of men accompanying their wives to consultations, having become aware via personal research or public campaigns on male infertility. Today, the presence of men in the gynaecologist's consultation room has become routine. This in turn has allowed infertility specialists to listen and hear men's grievances when faced with the difficulty of having a child 'naturally', which has enriched their practice as well as social science studies on infertility.

Patient Profiles and Financial Issues

Working in France and under French laws governing access to ART, Dr Neuraz has only treated heterosexual couples suffering from medically diagnosed infertility. Initial exploratory tests are fully financed upfront by the French Social Security system; in other words, patients consulting in public hospitals do not have to pay a cent in the process. There is an age limit for women (forty-three years of age) but not for men. Insofar as IVF is concerned, four cycles are fully financed upfront by Social Security. That being said, each cycle that is launched is not necessarily taken into account financially; only cycles that go as far as embryo transfer to the woman's uterus are counted. If ovarian stimulation is interrupted for any reason, or if it does not lead to any egg retrieval, or if no embryo is created or transferred, it does not count for the couple as a full cycle and they may start again from scratch.

Dr Neuraz's patients come from all walks of life and socio-economic categories: highly educated and cultivated upper-class or middle-class persons, business managers, civil servants, underprivileged persons and immigrants both legal and/or undocumented. However, concerning the latter category, since 2011 both legal and undocumented immigrants can no longer benefit from fully financed access to ART. They may access treatment legally, even if they are non-documented, but they must pay upfront and are not reimbursed.

As any ART practitioner, Dr Neuraz encounters patients whose request for access presents ethical dilemmas for her and/or her team. For example, the case of an elderly man (seventy years old) who consulted with his younger wife (thirty-five years old) who could not get pregnant raised issues of the future child's best interest. What responsibility did Dr Neuraz and her team feel when assisting a couple knowing that the father would probably die before the child became a young adult? Faced with such requests, along with her team Dr Neuraz decided to consider each request on a case-by-case basis; what was to predominate in their minds when evaluating the couple's request was whether the project to have a child was coherent, not dangerous and desired by both members of the couple, no matter the exterior and often unique factors. Though Dr Neuraz is part of a team made up of biologists, midwives, physicians and even administrative personnel, she has the last word as to whether or not she will accept patients. In thornier cases, the team brings in psychologists and social workers, and can also request advice from the Centre for Clinical Ethics based at Port Royal (http://ethique-clinique.com/). In addition, the team is not in a position of having to make a decision in a very short time; they are not in a medical emergency situation. Dr Neuraz and her team take time to receive couples and engage in dialogue over whatever length of time is necessary for the couples to be fully informed and the team to get to know them. For 'simple' cases, the procedure is quite straightforward, especially if the couple is referred to Dr Neuraz by another colleague specializing in fertility treatment and all the preliminary exploratory tests have been performed. This type of case rarely necessitates a discussion within her team. All other more difficult cases – a woman over thirty-five, an elderly man, a complex medical context – are systematically discussed among the members of her team and in conformity with French law. Dr Neuraz insisted on the fact that each centre benefits from a large degree of flexibility in accepting or rejecting a request, and in the event of a refusal, each centre can refer the couple to another centre.

The Evolution of Demand and Infertility Practices

For Dr Neuraz, there has been an enormous evolution in demand for access to ART and infertility practices themselves. Among some of the striking developments she has observed, the first lies in the techniques themselves, especially the progress made in detecting male infertility problems. When she began her practice, as mentioned earlier, the general consensus was that it was a 'woman's' problem. This is no longer the case, thanks to technological developments and innovation. Indeed, there have been incredible advances in ART diagnoses and treatment in only thirty years.

Insofar as patient demand is concerned, Dr Neuraz has noted stark changes. One of the main things she has noticed over the years is that couples are increasingly impatient to access ART. In the past, couples would have waited longer before consulting, whereas today patients turn to the medical community for help after only a few months of not becoming pregnant. She sees one of the explanations for this in the internet revolution. People in general and patients in particular have become more aware of a variety of issues by surfing the net. Even people living in rural or secluded areas are now as savvy as urban populations on a variety of issues thanks to the internet. As in any medical field, patients suffering from infertility are eager to learn of the latest techniques and innovations, what works and doesn't, and one finds an enormous amount of information on the internet. Of course, the problem is that the information does not necessarily pertain to a person's particular profile or case, yet they continue to amass information and come to consultations with preconceived ideas and/or erroneous readings of their own medical examinations.

This is a bias that, as a practitioner, Dr Neuraz has had to integrate in her consultations, but also in the profile of patients coming to see her. Though same-sex couples and single persons know they do not have legal access to ART in France, they consult for advice about where to go. Most of them have already mastered the legal complexities of what they seek to do (be it artificial insemination in Belgium, access to oocytes in Spain or to surrogacy in the US, Ukraine and elsewhere outside of France; see Chapter 8 in this book by Michael Stambolis-Ruhstorfer: 'Queer Families Online: The Internet as a Resource for Accessing and Facilitating Surrogacy and ART in France and the United States'), and in some cases, once a woman returns to France after benefiting from insemination or oocyte donation/IVF abroad, she can have her pregnancy followed up and financed within the French public health system. Dr Neuraz is convinced that prohibiting same-sex couples from accessing gamete donations and/or IVF is counterproductive as it only serves to increase the rates of cross-border practices. It is also, in her medical opinion, a dangerous undertaking not only from a legal standpoint but also from a public health perspective, when patients attempt to conceive and carry a future child 'solo' without proper supervision by a medical team.

When these particular patients come to Dr Neuraz's consultations, she tries to advise, inform and refer them as best she can. Most of her colleagues do the same, and recently in a French national widely-read daily evening newspaper, 130 ART practitioners called for an end to French prohibition and declared that when faced with persons who do not have legal access to ART in France, they do not hesitate to refer them to foreign colleagues.[1]

In the end, Dr Neuraz underlines both the positive and negative aspects of the French governance of ART, in both private and public practice. Among the most important positive aspects is of course the universal and 100 per cent free access to ART for any and all heterosexual couples suffering from infertility, and this for any existing technique or protocol. This does not exist anywhere else in the world. Of course, that being the case, the French government has always had its say in framing this access and has thus excluded single persons and same-sex couples. This has had negative effects, according to Dr Neuraz, the most deplorable being the increase in cross-border practices, which in the end are only available to well-off French citizens.

General Conclusion

The stark differences in ART access and practice between France and Belgium clearly come to the fore through these four experiences of ART practitioners. That neighbouring countries, both modern democracies sharing a language and often sharing a culture, present such different ART governance systems is testimony to the fact that ART and how it is framed depends on a specific national context: its own history, the relationship between the civil society and government, the weight (or absence thereof) of the scientific and medical communities, and so on. That being said, realities point to a high level of resistance to French law by the French population, and Belgium's proximity makes it the ideal place for those excluded from access to ART to go to. This clearly challenges the idea that a country can make laws in the realm of ART within a 'national bubble', in other words by choosing to ignore the globalized reality of today's economies in general and ART practices in particular. What France touts, and rightly so, as 'universal and free access to ART' is dampened by the growing number of persons who do not qualify to be a part of what France defines as 'universal', as we can see in a number of other chapters in this book. In addition, the fact that women (especially) who go abroad for sperm or egg donation and return to France and receive full coverage of their obstetrical costs and birth/delivery/maternal and neonatal care highlights the contradictions of French ART policy. Last but not least, the amount of money that France spends on ART practices almost equals the amount that French citizens have to spend on their own to access ART abroad, yet another contradiction that French authorities fail to take into consideration.

Jennifer Merchant is a professor of Anglo-American legal and political institutions at the Université de Paris II (Panthéon-Assas). She is a leading researcher in bioethical issues of comparative public policy with expertise in North American and European policy, and politics and regulation of medical technologies involving human reproduction. She is also an expert in French law and politics on embryo research and assisted reproductive technology.

Note

1. 'We, the Undersigned ART Practitioners, Have Helped Same-Sex Couples to Have a Child Even Though This Is Illegal', https://www.lemonde.fr/idees/article/2016/03/17/pour-la-creation-d-un-veritable-plan-contre-l-infertilite_4884871_3232.html. Accessed 29 June 2019.

References

Autin, Candice, et al. 2016. 'Au cœur du don, la dette? Étude exploratoire autour de la motivation des mères porteuses', *Dialogue*, no. 213.

Chevalier, Nicolas. 2016. 'Quel avenir pour nos centres d'assistance médicale à la procréation en France?', *Médecine de la reproduction* 18 (3), July–August–September: 164–165.

Chiland, Colette, et al. 2013. 'Pères d'un nouveau genre et leurs enfants', *La psychiatrie de l'enfant* 56 (1): 97–125.

De Sutter, Petra, et al. 2015. *Overleven: mijn strijd als transvrouw, arts & politica*. Holland: Manteau Publishers.

De Sutter, Petra, et al. 2017. *De maakbare baby: een onbegrensd verlangen?* Holland: Academia Press.

Jouannet, Pierre. 2014. 'Quand les hommes transsexuels souhaitent devenir père par don de sperme', in Laurence Hérault (ed.), *La parenté transgenre*. Presses Universitaires de Provence, pp. 117–25.

Schiffino, Nathalie. 2003. *Procréation médicalement assistée: régulation publique et enjeux bioéthiques*. Brussels: Bruylant Publications.

Chapter 5

Removing Anonymity for Egg and Sperm Donors?

(Re-)Igniting the Debate in Belgium

Cathy Herbrand and Nicky Hudson

Belgium has been at the centre of pioneering research and the application of new reproductive technologies since IVF was first developed in the 1970s. Its scientific and clinical communities have played a key role in donor conception, permitting and practising sperm donation widely for more than five decades and egg donation for more than two decades. Social science researchers in Belgium have also, correspondingly, been among the first to collect data on social attitudes on the issue of donor identification and disclosure to donor offspring. While the Belgian comprehensive law on medically assisted reproduction of 2007 reaffirmed the obligation for gamete and embryo donation to be anonymous, except in specific cases,[1] in recent years the possibility to ban anonymity has been raised and discussed in the Belgian Parliament. The debate on donor anonymity is therefore of timely political and cultural significance in Belgium and presents an interesting analytical moment for considering the issue of genetic origins and identifiability in the context of assisted conception.

Within the context of donor conception,[2] the significance of knowing about one's genetic origins and the moral and legal status of this information has been the subject of ongoing and vociferous debate in a number of Western countries. For a number of reasons, the importance granted to having information regarding identity, family history and susceptibility to certain illnesses has burgeoned in recent years, with the associated implication that the anonymity of donors and the issue of access to information about donors has been a major ethical, political and legal challenge. Arguments for a move towards more 'openness' in donation systems have also led on occasion to legislative changes, with a number of nations deciding to remove or ban anonymity in favour of identity-release systems[3] or those within which both anonymous and non-anonymous donations are possible.[4]

This chapter considers this wider socio-cultural context and examines how this, and a range of influencing factors, have ignited the debate about donor anonymity in the Belgian national context. It begins with a description of the current regulatory approach to gamete donation in Belgium, before examining the latest law proposals submitted to parliament. It then provides an overview of the recent international trends surrounding donor identification and information sharing within the context of shifting conceptualizations of personhood, genetics and identity. This is followed by a consideration of some key findings from social science research on perceptions of donor anonymity and the experience of disclosure in donor-conceived families in Belgium and other countries. The chapter concludes by arguing that greater attention should be given to social practices relating to gamete donation and highlights the need for more detailed future research to inform policy-making in assisted reproduction.

Belgian Regulation: The Reaffirmation of Gamete Anonymity

While medically assisted reproduction has been widely practised in Belgium since the 1960s, its regulation has been largely confined to that of professional oversight and guidance.[5] As a result, clinicians and researchers were granted a considerable degree of scientific autonomy and any bioethical and religious orientations were respected (Shiffino, Ramjoué and Varone 2009). It was in July 2007 that a comprehensive law on medically assisted reproduction and the disposition of supernumerary embryos and gametes was adopted in Belgium.[6] This law primarily aimed at formalizing existing clinical practices and limiting possible excesses. The law permits a broad range of reproductive techniques, such as *post mortem* insemination or preimplantation genetic diagnosis, and allows these techniques to be offered to any couple or single woman under the age of forty-eight.[7] This liberal law is in line with existing clinical practices and attitudes within some Belgian clinics.

The 2007 law also reinforced the obligation for embryo and gamete donation to remain anonymous, after an intense debate on this issue in Belgium. An exception was made for certain cases of gamete donation, where donors do not have to be anonymous provided they result from an agreement between the donor and the recipient. The aim of this exception was, it seems, in reality to facilitate the supply of egg donors, which constitutes a scarce resource, by allowing egg donation from a family member or a friend (Gallus 2009; Pennings 2007). Indeed, prior to this, it seems that most women in Belgium preferred to receive or donate eggs in circumstances where the donors and recipient knew one other (Baetens et al. 2000). This means that in the case of Belgian egg donation, some intending parents will know who the donor is from the start, which is different from the 'identity-release donation' system in place in several countries that allows donor-conceived offspring to access their donor's identity when aged eighteen. This possibility of 'known donation' is regarded and presented as an exception to the prevailing rule in Belgium, where clinics are obliged to guarantee the anonymity of donors by rendering inaccessible all information both identifying (e.g. names) and non-identifying (e.g. physical characteristics) relating to donors.

A crucial argument used to justify the maintenance of donor anonymity in Belgium was the priority given to the parents' autonomy (Gallus 2009). According to this principle, parents should be able to decide whether or not and how they wish to tell the child about the nature of their conception. In this model, anonymity goes hand in hand with the legislative will to privilege family ties based on parental commitment and daily involvement. In line with this argument was also the will to respect parents' rights to a private life and to protect their intimacy. The intention of Belgian policymakers was to help donor-conceived children integrate directly into their family without revealing the medical intervention needed for their conception and without the parents fearing the intrusion of the donor in their family. It also intended to prevent the possible disruption to the child and its parents caused by information about and contact with an additional parental figure. Likewise, an additional aim was to guarantee discretion towards the donor, who acted as a genitor and not as a parent. The law was therefore intended to protect the donor against the risk of parental obligations and intrusion into his/her private life at a later stage. The decision in 2007 to retain anonymity was also made to prohibit access to non-identifiable, non-medical information in order to avoid any genetic determinism, whereby the child's character, for example, might be attributed to the donor's genes (Belgian Chamber 2007). This differs from other countries, like the UK or the US, where the significance of genetics has potentially been reinforced through policies that appear to imply determining links between the genetics and personality of the donor (Turkmendag 2012), for example through providing the donor-conceived family with a personal and biographical description of the donor.[8] Finally, a position of anonymity was also justified in Belgium for practical reasons, since it also helped to preserve the number of donations and was therefore as important in avoiding a donor shortage.[9]

Current Debates and Challenges

Despite these changes, the issue of information sharing in gamete donation remains controversial in Belgium, against a growing significance of having information about one's genetic origins. The debate was reignited in 2014, when a law proposal (Lahaye-Battheu and Somers 2014) was submitted to the Belgian Parliament in order to implement five different possibilities in terms of information sharing about donation. These proposals offer a number of possible solutions to the question of donor anonymity in Belgium. They are as follows: (1) known donation; (2) access to non-identifiable information until the child is eighteen and then access to the donor's identity; (3) access to non-identifiable information only; (4) no information on the donor until the child is eighteen and then access to the donor's identity; and (5) anonymous donation. Within this proposal, the prospective parent could choose which donation option suits them best, while respecting the donors' preferences in terms of involvement. By offering more flexibility for all involved, this proposal also seeks to avoid significant gamete shortages. The primary aim of this recent law proposal is nonetheless to promote openness, which is illustrated by the suggestion that clinical counsellors be obliged to inform parents-to-be about the possible negative consequences of non-disclosure. In February 2015, a panel of experts were invited to share their views on these possibilities. The hearing was followed by the submission of two other, more radical law proposals, which aimed at banning donor anonymity and at creating a specific organization responsible for centralizing and organizing the sharing of donor information (Van Peel 2015; Van Hoof and Beck 2015). It is also worth mentioning that independent of the parliamentary debates, an international symposium on gamete donation was organized in August 2015 by researchers at the University of Ghent in Belgium, in which most presentations and discussions focused on the relative challenges and dilemmas associated with anonymous and non-anonymous donation.[10] These political and academic debates reflect the increasing and ongoing attention granted to this issue in Belgium and demonstrate the salience of the question of donor anonymity in Belgium in recent years. The next section briefly explores some of the possible reasons for these developments.

Shifting Mores in Relation to Disclosure and Donor Identification

The wider context regarding the privileging (or not) of information about genetic origins may offer some insights into the recent debates in Belgium. During the 1980s, a discourse in favour of access to information about one's genetic origins emerged in various Western countries. This discourse, which asserted the child's right to personal identity, first developed in relation to adoption in the US and Canada, where adoptees and birth parents were pushing for the removal of confidentiality in the adoption registry (Carp 1998). Not only did this movement lead to the creation of 'open adoptions' in the US and the UK, where biological and adoptive parents know their respective identity and can (under certain conditions) contact one another, but it also led to the adoption of international and national laws, giving adopted children the right to access information about their origins. Overall, this movement contributed to an increasing political and discursive shift in the significance given to knowing one's family origins.

This trend towards 'openness' progressively extended to the field of gamete donation on a number of grounds, including the need for knowledge about one's 'genetic' identity as well as a desire not to withhold information about a person's life story (Richards et al. 2012b: 1–2). Yet a number of authors have highlighted the substantial differences between adoption and gamete donation (Shenfield

1999; Blake et al. 2014). Donor-conceived children are planned by intending parents well before conception, while adopted children have, in contrast, been relinquished by their birth parents and as a result have been raised by another individual (Palacios and Brodzinsky 2010). In addition, adoptees often report feeling aware of the fact that they are not biologically related to adoptive parents due to physical differences within the family. They may also have to deal with the stigma associated with this lack of physical resemblance, unlike donor-conceived children who may have been conceived with the genetic material of one of the intending parents and may have increased resemblance to their parents due to any 'matching' done at the fertility clinic. While both adopted children and donor-conceived children may desire more information about their genetic origins, their conception circumstances are quite different and concerns may be distinct, especially in terms of disclosure and identity. It is well documented that some adoptees search for their birth parents in order to understand the context of and reasons for the adoption (Carsten 2000). Notwithstanding these differences in context, a parallel has been drawn between practices of information sharing in adoption in order to implore the need for more openness in gamete donation (Feast 2003).

This shift towards identification and greater information sharing in gamete donation has also been reinforced by the increasing attention given in recent times to genetics, especially in terms of medical history and family knowledge (Nelkin and Lindee 1995). With regard to medical progress on genetic disorders, the need to have access to or knowledge about one's own genetic and genealogical history is increasingly significant (Finkler 2000). This is also apparent in the proliferation of related phenomena such as 'popular genealogy', involving a search for one's ancestors and mapping of family trees (Cannell 2011) as well as the proliferation of direct-to-consumer genetic tests. This shift in thinking about origins as ultimately determinable has inflected public and policy discourses related to family relations, kinship and gamete donation.

The emergence of demand for non-anonymous donors among certain social groups has also added to the shifting landscape of donor anonymity. An increasing number of lesbian and single women have accessed reproductive technologies over the last two decades, creating family situations in which the biological (donor) father is not an active presence. For some of these women, having medical information about the donor as well as information about his interests and personality traits to provide to the future child was of significance (Baetens and Brewaeys 2001).

Changes in the uptake of egg donation may also have contributed to changes in practices around donor anonymity. As demand has grown and freezing technologies have advanced, egg donation has become more widely used and, in many contexts, the number of donated eggs is not sufficient to meet the increasing demand. This means that waiting times can be considerable, something which in turn has contributed to a rise in the number of women asking a close relative or friend to become their donor (Baetens et al. 2000), and indirectly has facilitated known donation and donor identification. Within this wider context, the culture of anonymity and non-disclosure that had once prevailed appears to have been subject to notable change, as disclosure and identification have increasingly been debated and encouraged in gamete donation, for example in countries like the UK and Sweden (Appleby, Blake and Freeman 2012). As a country at the heart of technological developments and ethical debates regarding assisted reproductive technologies, Belgium has also been exposed to these shifting values and trends regarding information about genetic inheritance. While these changes and concerns did not lead to a change of position on gamete anonymity policy in the 2007 law, donor conception parents may nevertheless have been influenced by these trends and may therefore be more likely to discuss with their children the circumstances of their conception. The implication of disclosure about donor conception under the current Belgian system is that the child will know about the lack of a biological tie with one of his or her parents, but will not be able to access any information regarding the donor.

The question of the regulation of donor anonymity was reignited amidst recent discussions about the opportunity to create a 'childbirth in discretion' ('accouchement dans la discretion'). This measure would facilitate surrogacy arrangements by allowing surrogates or any pregnant woman to give birth without being recognized as the child's legal mother, while keeping traces of her identity in a specific register that would be accessible to the child later on.[11] Regulatory changes in neighbouring countries have also influenced current debates in Belgium, in particular the case of open donation policies adopted in the Netherlands in 2004 following their use of a mixed system for seven years (Janssens et al. 2006). In recent years, it seems that there have also been a number of claims made by donor-conceived individuals in Belgium who have requested a ban on anonymous donation and access to the identity of the donor. These different elements have contributed to the re-emergence of the issue and the submission of law proposals aimed at partly or completely removing gamete anonymity. While discussions about the topic are likely to continue, it is worth highlighting insights gained from empirical research, as this has rarely been mentioned so far in the parliamentary and public discussions.

Donor Anonymity and Information Sharing in Families: An Overview of the Contribution from Research

In this section we consider key findings regarding the practices and attitudes of donor conception parents regarding donor anonymity and information sharing, by considering key studies conducted on this issue in several countries.[12] The intention is not to present a comprehensive review of these analyses but to highlight the main observations that can be drawn from these studies and to consider their implications for the Belgian case.[13] While accurate figures are not available given the difficulties in collecting data about children who have not been told about their donor conception (Nuffield Council on Bioethics 2013), the qualitative studies available provide noteworthy insights on perceptions of anonymity. There is still a significant gap in the evidence-base but these studies offer a valuable snapshot of the complex negotiations and variability surrounding decisions regarding disclosure and non-disclosure within donor conception families. They also offer the opportunity to gain improved understanding about the interplay between legal changes and social attitudes and practices regarding disclosure among donor families. Too often, a legal position of anonymity for gamete donors is conflated with a wider cultural practice of non-disclosure or 'secrecy' within families and, correspondingly, a legal position of identification is conflated with a culture of disclosure between parents and donor offspring. As existing research shows, it is important to clearly distinguish social practices from the legal position, as attitudes regarding the possible disclosure of the use of donor conception within families and communities are complex and diverse and do not necessarily align with the law.

Reporting on cases of known and anonymous egg donation in Belgium in 2000, a study by Baetens et al. (2000) indicated that two-thirds of a sample of 144 couples opted for known donation and one-third for anonymous donation. One of the main reasons to choose known donation was the fear of using unknown genetic material. Among the couples who used egg donation, the proportion of couples intending to disclose later on was similar to those who did not want to disclose (43 per cent) (Baetens et al. 2000). More recently, another European study on egg donation drawing on interviews with 135 recipient couples (almost half of whom resided in Belgium) reported similar rates of disclosure and non-disclosure among donor parents, regardless of whether they used an anonymous or identifiable donor (Laruelle et al. 2011). Half of parents using known donation (forty-two couples) and half of those using an anonymous donor (forty-five couples) did not want to tell the child about his or her conception because of the fear of stigmatization or rejection within their social circle, as well as to avoid jeopardizing the mother–child relationship. Disclosure was also sometimes regarded as a threat to the child's psychological well-being (Laruelle et al. 2011). This paper also indicates that 'among Europeans (90 couples), 50 per cent were in favour of disclosure compared with only 8.9 per cent of recipients from North or sub-Saharan Africa (45 couples)' (Laruelle et al. 2011). In some religious or ethnic communities, using gamete donation was taboo, and disclosing the information seen to be very harmful and stigmatizing not only for the child but also for the social father and the mother.[14] As a result, it remains unclear whether parents who can choose between an anonymous and a non-anonymous egg donor would prefer to disclose more information.[15] The authors therefore recommend 'maintaining access to different types of oocyte donation' (Laruelle at al. 2011: 382).

As for sperm donation, a qualitative study drawing on interviews with Belgian couples who had used an anonymous sperm donor has shown that once the child was born, most heterosexual couples 'avoided talking about the donor because it was perceived as disrupting men's growing confidence in their position as fathers' (Wyverkens et al. 2015: 203–16). This was not dependent on whether or not they had disclosed, but rather reflected the couples' priority to protect the father from possible reminders of the donor. By contrast, attitudes towards the donor among lesbian couples who were interviewed in the study were more diverse. While disclosure about donor conception was the norm, there were differences in the ways the donor was constructed, with some couples portraying him as a person, especially as the child grew older, and others only considering the male genetic progenitor as a means to the conception, tending to ignore him in discussions about family relationships (Wyverkens et al. 2014).

It is also interesting to look more broadly at the studies exploring the attitudes of donor conception parents and offspring in other contexts, as it provides insights on current wider trends and on the issues still at stake. The studies conducted to date on gamete donation practices demonstrate that despite a change of attitudes in professional counselling towards more openness, many heterosexual parents have not disclosed this information to their child or have expressed ambivalence or difficulty in doing so. For instance, in the UK, where gamete anonymity was removed in 2005, the ongoing longitudinal research conducted with donor-conceived families by Golombok et al. (2011) from Cambridge University shows that at age seven, only 28 per cent of sperm donation parents and 41 per cent of egg donation parents were in the process of disclosing information about their conception to their child. This trend seems to continue at age ten (Blake et al. 2014), with a majority of sperm donor parents in particular choosing not to disclose the conception to the child (Nuffield Council on Bioethics 2013). This study also highlights the need to distinguish between the initial intention to disclose and the actual process of letting the child know about the use of gamete donation. Indeed, while thirty-seven out of sixty-eight donation parents intended to disclose when the child was aged one, only about half of them had done so six years later (Readings et al. 2011). Moreover, for some of these parents, disclosure was only partial. They had told the child about the use of reproductive technologies, but not about the donor (Readings et al. 2011). The difficulty or reluctance of donor conception parents to disclose was also confirmed by a recent UK sociological study that describes how even in family situations where parents are in favour of openness (heterosexual and lesbian couples), telling the child about his or her conception may prove to be much more difficult than expected in practice, especially given the impact it has on the wider family (Nordqvist 2014).

Another study conducted by the team at Cambridge on donor-conceived children in several European countries showed that donor conception parents who had not disclosed to their children at age twelve tended not to do so later on. At age eighteen, only about a tenth of the children who had not been told at age twelve knew about the circumstances of their birth (Owen and Golombok 2009).

Overall, this means that a currently unknown proportion of donor-conceived children are therefore unaware that one or both of their legal parents is not their genetic parent. This proportion seems slightly higher among children conceived using sperm donation than egg donation (Readings et al. 2011). However, it is important to note that these trends differ in families formed by single mothers who used sperm donation in which, according to Murray and Golombok's 2005 study, 90 per cent of single mothers intended to tell their child (Murray and Golombok 2005). This proportion is even higher in donor conception families headed by same-sex couples, in which all parents, according to studies conducted in the UK, Belgium and the Netherlands, intended to disclose (Murray and Golombok 2005).

It is also worth noting that the impact of the legal change on disclosure in the families who have used gamete donation in the UK after 2005 is still unknown. However, according to the report from the Nuffield Council on Bioethics, 'preliminary findings from a study being carried out by Freeman T, Zadeh S, Smith V and Golombok S suggest that the removal of anonymity has not had an immediate impact on disclosure rates' (Freeman 2013). This study compared disclosure of donor conception to children between solo mother and two-parent families with children aged four to eight years conceived since the removal of donor anonymity in the UK, and found that 'parents will [not necessarily] tell their children about their origins or their entitlement to request the identity of their donor at the age of 18 years' (Freeman et al. 2016: 252).

Finally, studies also suggest that 'children who are not informed have positive relationships with their parents and develop normally, which shows that this specific family secret does not always have an impact on the child's life' (Raes, Ravelingien and Pennings 2016: 373). It is nonetheless important to emphasize that without more research it is difficult to demonstrate the impact that disclosure might or might not have for those involved, and moreover that access to the perceptions of those who do not know they are donor-conceived is of course impossible (Nuffield Council on Bioethics 2013).

Conclusion

Since the 2007 law confirming donor anonymity in Belgium, political approaches to donor identification and practices related to information sharing have evolved and are continually challenged by the diversity and complexity of family situations. In particular, whereas autonomy and freedom for intending parents have been maintained and prioritized, the implication of this is that those who want to use gamete donation to form a family have little choice with respect to donor characteristics and there is no possibility for donor-conceived individuals to access information about the donor, either at the time of donation or in the future.

In attempting to overcome these challenges, some commentators have argued for a 'double-track' approach to donation, in which more autonomy could be granted to parents and donors. It is argued that in this model, both parties would have the possibility to choose what suits them best and clinics would match donors and recipients according to their preferences (Pennings 1997). One of its main disadvantages, however, is the difference between the rights of offspring who have access to their donor's identity and those who do not, since the choice about which method to engage with still lies with the recipients and donors. This double-track system was temporarily adopted in the Netherlands and is now ongoing in Denmark. In both cases, it has not been implemented for a long enough period to draw conclusions on the implications at hand.

With respect to social practices, research about experiences and perceptions of donor identification and information disclosure remains limited. Almost all of what is known about those who are donor-conceived comes from small-scale studies, even though Belgium was a pioneer in this respect (Nuffield Council on Bioethics 2013). Given this, it is difficult to draw firm conclusions about the implications of donor identification. Current studies, however, do appear to illustrate more diversity regarding disclosure practices among families than has been suggested by various stakeholders in public debates. Despite this, the findings of such research have not, to date, played a significant role in shaping policy-making in Belgium, demonstrating a potential lack of effective and systematic dialogue between social scientists and law-making in this field. If legislative changes are to be made, it would seem important to make them reflective of and consistent with social practices and lived experiences.

Cathy Herbrand is a Reader in Medical Sociology at the Centre for Reproduction Research at De Montfort University (UK). She received her PhD in Sociology from the Université libre de Bruxelles, and has previously held posts at King's College London, London School of Economics and Political Science, and the University of Ottawa. Her research interests lie in the sociological and anthropological study of new family forms, biotechnologies, health and genetics, with a particular focus on reproductive decision-making and patients' needs. Her current work explores the interactions between scientific progress, policies and patients' lives, by examining the social and ethical issues surrounding mitochondrial donation techniques.

Nicky Hudson is a medical sociologist whose work is concerned with the relations between assisted reproductive technologies, subjectivities and social structures. She leads the Centre for Reproduction Research, an interdisciplinary centre of expertise dedicated to the production of scholarship on the social, cultural and political aspects of human reproduction based at De Montfort University. Nicky's research is characterized by a strong commitment to interdisciplinary collaboration and social translation. Her current work explores the social, political, economic and moral configuration of egg donation in Europe.

Notes

The authors note that portions of this chapter were taken from a previously published article, 'Information Sharing in Donor Conception: Comparing Regulations, Ethics and Cultural Practices in the UK and Belgium', published in the *Journal of Medical Law and Ethics* (JMLE) [2015/3], ISSN 2213-5405 (print); 2214-5354 (online); www.jmle-online.com. The Editorial Board of JMLE has given its full permission for the reprinted portions.

1. 'Known' gamete donation, which is distinct from 'identity-release' donation, is possible in Belgium when donation results from an agreement between donor and recipient (see below).
2. A means of achieving pregnancy via the use of a third-party donor who provides eggs, sperm or embryos for use by intended parents but who has no legal parental responsibility for the resulting offspring.
3. In an identity-release system, the donor-conceived child has the right to access identifying information about their donor at the age of majority. This is the case, for instance, in the UK, Sweden, Norway, Austria, Switzerland, the Netherlands and several Australian states (see Blyth and Frith 2015).
4. For instance in Denmark. For more details on the different systems, see Freeman, Appleby and Jadva 2012: 250–52.
5. The following three sections draw extensively on a previous paper (Herbrand and Hudson 2015).
6. A first law on *in vitro* embryos was nevertheless adopted in May 2003. It authorizes the procuring of stem cells from residual embryos,

therapeutic cloning and the creation of embryos for research purposes. Only reproductive cloning is forbidden.
7. For more details on the content of the law, see Pennings 2007.
8. Though it is also the case that this information is provided in order that donor families can incorporate this information into coherent 'conception stories'.
9. Although evidence suggests that donation, after initially dropping in countries where there was a legal shift in favour of open-identity donation, is on the increase again due to changing donor profiles and improvements in recruitment strategies, there is still a significant risk that the supply will not meet increasing demands (see HFEA 2014).
10. 'Donor Conception: An Unfamiliar Path to a Normal Family?', symposium organized by the research group on social and genetic parenthood from Ghent University, 27–28 August 2015.
11. This would be different from the 'anonymous childbirth' ('accouchement sous X') existing in France, in which no trace of the biological mother remains.
12. In this chapter we do not provide a broader discussion about donor-conceived children (see, for example, Richards, Pennings and Appleby 2012a), but instead focus specifically on the question of disclosure.
13. For a comprehensive review of the empirical studies on this topic, see Freeman 2015.
14. Ethnic and cultural differences in public perceptions of disclosure in gamete donation have also been noted in the UK context (see Hudson and Culley 2015).
15. This was also the conclusion of another study conducted later in the US on disclosure in egg donation (see Greenfeld and Klock 2004).

References

Appleby, J.B., L. Blake, and T. Freeman. 2012. 'Is Disclosure in the Best Interests of the Children Conceived by Donation?', in M. Richards, G. Pennings and J.B. Appleby (eds), *Reproductive Donation: Practice, Policy and Bioethics*. Cambridge, UK: Cambridge University Press, pp. 231–49.

Baetens, P., and A. Brewaeys. 2001. 'Lesbian Couples Requesting Donor Insemination: An Update of the Knowledge with Regard to Lesbian Mother Families', *Human Reproduction Update* 7 (5): 512–19.

Baetens, P., et al. 2000. 'Counselling Couples and Donors for Oocyte Donation: The Decision to Use Either Known or Anonymous Oocytes', *Human Reproduction* 15 (2): 476–84.

Belgian Chamber. 2007. *Rapport concernant le projet de loi relatif à la procréation médicalement assistée et à la destination des embryons surnuméraires et des gamètes*, Session 2006/2007: 41, 9 March 2007.

Blake, L., et al. 2014. '"I Was Quite Amazed": Donor Conception and Parent–Child Relationships from the Child's Perspective', *Children & Society* 28 (6): 425–37.

Blyth, E., and L. Frith. 2015. 'Access to Genetic and Biographical History in Donor Conception: An Analysis of Recent Trends and Future Possibilities', in K. Horsey (ed.), *Revisiting the Regulation of Human Fertilisation and Embryology*. Abingdon: Routledge, pp. 136–52.

Cannell, F. 2011. 'English Ancestors: The Moral Possibilities of Popular Genealogy', *Journal of the Royal Anthropological Institute* 17 (3): 462–80.

Carp, W.E. 1998. *Family Matters: Secrecy and Disclosure in the History of Adoption*. Cambridge, MA: Harvard University Press.

Carsten, J. 2000. '"Knowing Where You've Come From": Ruptures and Continuities of Time and Kinship in Narratives of Adoption Reunions', *The Journal of the Royal Anthropological Institute* 6 (4): 687–703.

Feast, J. 2003. 'Using and Not Losing the Messages from the Adoption Experience for Donor-Assisted Conception', *Human Fertility* 6 (1): 41–45.

Finkler, K. 2000. *Experiencing the New Genetics: Family and Kinship on the Medical Frontier*. Philadelphia: University of Pennsylvania Press.

Freeman, T. 2013. Personal communication, 11 February 2013, in Nuffield Council on Bioethics Report on 'Donor Conception: Ethical Aspects of Information Sharing'.

Freeman, T. 2015. 'Gamete Donation, Information Sharing and the Best Interests of the Child: An Overview of the Psychosocial Evidence', *Monash Bioethics Review* 33 (1): 45–63.

Freeman, T., J.B. Appleby, and V. Jadva. 2012. 'Identifiable Donors and Siblings: Implications for the Future', in M. Richards, G. Pennings and J.B. Appleby (eds), *Reproductive Donation: Practice, Policy and Bioethics*. Cambridge, UK: Cambridge University Press, pp. 250–69.

Freeman, T., et al. 2016. 'Disclosure of Sperm Donation: A Comparison between Solo Mother and Two-Parent Families with Identifiable Donors' *Reproductive Biomedicine Online* 33 (5): 592–600.

Gallus, N. 2009. 'Le droit de la filiation: Rôle de la vérité socio-affective et de la volonté en droit belge', Doctoral thesis. Brussels: Université Libre de Bruxelles.

Golombok, S., et al. 2011. 'Children Conceived by Gamete Donation: Psychological Adjustment and Mother-Child Relationships at Age 7', *Journal of Family Psychology* 25 (2): 230–39.

Greenfeld, D.A., and S.C. Klock. 2004. 'Disclosure Decisions among Known and Anonymous Oocyte Donation Recipients', *Fertility and Sterility* 81 (6): 1565–71.

Herbrand, C., and N. Hudson. 2015. 'Information Sharing in Donor Conception: Comparing Regulations, Ethics and Cultural Practices in the UK and Belgium', *Journal of Medical Law and Ethics* 3 (3): 175–92.

HFEA. 2014. *Egg and Sperm Donation in the UK: 2012–2013*. London. http://pmanonyme.asso.fr/wp-content/uploads/2014/03/Egg-and-sperm-donation-in-the-UK-HFEA-report.pdf Accessed 30 June 2019.

Hudson, N., and L. Culley. 2015. '"Knock Knock, You're My Mummy": Anonymity, Identification and Gamete Donation in British South Asian Communities', in K.R. Hampshire and B. Simpson (eds), *Assisted Reproductive Technologies in the Third Phase: Global Encounters and Emerging Moral Worlds*. Oxford: Berghahn Books, pp. 214–29.

Janssens P.M.W., et al. 2006. 'A New Dutch Law Regulating Provision of Identifying Information of Donors to Offspring: Background, Content and Impact', *Human Reproduction* 21 (4): 852–56.

Lahaye-Battheu, S., and I. Somers. 2014. 'Proposition de loi du 13 novembre 2014 modifiant la loi du 6 juillet 2007 relative à la procréation médicalement assistée et à la destination des embryons surnuméraires et des gamètes, en ce qui concerne l'anonymat dans le cadre d'un don de gamètes', Chambre des représentants belge, Doc. 55/0618.

Laruelle, C., et al. 2011. 'Anonymity and Secrecy Options of Recipient Couples and Donors, and Ethnic Origin Influence in Three Types of Oocyte Donation', *Human Reproduction* 26 (2): 382–90.

Murray, C., and S. Golombok. 2005. 'Going It Alone: Solo Mothers and Their Infants Conceived by Donor Insemination', *American Journal of Orthopsychiatry* 75 (2): 242–53.

Nelkin, D., and S.M. Lindee. 1995. *The DNA Mystique: The Gene as a Cultural Icon*. New York: Freeman and Company.

Nordqvist, P. 2014. 'The Drive for Openness in Donor Conception: Disclosure and the Trouble with Real Life', *International Journal of Law, Policy and the Family* 28 (3): 321–38.

Nuffield Council on Bioethics. 2013. *Donor Conception: Ethical Aspects of Information Sharing*. London. http://nuffieldbioethics.org/project/donor-conception. Accessed 30 June 2019.

Owen, L., and S. Golombok. 2009. 'Families Created by Assisted Reproduction: Parent-Child Relationships in Late Adolescence', *Journal of Adolescence* 32 (4): 835–48.

Palacios, J., and D. Brodzinsky. 2010. 'Review. Adoption Research: Trends, Topics, Outcomes', *International Journal of Behavioral Development* 34 (3): 270–84.

Pennings, G. 1997. 'The "Double Track" Policy for Donor Anonymity', *Human Reproduction* 12 (12): 2839–44.

Pennings, G. 2007. 'Belgian Law on Medically Assisted Reproduction and the Disposition of Supernumerary Embryos and Gametes', *European Journal of Health Law*, 14 (3): 251–60.

Raes, I., A. Ravelingien, and G. Pennings. 2016. 'Donor Conception Disclosure: Directive or Non-Directive Counselling?', *Journal of Bioethical Inquiry* 13: 369–79.

Readings, J., et al. 2011. 'Secrecy, Disclosure and Everything In-Between: Decisions of Parents of Children Conceived by Donor Insemination, Egg Donation and Surrogacy', *Reproductive Biomedicine Online* 22 (5): 485–95.

Richards, M., G. Pennings, and J.B. Appleby (eds). 2012a. *Reproductive Donation: Practice, Policy and Bioethics*. Cambridge, UK: Cambridge University Press.

Richards, M., G. Pennings, and J.B. Appleby. 2012b. 'Introduction', in M. Richards, G. Pennings and J.B. Appleby (eds), *Reproductive Donation: Practice, Policy and Bioethics*. Cambridge, UK: Cambridge University Press, pp. 1–12.

Schiffino, N., C. Ramjoué, and F. Varone. 2009. 'Biomedical Policies in Belgium and Italy: From Regulatory Reluctance to Policy Changes', *West European Politics* 32 (3): 559–85.

Shenfield, F. 1999. 'Truth or Dare? Anonymity: The Case For', *Progress in Reproduction* 3 (1): 8.

Turkmendag, I. 2012. 'The Donor-Conceived Child's "Right to Personal Identity": The Public Debate on Donor Anonymity in the United Kingdom', *Journal of Law and Society* 39 (1): 58–75.

Van Hoof, E., and S. Beck. 2015. 'Proposition de loi du 6 mai 2015 modifiant la loi du 6 juillet 2007 relative à la procréation médicalement assistée et à la destination des embryons surnuméraires et des gamètes, réglant le don anonyme de gamètes et instaurant un droit à l'identité pour les enfants issus d'un don', Chambre des représentants belge, Doc. 55/1066.

Van Peel, V. 2015. 'Proposition de loi du 11 mars 2015 créant un Institut pour la conservation et la gestion des données relatives aux donneurs', Chambre des représentants belge, Doc. 54/0952.

Wyverkens, E., et al. 2014. 'Beyond Sperm Cells: A Qualitative Study on Constructed Meanings of the Sperm Donor in Lesbian Families', *Human Reproduction* 29 (6): 1248–54.

Wyverkens, E., et al. 2015. 'The Meaning of the Sperm Donor for Heterosexual Couples: Confirming the Position of the Father', *Family Process* 56 (1): 203–16.

Part III

Same-Sex Families and Surrogacy

Chapter 6

When French Couples Become Parents through Surrogacy

Examining the Relationship with the Surrogate

Jérôme Courduriès

Surrogacy made its first explosive appearance in the media during the UK's 'Baby Cotton' case in 1985, and again during the 'Baby M' case three years later in the United States. In each of these cases, the surrogacy involved a couple consisting of a man and an infertile woman, who sought another woman to conceive and carry their child using the sperm of the intended father (Merchant 2011). In 1990, a French television programme made public the cases of two 'surrogate mothers', as they were called. The first woman, who had carried and given birth to her twin sister's child, reported to be very happy with the arrangement, while the second, who had carried a child for an infertile couple in exchange for compensation, said that she was miserable, namely because she had ceased to receive news from the couple and the child following the birth (Fine 1991). Despite their sensational depictions in the media, these cases were by no means new.

In ancient Rome, for example, a citizen whose wife was fertile could lend her to another man with a barren wife. The child born of this ephemeral sexual union would then belong to the second man, and would subsequently be raised by the infertile couple (Héritier-Augé 1985; Trimmings and Beaumont 2013). In a column for *La*

Repubblica, Claude Lévi-Strauss cited the example of the Samo of Burkina Faso. Girls in the Samo community, who usually married very young, were required to have an official lover before marrying their husband, the latter of whom would become the father of any child born of the union between his wife and her previous lover. Lévi-Strauss also cited the custom in certain African communities which dictated that a husband who left his wife or wives retained the right to become the father of any children they would later have, provided that he was present for the first post-partum report. A man married to an infertile woman could even 'obtain a fertile woman, either for free or in exchange for payment' in order to become a father. These three cases forced Claude Lévi-Strauss to make a clear distinction between the man who inseminated the woman and the father of the child. In the third case, he included 'the woman who lends her womb to another man or a childless couple' (Lévi-Strauss 2013: 95). In his analysis of ART in the state of Haryana in India, Aditya Bharadwaj (2012: 252) revealed that the participants he met often compared surrogacy to the traditional practice of levirate marriage,[1] which ART would come to replace. However, these traditional practices, though used in order to relieve childlessness, should not be considered as strict equivalents of what British anthropologists began to call 'New Reproductive Technologies' by the late 1980s (Edwards et al. 1993). Nevertheless, all of the above-mentioned societies offered infertile couples the opportunity to become parents by separating procreation from filiation.

Today, surrogacy has become even more complex, not only because of the techniques involved, but also because of the number of participants involved in the process. The World Health Organization considers surrogacy as a medically assisted procreation technique (Zegers-Hochschild et al. 2009). This is also the case in many countries like Brazil, where surrogacy is not subject to parliamentary legislation, but was nonetheless given a legal framework by the Federal Council of Medicine in 1992.

In terms of kinship practices, these techniques have the same effects. In terms of conceptions of reproduction, filiation and personhood, however, assisted reproductive techniques (Courduriès and Herbrand 2014) have come to blur the boundaries between the natural and the cultural, as well as the biological and social. When gametes do not meet in the uterus, but are introduced *in vitro* by a lab technician, the biological process that unfolds is generally perceived as 'natural', but nevertheless takes place in a high-tech environment (Strathern 1992a; Edwards 2009).

Technological progress has allowed for a division that would have previously been impossible in the field of reproduction. These days, in the case of heterosexual couples who use a surrogate, we identify not only the woman who donates the egg and the woman who carries and gives birth to the child, but also a third woman who conceived the parental project, and who will raise the child as his or her mother. Conception is thus represented in three phases, which often overlap: the desire to become a parent (which must be made explicit in order to access both reproductive assistance and adoption), conception and gestation. To better reflect contemporary developments, Flávio Tarnovski has proposed to complete the definition of the first parental function as identified by Esther Goody (1982), 'to conceive and give birth', with 'the intention of becoming a parent, and the implementation of a project to reach this end' (Tarnovski 2010: 251). In a society like France, where motherhood seems indivisible both in terms of general representations and in the Civil Code, the notion of more than two adults (and sometimes more than one woman) is almost impossible to imagine (Fine 1991; Théry and Leroyer 2014). The terms used today to describe each of the participants in the conception of a child through an assisted reproductive process focus on the function he or she performs: the sperm donor, the egg donor, the surrogate, and the intended parents. These descriptive terms, however, fall short of addressing the many questions attached to each participant's role. In this chapter, we will explore the role of the woman who carries and gives birth to the child, as well as that of the woman who donates her egg. Are these women mere adjuncts to the process? Are they simply fulfilling a contractual obligation? Do they become friends with the intended parents? Or do they perform the parental functions identified by Esther Goody alongside the intended parents, acting in the periphery of the relationship between the intended parents and their children? We will attempt to address these issues without losing sight of the importance of context when a surrogacy takes place in a different country and culture than that of the intended parents. Indeed, since the early 1990s, empirical research on surrogacy has been conducted in various national contexts, including in the United States, Israel and India. These studies have reported practices that change according to the time periods and cultural contexts in which they take place.

The evolution of technology in the domain of procreation has produced a division that, up until now, would have been not only impossible, but even unthinkable. Assisted reproduction with donor gametes differentiates the woman who carries the baby for nine months and gives birth from the woman who donated her oocyte. As of now, in the case of heterosexual couples who resort to gestational surrogacy, not only are these two women distinguishable, but also a third who conceives the project, who rears the child and is the mother. Here, procreation is a three-dimensional procedure of different projects that usually merge, exposing the desire of parenthood (which is always made explicit in procedures for assisted reproductive technology and for adoption), conception and gestation.

Surrogacy is prohibited in France. First, in 1991 the Court of Cassation condemned the practice of surrogate mothers on the grounds that 'there are things that come under business that can be the subject of agreements' (Article 1128 of the Civil Code). The judgement of 29 July 1994 explained the prohibition, arguing that 'any agreement concerning procreation or gestation on behalf of another is void' (Article 16-7 of the Civil Code). The Penal Code, meanwhile, provides no sanction against the 'surrogate mother' or against the applicants, but against the intermediary.

A number of prohibitions affect assisted reproduction techniques in France, such as access to medical assistance for procreation for couples of women and single women, trans people, or women over forty-three years of age, or recourse to surrogacy. This does not mean that French people in these situations will never have a child as close to them as possible in terms of biogenetical links. A number of them turn to other countries with more liberal, or at least less repressive, legislation. French people who resort to surrogacy abroad, in a country that does not prohibit but authorizes and supervises this technique, do this despite the French law. Once the child is born on foreign soil, except in rare cases, his/her birth is not recorded in the Civil Register, and thus the child is excluded from the national community. Refusing to frame surrogacy in France and recognizing children born of surrogacy abroad, French people still resort to surrogacy and many children are born abroad. This leads the families I interviewed to a form of unprecedented distortion between descent and nation (Courduriès 2017; Giroux et al. 2017). Most of these children have a foreign birth certificate and the nationality of their birth country.

Surrogacy is the subject of many ethical, moral and political discussions. The important questions that surrogacy raises concerning the availability of the human body and the commercial aspect of this practice in certain countries obscure other issues that summon the curiosity of an anthropologist interested in kinship and definitions of being. This chapter discusses how surrogacy, a medical technology and at times a commercial operation, is also a practice that establishes kinship.

The Maternal Role of the Woman Who Carried the Child

My research on surrogacy is currently in progress.[2] So far, I have conducted interviews with twenty families in France. In thirteen of these cases, the families were started by a male couple; in six cases, the parental couple was heterosexual; and in one case, the surrogate's help was enlisted by a single gay man. One couple sought a surrogate in Russia, one couple in Poland and another in India; in the other cases, the surrogates were found in North America (mainly in the US, but also in Canada). The conversations we had lasted several hours, and I had the opportunity to meet with some of the parents several times.

One male couple, parents of a two-year-old boy, felt that the woman who had carried their child was 'a kind of mother' as the child had 'grown in her belly'. Here, the woman who carried the child was attributed a maternal quality, unlike in a previous case in which the couple ignored the woman who donated her eggs (and therefore passed her genes on to the child), contradicting the notion that a parent is first and foremost a genitor. Of the two physiological components that make up the maternal function of procreation, pregnancy is given slightly more value in this case. In other words, *quasi-maternity* seems to be based on the bodily experience of pregnancy and childbirth, rather than procreation *in vitro*. In a context where surrogacy alone represents the by-product of an artificial and disembodied procreation in the minds of its critics, the woman who carries and gives birth to the child preserves the 'natural' image of procreation. Among the men in this case, the surrogate mother is 'a kind of mother' with whom they maintain regular contact and exchange family news. They send her photographs of their child. They also began to show their little boy pictures of her as early as his very first weeks after their return to France, explaining that it is 'thanks to her' they 'were able to have a child'. They have also told the child about the egg donor, though they waited many years before doing so. In the male couple's family, a place in the child's life appears to be available for the surrogate, this 'sort-of mother', but it is a place that she does not have to share with the egg donor. There are, of course, logical explanations for this: although the egg donor's identity can be revealed at the request of the child after he turns eighteen, in this case (as in many other), the donor declined to meet the intended parents. Moreover, the couple's relationship with the surrogate is as predominant as it is friendly.

Arthur and Gerald,[3] another couple in the study, felt that their eight-month-old son also had two mothers: one who gave birth, and another who facilitated the pregnancy by donating her eggs. From this point of view, their case was quite exceptional in this study's population. In the little book they put together to help tell their child the story of his birth, each woman wrote a message to the boy and signed, respectively, 'belly mummy' and 'luv Mummy'. The two fathers said that for the surrogate mother, who was already a mother before the birth of their child, this is another kind of maternity to experience, a maternity that while present every day, is also less emotionally involved. In the same way that Arthur and Gerald say that she, her husband and her son are their 'American family', the surrogate mother says that the couple and their son are her 'French family'. Here, the surrogate mother has joined the fathers of the child she carried as part of the family, and vice versa, a situation which is not the case with the egg donor, who while designated by a familial term, had a much more limited relationship with the family during and after the pregnancy.

Both cases highlight, in a relatively new way, how the work of providing gametes and the work of carrying a child both come back to a biological perspective of motherhood. In short, the way the two women are addressed highlights that for intended parents, this woman is not a stranger, but is not their child's parent either. Moreover, surrogacy can create, under certain conditions, real parental links with the woman who bore the child and, to a lesser extent, the woman who provided her eggs, as the first case demonstrates (Ragoné 1996; Teman 2010; Courduriès 2016).

In Europe and America, there are many obstacles that prevent us from imagining that the maternal function of procreation can be shared. The first is the way in which we refuse to imagine that parental attributes – as outlined by Esther Goody – can be shared by several adults. Yet this division is already at work in many family situations and on every continent; we already accept, for example, foster families, adoption, family recomposition and the use of third parties (e.g. sperm donors) in order to become parents. Agnès Fine (2001) has proposed that we reflect on these situations within the framework of pluri-parenthood (*pluriparentalité*), a concept that includes situations where more than two adults have contributed to the child's existence, whether through the development of the parental project or the creation and/or birth of the child.

Parental attributes, at least in terms of procreation, can now be spread among several people. However, the definition of what exactly a parent is according to French society and, more broadly, in all societies in which family ties are traditionally organized according to the principles observed by David Schneider in North America, suggests that parents suffer from little to no competition. The logic of elective filiation has long existed in these societies. Nevertheless, it is generally considered that parents must be connected to the child by a biogenetic relationship, or, to be more precise, that children should ideally be the product of both parents' sexuality (Schneider 1968). Moreover, although the father can access paternity by recognition or marriage to the mother, motherhood, in turn, seems to be rooted in the bodily experience of childbirth.

In both situations, the principle of exclusive filiation is slightly modified, but still respects the essential elements. In his or her daily life, the child has two parents. In a family with two fathers, however, a more substantial exception is made when it comes to another traditional principle: that of heterosexual filiation. Because of their concern about questions that their son will eventually ask, and perhaps in an effort to demonstrate to the interviewer that they adhere to the familial norms prescribed by French society, the parents explain that the surrogate is a 'kind of mother'. When I met the couple, the child was not legally recognized by French civil status. On the birth certificate issued by the judge on American soil, two fathers were listed, but no mother.

Between a Mother and a Stranger

None of the mothers I met in the study said that they recognized the woman who carried their child as 'a kind of mother'. There are certainly many reasons for this, but one reason in particular is especially significant: for a gay couple, the goal of having a framework for raising the child that closely conforms to prevailing familial norms can be achieved by choosing to perceive the woman who carries the child as a mother figure. A woman who seeks the aid of another woman to carry her child, on the other hand, is required to deny any and all maternal qualities to this woman. The mother must construct her own motherhood without having carried, given birth to, or perhaps even conceived her child, a task that is made all the more difficult by the fact that surrogacy is denounced by many as morally suspect. Her motherhood is weakened and even challenged in France by civil status documents and judicial decisions. In a society that cannot seem to tolerate an additional mother or father in a family, the intended mother's maternal status is unable to withstand the least bit of competition.

Nevertheless, not wanting to see the surrogate as another 'kind of mother' for fear of encouraging the dominant representations of motherhood based on pregnancy and childbirth does not necessarily mean that there is a total absence of recognition of the role played by the woman who carried the child. On the contrary, all of the mothers I spoke with during the study (as did all the fathers, gay and straight) stressed the important role of the surrogate in achieving their goal of starting a family, and integrated her into the story of their family that they tell (or will tell) to their child. This family story, told to the child (as well as the extended family, friends, and the researchers who conducted this study), has several functions. It puts the child's history into words, and marks its beginning at the child's conception, or even at the parents' decision to start a parental project (Delaisi de Parseval 2008). It gives the child many elements to which he or she can later refer, as well as the ability to stay in touch with (or contact at a later time) the woman who gave birth to him or her. It also protects the parents against any accusations that they have lied to their child, or denied him or her insight into the corporeal aspect of their own creation. Finally, this story serves to recognize the different people who played a role in creating the child, and thus serves as an act of recognition to all involved.

The women in my corpus who, along with their husbands, had sought the aid of a surrogate never reported seeing the woman who had carried their child as a maternal figure. Some presented her as a friend. This was the word that was used by Nadine and her husband, who had turned to a California agency that eventually helped them find a surrogate, sending the records of several possible surrogates to Nadine and her husband. Several years later, when her children, both born of the same surrogacy, were ten years old, Nadine said that she and the surrogate shared many common interests, that their time together had been a rich experience, and that they remained great friends.

For some parents, the surrogate, much more than a simple supplier of children, has become part of the family. In Helena Ragoné's pioneering study on surrogacy in the United States in the late 1980s and early 1990s, in which she studied surrogates as well as the women she described at the time as adoptive mothers (Ragoné 1994), she showed that the consistent logic in bringing the surrogate into the family of the intended parents is also initiated by the surrogates themselves.

A Nanny, the Children's Guardian

Years ago, at the initiative of members of an association of infertile persons who were anxious to find a role for the woman who had helped them achieve their desire for motherhood, a word was diverted from its usual meaning: the surrogate became a *nounou* ('nanny', or 'nurse'). When discussing her first meeting with her surrogate, for example, Nadine exclaimed: 'We had found our nanny and she was great!'

We do not know if the term *nounou* is widely adopted outside of the heterosexual couples that we met in our study, but the term nevertheless has several dimensions. By evoking the image of a woman employed to care for the child, it makes the monetarized relationship between the intended parents and the surrogate mother (as the former are indeed providing the latter with a financial payment or compensation) more acceptable from the points of view of those involved. The term *nounou* also adds value to the role of the woman who carried the child, but without going so far as to consider her a mother. At the same time, the term recognizes the surrogate as the holder of one parental attribute (again, in the sense of Esther Goody), that of 'nurturing' the child. The *nounou* is the one to whom the parents entrust the child, the guardian; this is the notion that parents attribute to this metaphor. Though the traditional role of the nurse is to nurture the child with whom she is entrusted, no parents in the study mentioned the actual nurturing role of the surrogate mother. The child and his nurse are connected to each other through the transmission of a nourishing substance. In many non-European and North American societies and, at one time, in some European societies, this nutritive consubstantiality was at the basis of parental ties (Carsten 2003; Vernier 2006). In a general sense, it is because the nurse's relationship to the child is integral to kinship, and especially, according to the 'ideology of motherhood', to the relationship between mother and child, that some mothers undergo hormonal treatments in order to produce milk and breastfeed after birth (Teman 2010: 151). Returning to the surrogate, the question arises of the nutritive consubstantiality of the child and the woman who carried and gave birth to him/her. Qualifying this woman as a *nounou* allows the intended parents to value her contribution and, at least for some parents, allow her to take on the historical image of the nurse, hovering at the edge of kinship. At the same time, assigning to this woman the role of the nanny, in the sense of someone who watches and cares for the child, could also echo a desire on the part of the intended parents to minimize her physical and biological role in having created the child. Similarly, the surrogate herself often tries to minimize her own role and reduce it to a simply functional role, thus highlighting the intended parents' intention, care and education of the child, and enhancing the link between the child and his mother (Ragoné 1996: 360). The surrogate, far from being a kind of mother, is really more of a maternity facilitator. It is almost certain that it was this idea that many of the surrogates that Elly Teman encountered in Israel wished to highlight. They themselves admitted, not only to the anthropologist but also to their own children, that they considered themselves as a 'babysitter' for the child they had carried for another woman. Not considering themselves as a 'kind of mother' was a way to leave space for the intended mother, but also to demonstrate to their own children the boundary between their family and the family of the child they had carried for someone else (Teman 2010: 56).

Participants Bound by Contract

Among the people I met, some explained that they saw the surrogate as simply a person to whom they were bound by contract. Two of these people, Nicolas and Didier, are the parents of a three-year-old boy who was born thanks to a Polish woman whose help his fathers sought. The contract was drawn up in Poland (the native country of one of the fathers), and every stage of the surrogacy took place in that country with the exception of the birth, which took place in France. If, at that point, authorities had suspected that the couple had enlisted the help of a surrogate, the family would have faced criminal prosecution, as surrogacy is illegal in France. For Nicolas and Didier, however, the benefits seemed to outweigh the risks at the time. They were mainly motivated by the health of their child, but also by the legality of his birth, as the birth itself was achieved by natural means: the woman who gave birth and the biological father were both registered as the child's parents. The two fathers, one of whom speaks Polish, continue to exchange news regularly with the surrogate, but they have not seen her since their last meeting on the first birthday of the child.

Patricia and Daniel have a six-year-old daughter. To become parents, they found a surrogate in Russia. The woman who carried the child also provided her eggs, and gave birth in her own country. Direct contact with her was limited, and always mediated by an interpreter, a situation that would not change over the course of the surrogacy. Two or three times a year, on their daughter's birthday or the New Year for example, they send her photographs and exchange news in English. During our discussions, Patricia and Daniel expressed their gratitude for the surrogate and explained that without her help they would not have been able to have their daughter. They are undoubtedly grateful, but also believe that they helped her in return, as she was able pay for her son's education with the financial compensation she received for carrying the child. Aside from this feeling of gratitude, Patricia and Daniel have no particular personal connections with the surrogate, but said that if their daughter ever expressed interest in meeting her, they would arrange a meeting.

Valentin is the father of a four-year-old girl. He now lives with his daughter and his partner. When he began the surrogacy process in the United States, however, he was single, and therefore founded and developed his plans to have a child alone. Throughout our conversations, he used words and phrases that clearly established the strictly contractual nature of his relationship with both the egg donor and the surrogate. They were all bound by contract, and were each provided with specific obligations and commitments: one woman donated her eggs, a second agreed to carry a child for him, and Valentin paid both women a sum of money, the amount, different for each, having previously been established in the contract. This was how he explained the process to me. He had never met the egg donor, who wished to remain anonymous, and had never been in direct contact with her either. He had met the woman who bore his child several times, however, and sends her news of his daughter once or twice a year. Between them, it was agreed that 'when she is older, and if she needs to', his daughter can meet and talk to the woman who carried her. During our interviews, Valentin never used kinship terms to describe the woman who gave birth to his daughter (or the woman who donated her eggs) and insisted that he had not begun a friendship with her either. He has a strict vision of what he considers to be an injunction, both on the part of certain organizations and intellectuals, to not view surrogacy within the framework of a friendly interpersonal relationship.

Valentin, Patricia and Daniel, and Nicolas and Didier have all begun to tell their children the story of their birth. For Amelia, the daughter of Patricia and Daniel, the woman who gave birth to her was described by her parents as a 'nice lady who stood in for mom when she could not carry you in her womb'. In these three families, as in others, a photo album with pictures of the donor and surrogate serves as a visual aid to this story, and is available at home for the children to consult, either alone or with their parents. When these three families were asked about the surrogate, however, they did not use any kinship terms. This was also the case with the egg donor. These experiences with surrogacy, rarely recorded in other empirical research, contrast with the perspectives expressed by people we met elsewhere.

It is interesting to note, however, that these couples insisted upon the contractual aspect of surrogacy, in so much as it is implemented in a society in which most exchanges are negotiated according to market logic. These parents go up against the current flow of contemporary debates on surrogacy in France. Critics of the practice often equate the financial compensation of a surrogate with the renting out of her uterus, or worse, the purchase of a child. In order to avoid these kinds of accusations, advocates of the regulation and supervision of the practice try to both limit its scope and highlight the human and emotional relationship between those participating in the surrogacy, especially in the case of transatlantic surrogacies. They do this, however, while acknowledging the existence of financial compensation in the majority of the states in which surrogacy is legal. Valentin thinks of himself as having found a compromise, a middle ground that both insists upon the contractual nature of the surrogacy and shows great respect for the women who helped him to become a father.

The Relationship with the Surrogate and Cultural Distance

According to the testimonies of the intended parents I met, as well as those found in other studies, it seems that in North America, surrogacy, while certainly not a casual practice, does not place the kind of taboo on surrogates that would prevent them from discussing the process with their friends and family, or establishing and maintaining a relationship with those for whom she carries the child.

Other cross-border surrogacies can bring together people who live in worlds where kinship norms, local theories on reproduction, and roles of men and women are very different. Sometimes, significant economic differences and, of course, geographical distance and the lack of a common language can add to the cultural rift, making it difficult or impossible to build and maintain personal relationships without the help of an intermediary. As part of her doctoral research, Delphine Lance, who led a double study in the United States and Ukraine, has demonstrated that surrogacy in Ukraine, while legal, is very socially maligned, and surrogates are reluctant to speak about their experience of carrying another person's child (Lance 2017). This observation echoes the experiences of the surrogates who helped Nicolas and Didier in Poland, and Patricia and Daniel in Russia.

Amrita Pande has also shown that in Anand, a town in western India's state of Gujarat, very few surrogates involved in cross-border surrogacy maintained direct and regular contact with the intended parents of the child they were carrying or had carried (Pande 2014). In addition to the inherent differences in these cross-border relationships, the very structure of the surrogacies observed was found to be very hierarchical. The fact that these surrogacies were organized by commercial and medical intermediates, themselves assisted by matchmakers and 'hotel' staff in the dormitories where the surrogates spent all or part of their pregnancies, rendered any direct relationship between the surrogates and the intended parents nearly impossible. The surrogates, for whom the procedure meant five years of steady income for their families, are often wary of the intended mother, whom they see simply as a person who sends them a significant amount of money in order to 'rent out' their wombs. This perception is no doubt encouraged by the commercial surrogacy industry (Rudrappa 2015).

Conclusion

Surrogacy is a medical procedure (and in some countries a commercial procedure), but it is also a kinship practice, which gives childless men and women a child, and can lead to the creation of new kinds of relationships on the margins of kinship for the child. Marcin Smietana (2017) shows that in the North American context, circulation of money between intended parents on the one hand and the surrogate mother on the other facilitates making kin ties between parents and children and on the contrary allows de-kinning surrogates as mothers.

The intended parents we observed in the study, whether gay or heterosexual, desired the child, raised him or her, and defined themselves as the child's parents. The intended parents' community also saw them as such; the child, friends, family, the child's school, doctors, and sometimes even the government, all recognized them to be the parents of the child who was born of the surrogacy.

As for the woman who carries a child for another woman, she helps people who cannot conceive a child through sexual union so as to pass down their respective lines of descent. The question remains, however, to what extent the many relationships in the 'surrogate family' (Delaisi de Parseval and Collard 2007) and the family founded by the intended parents are constructed, as the ties that develop on both sides do not always fall under the definition of parenthood. Thinking about this question can help us to understand under what conditions a direct, respectful and sustainable link can be formed between the intended parents and surrogate. These questions must be asked by anthropologists, as they can also help us to understand whether the links established in surrogacy can go beyond merely contractual relationships, creating solid friendships and even family ties between the two families.

Jérôme Courduriès is an anthropologist and Associate Professor in the Department of Anthropology in Toulouse Jean Jaurès University, member of LISST (Laboratoire Interdisciplinaire Solidarités, Sociétés, Territoires; Interdisciplinary Solidarity, Society, and Territory Studies) – CAS (Centre d'Anthropologie Sociale; Center for Social Anthropology) (UMR 5193). His research focuses on the anthropology of kinship and gender.

Notes

A portion of these analyses were published in Courduriès 2016. Permission was granted for reprint by the *Journal des Anthropologues* of a portion of 'Ce que fabrique la gestation pour autrui: Les relations entre la femme porteuse, l'enfant et ses parents', 144–45: 53–76.

1. In some societies, a widow, especially if she is childless, must marry a brother of her deceased husband or, failing that, one of his paternal cousins.
2. My research work forms part of the collective programme ETHOPOL funded by the French ANR (n°ANR-14-CE29-0002).
3. I have changed all the interviewees' names to pseudonyms and removed other identifying details.

References

Bharadwaj, A. 2012. 'The Other Mother: Supplementary Wombs and the Surrogate State in India', in M. Knecht, M. Klotz and S. Beck (eds), *Reproductive Technologies as Global Form: Ethnographies of Knowledge, Practices, and Transnational Encounters*. Frankfurt: Campus Verlag.

Brunet, L., J. Courduriès, M. Giroux and M. Gross. 2017. *Le recours transnational à la reproduction assistée avec don: Perspective franco-québécoise et comparaison internationale*, Rapport remis à la Mission de recherche Droit et Justice.

Carsten, J. 2003. *After Kinship*. Cambridge: Cambridge University Press.

Courduriès, J. 2016. 'Ce que fabrique la gestation pour autrui: Les relations entre la femme porteuse, l'enfant et ses parents', *Journal des Anthropologues* 144–45: 53–76.

Courduriès, J. 2017. 'La lignée et la nation: État civil, nationalité et gestation pour autrui', *Genèses* 108: 29–47.

Courduriès, J., and C. Herbrand. 2014. 'Genre, parenté et techniques de reproduction assistée: bilan et perspectives après 30 ans de recherche', *Enfances Familles Générations* 21: 1–27.

Delaisi de Parseval, G. 2008. *Famille à tout prix*. Paris: Éditions du Seuil.

Delaisi de Parseval, G., and C. Collard. 2007. 'La GPA', *L'Homme* 183: 29–54.

Edwards, J. 2009. 'The Matter in Kinship', in J. Edwards and C. Salazar (eds), *European Kinship in the Age of Biotechnology*. New York: Berghahn Books, pp. 1–18.

Edwards, J., S. Franklin, E. Hirsch, E. Price and M. Strathern. 1993. *Technologies of Procreation: Kinship in the Age of Assisted Conception*. Manchester: Manchester University Press.

Fine, A. 1991. 'Des parents "en plus" ', in G.R.I.E.F. (Groupe de Recherches Interdisciplinaire d'Etude des Femmes), *Se reproduire, est-ce bien naturel?* Toulouse: Presses Universitaires du Mirail, pp. 29–46.

Fine, A. 2001. 'Pluriparentalités et système de filiation dans les sociétés occidentales contemporaines', in D. le Gall and Y. Bettahar (eds), *La pluriparentalité*. Paris: PUF, pp. 69–93.

Giroux, M., J. Courduriès, M. Gross. 2017. *Le recours transnational à la reproduction assistée avec don: Perspective franco-québécoise et comparaison internationale*. Rapport au GIP Mission de recherche Droit et Justice, July 2017.

Goody, E. 1982. *Parenthood and Social Reproduction: Fostering and Occupational Roles in West Africa*. Cambridge: Cambridge University Press.

Héritier-Augé, F. 1985. 'La cuisse de Jupiter. Réflexions sur les nouveaux modes de procréation', *L'Homme* 94 (25): 5–22.

Lance, D. 2017. 'Mettre à distance la maternité: La gestation pour autrui en Ukraine et aux Etats-Unis', *Ethnologie Française* 3: 409–20.

Lévi-Strauss, C. 2013. 'Problèmes de société: excision et procréation assistée', in *Nous sommes tous des cannibales*. Paris: Éditions du Seuil, pp. 81–101.

Merchant, J. 2011. 'Procréation et politique aux Etats-Unis: le cas de la GPA', in G. David et al. (eds), *La GPA: Rapport de l'Académie nationale de médecine*. Paris: Lavoisier, pp. 213–24.

Pande, A. 2014. *Wombs in Labor: Transnational Commercial Surrogacy in India*. New York: Columbia University Press.

Ragoné, H. 1994. *Surrogate Motherhood: Conception in the Heart*. Boulder, CO: Westview Press.

Ragoné, H. 1996. 'Chasing the Blood Tie: Surrogate Mothers, Adoptive Mothers and Fathers', *American Ethnologist* 23 (2): 352–65.

Rudrappa, S. 2015. *Discounted Life: The Price of Global Surrogacy in India*. New York: New York University Press.

Schneider, D.M. 1968. *American Kinship: A Cultural Account*. Englewood Cliffs, NJ: Prentice Hall.

Smietana, M. 2017. 'Affective De-commodifying, Economic De-kinning: Surrogates' and Gay Fathers' Narratives in US Surrogacy', *Sociological Research Online* 22 (2): 5. http://www.socresonline.org.uk/22/2/5.html. Accessed 2 July 2019.

Strathern, M. 1992a. *Reproducing the Future: Essays on Anthropology, Kinship and the New Reproduction Technologies*. Manchester: Manchester University Press.

Strathern, M. 1992b. *After Nature: English Kinship in the Late Twentieth Century*. Cambridge: Cambridge University Press.

Tarnovski, F. 2010. Être *père et homosexuel dans la France contemporaine, thèse de doctorat en anthropologie*. Toulouse: EHESS.

Teman, E. 2010. *Birthing a Mother: The Surrogate Body and the Pregnant Self*. Berkeley: University of California Press.

Théry, I., and A.-M. Leroyer. 2014. *Filiation, origines, parentalité: Le droit face aux nouvelles valeurs de responsabilité générationnelle*. Paris: Odile Jacob.

Trimmings, K., and P. Beaumont. 2013. 'General Report on Surrogacy', in K. Trimmings and P. Beaumont (eds), *International Surrogacy Arrangements: Legal Regulation at the International Level.* Oxford: Hart Publishing, pp. 439–550.

Vernier, B. 2006. 'Du bon usage de la parenté construite avec des humeurs corporelles (sang et lait) et quelques autres moyens', *European Journal of Turkish Studies* 4. http://ejts.revues.org/623. Accessed 30 June 2019.

Zegers-Hoschschild, F., G.D. Adamson, J. de Mouzon, O. Ishihara, R. Mansour, K. Nygren, E. Sullivan and S. Vanderpoel (on behalf of ICMART and WHO). 2009. 'The International Committee for Monitoring Assisted Reproductive Technology (ICMART) and the World Health Organization (WHO) Revised Glossary of ART Terminology', *Human Reproduction* 24 (11): 2683–87.

Chapter 7

Using ART or Surrogacy

Designating Third Parties in the Reproductive Process, and Representing Family Ties in Same-Sex Families

Martine Gross

In this chapter, we will focus on same-sex couples who have chosen to start a family by using a third party in the reproductive process. For women, this third party can be an anonymous or semi-anonymous donor through medically assisted reproduction with a sperm donation.[1] This third party is sometimes a friend who has agreed to contribute to the creation of a child, but chooses not to claim his paternity – this kind of donor will hereby be referred to as a 'known donor'. The third party can also be a father or two fathers who choose to co-parent.[2] Same-sex co-parenting occurs when a man and woman (usually both homosexual) who are not romantically involved reproduce and raise their children in their respective homes: the maternal home and the paternal home. In this case, there can be two to four people involved in the parenting of the child, depending on whether the partner(s) of the mother and/or father are also involved in the parental project.[3] In order to procreate, male couples need a woman to carry their child, as well as an egg donor if they choose to use a surrogate; they may even wish to include a mother or two mothers in the parenting of the child. As medically assisted procreation has been reserved for heterosexual couples suffering from fertility problems since the French Parliament adopted the bioethics laws in 1994, French female couples often go abroad, usually to Belgium and Spain (more rarely, the Netherlands and Denmark), to use artificial insemination via a sperm donor. Surrogacy is also prohibited in France, so men who use this practice must travel to countries where it is legal (usually to the United States and Canada, and in rarer cases to Russia, Ukraine or India).

While the May 2013 law allowed same-sex couples to marry and adopt children together (or adopt those of a spouse), it has not opened access to medically assisted procreation to female couples, nor has it legalized the use of a surrogate. Hence, before the new law was passed, a child born to a gay couple could not legally have two same-sex parents; now, the partner of a mother or father can establish filiation with the child through marriage and adoption. Using several surveys of men and women who have chosen to include a third party in the procreation of a child, this chapter will explore their perceptions and representations of what it means to be a parent by examining the establishment of family ties with the child, terms of address, and discussions surrounding third-party reproduction.

Three questionnaires were conducted in 1997, 2001 and 2005 among 30, 221 and 270 members, respectively, of the Association of Gay and Lesbian Parents and Future Parents (APGL). In 2012, the Survey of the Family and Conjugal Function of Same-Sex Families (the FHP Survey) was conducted among 624 lesbian and gay parents, half of whom were not members of an association. Interviews were conducted with approximately forty families. Data from these surveys are not intended to represent all LGBT families in France; obtaining a representative sample is impossible because the reference population is unknown. Within the surveyed population, however, these questionnaires allowed us to explore different types of parental projects (whether of an individual or couple), methods of designating the partner of the legal mother or father, and the terms used by children to address their non-statutory parents, as well as those used to discuss the third party (sperm donor, surrogate or egg donor) that helped to create the child (Gross 2008, 2012).

Families with Lesbian Mothers: Terms of Address

Between 1997 and 2005, the ways in which children addressed (or were encouraged to address) the partner of their legal mother changed significantly (see Table 7.1). The spiritual and/or religious term *marraine* ('godmother'), still widely used in the 1990s, was approaching extinction by 2005. In the most recent survey, most female partners referred to themselves with a maternal nickname: *mamou, mamina,* or another word that means 'mother' in another language. Using the first name as a term of address is becoming less and less common, while the term *maman* ('mum'), either alone or followed by a first name, has grown in popularity. The most recent qualitative survey conducted by FHP confirms this trend.

It is worth noting that during this period, the preferred methods of starting a same-sex family also evolved. By 2005, more women were deciding not to co-parent with a father (or two fathers), opting instead to go abroad for artificial insemination, and placing more importance on the role of their relationship as a couple in their parental project. As a result, the ways in which the legal mother's partner is involved in the child's parenting have changed. This observation is supported by the answers of the partners of legal mothers to the question 'How do you see your role in the parenting of the child?' (see Table 7.2). The answer 'As that of a future parent', which was already a common response in 2001, continues to grow in popularity, while the answer 'As involved in the parenting, but not as a parent' is in decline. In the FHP Survey, the eldest child

Table 7.1. Terms of address used.

	1997 (n=30)	**2001 (n=221)**	**2005 (n=270)**
First name	50%	34%	23%
Marraine	40%	7%	4%
Nickname	n/a	46%	39%
Maman + first name	10%	9%	16%
Maman	0%	4%	17%

Table 7.2. How do you see your role in the parenting of the child?

	2001 (n=62)	**2005 (n=85)**	**2012 (n=276)**
unwilling	3%	1%	0%
involved but not a parent	16%	6%	3%
as a parent	81%	93%	96%

of the surveyed couples was co-parented from birth in 96 per cent of families with lesbian parents, while in 3 per cent of cases the child was born to a single parent. In less than 1 per cent of cases, the child was born to a parent whose partner was unwilling to participate in the parenting of the child.

The surveys conducted in 2001 and 2005 showed an increase in the percentage of respondents who were partners of a biological mother and saw themselves as a parent (from 81 per cent to 93 per cent), while the percentage of respondents who described themselves as either unwilling to participate in the parenting of the child, or involved in the parenting of the child but not a parent, decreased from 19 per cent to 7 per cent. In the FHP Survey, of the 354 families with lesbian parents in which the eldest child was not born from a previous relationship, 94.4 per cent responded that their parental project was founded as a couple.

In other words, among the families with lesbian parents surveyed, artificial insemination (AI) with a sperm donor was increasingly used not only as a means of having a child, but as a way for lesbian couples to start a family together. The partners of legal mothers are also steadily becoming more invested in the parenting of the child, and are becoming more likely to consider themselves as a parent of the child.

Designating Family Ties

While analysing the designation of family ties in families with lesbian parents, I was particularly interested in the gendered or neutral nature of the terms used (e.g. parent vs. mother) in the answers to the question 'When speaking to your child about their life, how do you explain the story of his/her conception?' Indeed, the answer 'We are both his/her mother' does not have the same effect as saying, 'We are both his/her parents'. Unlike 'two mothers', the phrase 'two parents' is not gendered. The decision to use the phrase 'two parents' reflects a compromise with the standard definition of a family; by identifying themselves as two 'parents', a female couple can comply with the two-parent standard without directly challenging the heteronormative notion that a family consists of 'one woman/mother and one man/father'.

Among the women surveyed, the neutral term 'parents' was often accompanied by some kind of differentiation or individuation for each party when it came to the preferred terms of address. In fact, the neutrality of the term 'parent' can lead to a scenario in which the child is actually encouraged to distinguish between his/her legal and non-legal mother.[4] In this case, the child often addresses the mother's partner with a nickname or by their first name, while the biological mother is called *maman* (mommy).

However, when the terms of address are gendered, as was the case for most respondents (e.g. 'he has two mums') they are necessarily symmetrical. Children often address the partner of their custodial mother as *maman*, or *maman* followed by their first name.

Some of the mothers we interviewed explained that they were afraid to confuse the child, or that the child might not be able to tell them apart. The decision to tell a child that he/she has just one mother or 'two parents', rather than 'two mothers' or 'two mums', likely reflects adherence to the traditional family structure, in which the one and only mother (or mum) is the woman who gives birth. Women who associate the word 'mother' with biological motherhood often prefer that their child call their partner by another term of address. Within this paradigm, the child can have two 'parents', because the word 'parent' may entail functions such as education and nurturing. To have 'two mothers' (or 'two mums'), however, is impossible, because the terms 'mum' and 'mother' focus on a unique biological phenomenon.

The Man Who Helped to Create the Child: A Father, a Nice Man, a Donor, or a Parent?

Lexical analysis of the write-in responses to the question 'How do you explain to your child the story of his/her conception?' in the 2005 survey also explores the designation of the man who helped to create the child.

Even when the genitor has no role in raising the child, the prevalence of representations attributing paternity is apparent in the ways in which he is discussed. However, these representations differ significantly depending on whether or not the genitor is known by the child, or is involved in his or her parenting. Here we must take into account the three possible scenarios that can include a third party: the situation in which the donor co-parents the child, the situation in which the donor is simply known by the family, and artificial insemination by an anonymous or semi-anonymous donor.[5]

In the case of the co-parenting scenario, the donor is the legal father of the child, and is involved in the child's upbringing on a daily basis. According to a series of interviews carried out in 2005, this man can be called 'the father', 'the biological father' or 'a relative'. These accounts never described two mothers, and showed a clear hierarchy between the legal parents and their partners (e.g. 'A dad and a mum for the conception, plus two more parents'). Only the biological mother was called *maman* by the child, and never her partner.

The 'known donor' is usually a friend who has agreed to donate his sperm in order to help to create a child. He is not, however, the child's legal father as he has not claimed the child as his own – and he usually has no intention of doing so. Depending on the situation, he occupies a position of varying importance in the daily life of the child. In the vast majority of accounts in which the child is conceived using a known donor, the sperm donor has no legal ties to the child, and is often uninvolved in his/her daily life – and is yet addressed with a familial term. He can be called 'the father who planted the seed', 'the donor who is one of the parents' or, more simply, 'the father who helped us'. Two of the three different kinds of links that influence our representations of parenthood – the biological or genetic link, the legal name, and the emotional bond – are absent from this kind of situation, namely the legal and emotional connections. His biological link with the child (since the known donor is, by definition, not anonymous) nevertheless seems to suffice in order for the sperm donor to be qualified by his paternity.

When it came to the terms of address used in situations where the donor is known, it seems that non-statutory mothers in the study were often called by their first name or a nickname, and never by *maman* or *maman* followed by a first name. Once the genitor is known, whether just as a known donor or as a father involved in the co-parenting of the child, he regains the status of 'parent' – which makes it less likely for the legal mother's partner to be identified as a second mother. Even if the known donor only plays a tenuous role in the life of the child or the couple, the hierarchy of biological and social ties in the representations of what makes a 'real' parent reappears in full force with his presence. As a result, there is no room left for the statutory mother's partner to be considered a parent.

In the case of artificial insemination, the donor is not known. In interviews collected in the study, the contribution of a man was always mentioned, with terms ranging from 'seed donor' or 'dad' to 'genitor' and 'biological father'. When children were young, donors were often referred to as 'a nice man who gave his seeds', and sometimes as 'a father we don't know' or 'an unknown father who helped us or gave us the seeds', but rarely as 'a donor', a term that was often thought to be too technical.

In the 2005 study, it is clear that as soon as the genitor – whether the father in co-parenting, the known donor or the anonymous donor – is identified by a kinship term, as soon as he is designated as the biological father or an unknown father, the two women cease to call themselves *maman*, and no longer think of themselves as two mothers. Designating the man who helped to create the child with a paternal term, even if he lacks a daily paternal role, reflects the implicit acceptance of the exclusive family model, which prescribes 'a father, a mother, and no one else' and prohibits two mothers for one child.

When two women or two men decide to build a family together, they challenge the filiation system that 'drives not only the idea that filiation is a fact of nature, but also a standard of exclusive filiation, i.e. the idea that each individual is the son or daughter of a single man and single woman' (Ouellette 1998: 160). Since the order of July 2005, a woman who gives birth in France no longer needs to legally claim the child she brought into the world; maternity is automatically given to the woman whose name is recorded on the birth certificate. In a way, 'the birth makes the mother'.[6] Also, with this model, declaring oneself the mother without having given birth to the child, or when there is already a declared birth mother, is impossible. Declaring oneself the father of the child when another has already been recorded on the birth certificate is also impossible. A same-sex couple who identify themselves as 'two mothers' or 'two fathers' undermine this exclusive model of filiation. Same-sex parents, however, are not the only ones to challenge these two exclusive models of filiation – 'one father, one mother' on one hand, and the naturalness of maternal descent on the other. This is evidenced by the difficulty of addressing not only the different aspects of surrogacy, but also the status given to third parties in step-families, as well as the question of a child's access to the identity of the donor who helped to create him or her. With the exclusive, procreation-based system of filiation in France, declaring oneself the mother of a child without having given birth, or when there is already a birth mother, is difficult to imagine, as is declaring oneself the father of the child when another has already been listed as the father on the birth certificate. A same-sex couple who identifies themselves as 'two mothers' or 'two fathers' undermines this exclusive French model of filiation. Indeed, with the present state of the law at the time of this study, only a man can declare himself a parent alongside the biological mother of the child. The parental commitment that establishes filiation through the recognition or presumption of relation through marriage (as presumption of paternity for married men) is not accessible to the partners of lesbian mothers. Since 2013, however, they have had the opportunity, due to the vote of the law opening marriage and adoption to same-sex couples, to adopt their spouse's child.

Families with Two Gay Fathers

Let us now examine the situation of men who have chosen to co-parent or to turn to surrogacy to start a same-sex family. In 2011, a qualitative interview survey collected the testimonies of around forty men who had used a surrogate, as well as those of a dozen men who were involved in the co-parenting of a child (Gross 2012; Gross and Mehl 2011). As with female couples, the conjugal aspect was often present. This spousal dimension of the parental projects observed in the survey differs from the results revealed by the surveys of the members of APGL in 1998 and 2005, where even as a couple, men were more often leading individual parental projects, and rarely identified themselves as two fathers (Gross 2006). Does raising and co-parenting a child with a couple of women, or raising a child without a daily maternal presence (as in the case of surrogacy), have an impact on how each man is named and identified by the children? How do gay fathers talk about the woman who carried their child?

Co-parenting

The male couples in the survey who had started families as co-parents with a woman or two women did not all talk about a joint parental project; more often than not, one man served as the leader in parenting, while the other served a more secondary, supportive role in the parenting of the child.

The men in the survey who had chosen to co-parent tended to identify biological origins and kinship. Some justified their choice of co-parenting by explaining that they wanted their child to have a biological heritage, or that they wanted to be able to tell the child where he or she came from. Yves, a single 45-year-old father and co-parent of two children, stated: 'I think a child should have a known and recognized biological father and mother so he knows where he comes from'. With co-parenting, procreation and filiation coincide. According to some of the men surveyed who had chosen this way of parenting, biological origins and parents are interchangeable terms. Concerning the designation of parental links, some couples actually insisted that there is one dad and one mum in their family, rather than two dads.

Surrogacy

In the early 2000s, at least within the APGL, there were very few men who turned to surrogacy as an option for having a child, discouraged not only by the method's financial costs but its social costs as well. Seeking the aid of a surrogate meant accepting the risk of being seen as contributing to the commercial exploitation of women's bodies, not to mention disregarding a legal ban on the arrangement. Added to this social stigma is the accusation of depriving a child of a mother who is involved in the child's daily upbringing. In a 2008 study, Emmanuel Gratton remarked that 'depictions of a child who has been deprived of his or her mother, or of a mother who rents out her uterus and makes the decision to give up her child, are generally very guilt-inducing. Women who make this decision are freed from this kind of guilt and prejudice' (Gratton 2008: 26).

The 2011 survey conducted with gay fathers who had used a surrogate revealed another reality: more and more gay men in APGL are resorting to surrogacy, choosing to pursue their desire for children as the product of their partnership, defining themselves as two fathers, and calling themselves *papa* and *daddy* (or even *papa* and *papa*). What is new in surrogacy is the conjugal nature of parental projects where two men decide to become fathers (with only one partner participating in the creation of the child).

Being able to declare that 'we' will live as two fathers, even if only one parent assumes legal paternity, is a strong motivation for a couple to choose surrogacy and start a family as an extension of their relationship, even if the child is not the biological product of the couple. This is the same motivation that inspires lesbians to travel abroad to use a sperm donor. Among gay men, however, it appears to happen later than with lesbian couples. The question of 'we' includes not only the domestic aspect of the parental project, but also identifies who the parents are. With the exception of two, all of the couples in the survey who felt that a child could only have one father and one mother evoked the parental 'we' and identified themselves as two fathers. Some fathers both called themselves *papa*, and others used a fatherly-sounding name for the other father such as *papou*, or the equivalent of dad in another language, like *daddy*. The diversity of these names reflects the wide range of nuances in the representations and personal definitions of kinship that these men give themselves.

The Surrogate Mother and Egg Donor: Two Mothers, One Mother, or No Mother?

The gay fathers in the study had many different ideas and representations of family and fatherhood. Forced to innovate, they often hesitated, having to move from the biological representation of parenthood (in which a child can only have one father and one mother) to a representation that is more focused on parenting (and thus allows for two fathers and no mother). These representations are not mutually exclusive, however, and respondents often combined them. Some explained, for example, that their child has two fathers (as they are both involved in the daily parenting of the child), as well as one or two mothers (the women who contributed to the birth of the child).

We found great diversity in the respondents' perspectives on the status and designation of the women who made them fathers. Most of the men in the survey had found surrogates in the United States, and in the majority of cases, two women contributed to the production of the child. In this kind of situation, the woman who contributes her genetic material is the egg donor, and another woman carries the child, who was conceived using sperm from one of the two men and the donor's egg. The couples in the study often called the woman who carried the child *maman* ('mum'), *la mere porteuse* ('the surrogate mother'), *la porteuse* ('the surrogate'), *la gestatrice* ('the gestational carrier'), *la surrogate*, or just used her first name. The egg donor was often identified by the terms *mère donneuse* ('donor mother'), *donneuse* ('donor') or her first name, if she was not anonymous. These designations reflect the ambiguity of what is meant by the term 'mother': is a woman a mother if she brought the child into the world, but does not raise him/her? Can she be a mother if she passed her genetic heritage down to the child, but did not carry him/her?

There are those who believe that in this kind of situation, there can be no mother, no mum. They consider that a mother is above all someone who has not only given birth to a child, but is also involved in the child's daily care and upbringing. Regardless of what she is called, the woman who helps two men become fathers often plays a role after the birth; she will always have a face and a name. The fact that these women are not mothers does not bar one or both of them (though it is usually the surrogate) from building a relationship with the couple whose child they helped create. These relationships are not limited to the time of pregnancy; they often persist and sometimes introduce a link that is considered familial by the fathers and even the surrogates. Surrogacy, therefore, is not comparable to anonymous sperm donation.

Two parameters affect the terms used to describe women who help men to become fathers. First, the decision whether to use just one woman or two women affects the terms used. When the same woman donates her egg and carries the child, she is often referred to by a maternal term such as 'mum', 'mother', 'biological mother' or 'birth mother', and thus considered the mother of their child. Next, the importance placed on the biological link also contributes to the designation of the donor. Some may consider her to be a 'real' mother, the biological mother or the donor mother, while others would consider the donor as without any maternal connotations.

Most of the men interviewed had found a surrogate in the United States, and had established a strong connection with her. Sometimes they were not only close to her, but to her husband and their children as well, who called the newborns 'surrogate brother (or sister)'. Anne Cadoret (2000 and 2002) and Geneviève Delaisi de Parseval (2008) had already noted this intense relational dynamic between gay fathers and surrogate mothers. When a heterosexual couple uses a surrogate, a very close, almost symbiotic relationship can arise between the surrogate mother and the intended mother during pregnancy (Teman 2010). It is rare, however, that these relationships maintain their intensity after the birth of the child. Among male couples, no intended mother comes to occupy a maternal space, which can thus be reserved for the surrogate. Ely Teman (2010) and Shireen Kashmeri (2008) have both reported that some women say they prefer to carry a child for a male couple because this kind of relationship is less stressful.

For male couples, considering the women who have contributed to the creation of their children as mothers, and maintaining close relationships with these women, does not seem to have any impact on how the two men choose to represent their paternity. With the exception of a few respondents who attributed a certain level of importance to the birth in their representation of what makes a father and a mother, most identified themselves as two fathers because they placed paternity in the realm of emotional connection and childcare.

Final Considerations

Listening to these men, it seems clear that their perceptions of the women who helped them become parents are different from those that we heard in the survey of lesbian mothers who had used sperm donors. The lesbian couples surveyed were able to easily separate the notions of 'father' and 'genitor', especially when the latter was not known. Gay fathers, on the other hand, were not able to make the distinction between the mother and the surrogate as easily. The lesbian mothers in the study whose parental project was started as a couple, and who both called themselves *maman*, almost never identified the sperm donor with a term from the kinship lexicon. Instead he was a 'genitor' or a 'donor', because a father, they said, is someone who is involved with the child. On the other hand, several gay fathers who had used a surrogate referred to her with a maternal term such as 'the mother', 'the surrogate mother', 'the birth mother', and sometimes 'the biological mother' or 'the donor mother'. Why do men seem to adhere to more common representations of procreation and kinship? Why do gay fathers and lesbian mothers address these 'third parties' differently? Is it possible that representing the progenitor as a father affects their perception of their relationship? The physical implications of sperm donation are minimal compared to those required in egg donation or surrogacy. Once conception has been achieved, the presence and involvement of a man is no longer required to make a woman a mother. This is not the case for men, however, who must accept the aid of a woman in order to go from being simple genitors to becoming fathers. Under French law (except in the case of adoption), a man cannot become a father without having identified the woman who gave birth to the child. Naming the birth mother, or having some sort of relationship with her, is the condition of his paternity.

Where do sperm donors, egg donors and surrogate mothers stand with regard to the children they helped to create? In his study of reproductive third parties in the United States (2011), Rene Almeling showed that sperm donors, even if they are not bound by any right or duty to the children born of their donation, often consider the children as their own, and themselves as fathers. On the contrary, egg donors and surrogate mothers tend to proclaim loud and clear that they are not mothers, and that they are only helping to create the child. While men declare their paternity as soon as they know they have created life, and do not feel that any further involvement is necessary, women cannot identify themselves as mothers without being automatically assigned to maternal duties (unless, of course, they are content to be called a 'bad mother'). To escape this judgement, as well as the guilt of having abandoned a child, their only recourse is to renounce their claim to motherhood, even if they have played a major role in bringing the child into the world. This renunciation is facilitated by the fact that motherhood is generally split into three separate spheres: gestational, genetic and emotional. Being only involved in the pregnancy or egg donation allows women to choose not to become the mother of the children to whom they have given birth.

Could the Explanation Be Linked to the Body?

In the case of gay male parents, the third party, whether a surrogate or donor, is a person whose existence is real and concrete, but whose contribution remains outside of the men's bodies. Since she has already forfeited her maternal status, the men take no risk in identifying the woman, starting a long-term, reciprocal relationship with her, or calling her the child's mother. For lesbian couples, on the other hand, cultivating a concrete relationship with a non-anonymous donor – a man whose sperm has been introduced into one of the two women's bodies, and who could eventually begin to think of himself as a father – could undermine the integrity of their relationship. Alain Ducousso-Lacaze (2004), for example, has highlighted the existence of heterosexual fantasies within some lesbian couples which involve the sperm donor.

When heterosexual couples maintain a relationship with the surrogate, they generally have no information identifying the egg donor unless she is the intended mother. Most of the gay men observed in the survey had taken steps so that the child could not only access the identity of the women involved in his birth, but also meet them face to face if the child ever expressed the desire to do so. Are these couples less threatened by the child's knowledge of the female donor's identity because they believe the 'social' infertility of the gay couple is less upsetting than the pathological infertility that affects heterosexual couples? Are gay fathers more concerned about their children eventually trying to discover their roots? Are they wholly motivated to give their child an account of his or her birth in the most accurate way possible, giving them the sense of being part of a common humanity, and thus reducing any possible feelings of having been born outside the norm?

An Israeli study (Landau et al. 2008) has found that using a homologous gamete donation is as difficult to accept for women as it is for men. Sperm donated to heterosexual couples, for example, is more likely to threaten the intended father than the intended mother. Conversely, an intended mother is more likely to feel threatened than an intended father in the case of an egg donation, since the process can put her parental link to the child in question. In other words, the biological and social ties developed by gay fathers differ significantly from those of infertile heterosexual couples. Firstly, the gestational donation and egg donation that help two men to become fathers are not homologous donations, and as a consequence, neither of the men is threatened. On the other hand, these donations do not have the effect of making the couple a reproductive couple. However, in order to represent their dual paternity, male couples must value the emotional and social links between the child and the father who is neither his biological nor legal parent. To do this, they sometimes go so far as to hide or deliberately ignore the biological nature of the relationship in order to avoid creating too great an imbalance between themselves and in the eyes of others. Female couples, in turn, cannot use this strategy, as it is much harder to hide having carried a child. If they want to be 'two mothers' and place importance on their elective maternity, they must value the conjugal dimension of their parental project, which the daily presence of a father, if only in speech, may weaken.

Martine Gross is a social science research engineer at the Centre d'études en sciences sociales du religieux (CéSor) attached to the Centre national de la recherche scientifique (CNRS) in France. She has devoted most of her work to gay and lesbian parenting and has published or edited many books on the subject.

Notes

This text draws from the article 'Les tiers de procréation dans les familles homoparentales' published in the journal *Recherches familiales*, no. 11, 2014, and has been submitted to Berghahn with the Editorial Board's full permission.

1. In a semi-anonymous donation, the donor agrees to have his identity revealed to the child if the latter asks and is no longer a minor.

Semi-anonymous donation is practised in the Netherlands, and is offered by some fertility clinics in Belgium.

2. I use the terms 'mother' and 'father' when the respondents consider and identify themselves as such.
3. The term 'parental project' implies the intention of becoming a parent, the means by which one chooses to become a parent, and the way in which one represents oneself as a future parent.
4. I use the adjectives *légal* (legal) and *statutaire* (statutory) interchangeably to describe the partner in a same-sex couple with whom the child's filiation has been established (these adjectives have also been used by Virginie Descoutures [2010]). The other partner is simply a 'social' parent. When the survey was being carried out, it was still impossible for a child to have two statutory (or legal) parents of the same sex. At most, the legal parent could share parental authority with the social (non-statutory) parent. Since the *Mariage pour tous* ('Marriage for All') law was passed, it has been possible to have two legal parents: a birth parent and an adoptive parent.
5. Although in some cases (notably in the Netherlands and Denmark), the child is able to access, if he or she wishes, information regarding the identity of the donor, we still consider the donor to be unknown in this case, as he cannot meet the child until the latter is no longer a minor.
6. In the case of anonymous childbirth, which in France allows a woman to decide not to be the mother of the child to whom she gave birth, the delivery of the child is considered (at least officially) as having never taken place.

References

Almeling, A. 2011. *Sex Cells: The Medical Market for Eggs and Sperm*. Berkeley: University of California Press.

Cadoret, A. 2000. 'L'homoparentalité, construction d'une nouvelle figure familiale', *Anthropologie et Sociétés* 24 (3): 39–52.

Cadoret, A. 2002. *Des parents comme les autres*. Paris: Odile Jacob.

Delaisi de Parseval, G. 2008. *Famille à tout prix*. Paris: Seuil.

Descoutures, V. 2010. *Les mères lesbiennes*. Paris: PUF.

Ducousso-Lacaze, A. 2004. 'A propos du père dans la parentalité lesbienne', *Divan Familial* 13: 29–42.

Gratton, E. 2008. *L'homoparentalité au masculin: Le désir d'enfant contre l'ordre social*. Paris: PUF.

Gross, M. 2006. 'Désir d'enfant chez les gays et les lesbiennes', *Terrain* (46): 151–64.

Gross, M. 2008. 'Deux mamans ou deux parents: Évolution de la désignation des liens dans les familles lesboparentales', in D.L. Gall (ed.), *Identités et genres de vie: Chroniques d'une autre France*. Paris: L'Harmattan, coll. 'Sociologies et environnement', pp. 199–216.
Gross, M. 2012. *Choisir la paternité gay*. Paris: Eres.
Gross, M. 2014. 'Les tiers de procréation dans les familles homoparentales', *Recherches familiales* 11: 19–30.
Gross, M. 2015. 'L'homoparentalité et la transparentalité au prisme des sciences sociales: révolution ou pluralisation des formes de parenté?', *Enfances, Familles, Générations* 23: i–xxxvii.
Gross, M. 2018. *Idées reçues sur l'homoparentalité*. Editions le Cavalier Bleu.
Gross, M., and D. Mehl. 2011. 'Homopaternités et GPA', *Enfances, Familles, Générations* 14: 95–112.
Gross, M., et al. 2019. 'Paternité gay et GPA: entre lien génétique et lien affectif', *Enfances, Familles, Générations* 31.
Kashmeri, S. 2008. 'Unraveling Surrogacy in Ontario, Canada: An Ethnographic Inquiry on the Influence of Canada's Assisted Human Reproduction Act (2004), Surrogacy Contracts, Parentage Laws, and Gay Fatherhood', Master of Arts thesis. Montreal, Quebec, Canada: Concordia University.
Landau, R., et al. 2008. 'A Child of "Hers": Older Single Mothers and Their Children Conceived through IVF with Both Eggs and Sperm Donation', *Fertility and Sterility* 90 (3): 576–83.
Ouellette, F.-R. 1998. 'Les usages contemporains de l'adoption', in A. Fine (ed.), *Adoptions: Ethnologie des parentés choisies*. Paris: Editions de la Maison des sciences de l'homme, pp. 153–76.
Teman, E. 2010. *Birthing a Mother: The Surrogate Body and the Pregnant Self*. University of California Press.

Chapter 8

Queer Families Online

The Internet as a Resource for Accessing and Facilitating Surrogacy and ART in France and the United States

Michael Stambolis-Ruhstorfer

In 2012 and 2013, as French legislators contentiously debated same-sex marriage and adoption, several American for-profit agencies offering assisted reproductive technologies (ART), including fertility treatments and surrogacy, held private seminars in Paris. They advertised their services to potential French and European parents, many of whom were gay and lesbian. Building on an already tense social climate marked by massive demonstrations against the proposed legislation, protest leaders of the Manif pour tous (Protest for All) publicly denounced the seminars. In addition to their fundamental opposition to parenting by same-sex couples more generally, they specifically decried the American 'commercialization' of ART, which they deemed threatening and un-French (Kovacs 2013). That these American organizations could advertise their services as 'products' to future clients – and to gay and lesbian people to boot – went against the public, free and heteronormative imperatives of the French ART system. Yet, on the other side of the Atlantic, these recruitment and marketing activities are normal and ordinary. Indeed, in the United States, even strong opponents of queer families, such as the lawmaker authors of a federal court *amicus curiae* in support of same-sex marriage bans, take it for granted that gays and lesbians access ART and other means of becoming parents. For example, even as they argued against same-sex marriage, the authors noted that 'same-sex couples now raise children together by virtue of artificial insemination, surrogacy, and adoption', and they mentioned the websites of several well-known agencies these couples use (Brief of *Amici Curiae* 2013).

The contrast between these examples illustrates the nationally specific circumstances between France and the United States that shape the challenges and opportunities same-sex couples face on their paths to parenthood. Since the legalization of same-sex marriage and adoption in 2013, French same-sex couples can jointly adopt or adopt the children of their spouses. Yet the ongoing restriction of fertility treatments to 'medically infertile' long-term heterosexual couples and a blanket ban on surrogacy means that lesbians and gay men must leave France in order to get the services they need, which requires money and means. Otherwise, their only local legal option is to search for people willing to engage in non-medical forms of reproduction, such as co-parenting or known-donor at-home insemination.

In contrast, in most states in the US, same-sex couples can adopt, use tissue banks, fertility clinics and surrogacy agencies. All of these forms of access to parenting – including, perhaps surprisingly, adoption – charge various fees, many of which clients must pay for out of pocket (Almeling 2011; Swanson 2014). This system of ART as a private, for-profit service open to all, regardless of family structure, has long helped to normalize queer parenting in the United States more generally. It has allowed same-sex couples to create families more easily and with more visibility than in France. The increasing banality of gay families is also reflected in polling data. For example, in May 2009, although only 40 per cent of US respondents in a national survey supported same-sex marriage, 54 per cent supported same-sex adoption (Swift 2014). In contrast, in France, only 46 per cent of respondents supported same-sex adoption in a December 2012 poll taken during the parliamentary debates, even as the majority supported same-sex marriage (IFOP 2012).

Unlike many of their French peers, who frame the legalization of same-sex couples' access to parenting as a threat to children or as the 'commercialization' of life and the human body, many American policymakers consider these practices as unremarkable.[1] In fact, in some circumstances, public agencies specifically target same-sex couples in order to encourage them to become parents. For example, in November 2015 in celebration of National Adoption Month, adoption services in Los Angeles posted banners on lampposts advertising an interracial gay couple with their adopted son (see Figure 8.1). They did so in part to encourage same-sex couples to become adoptive parents because, in contrast to France, there is a dearth of potential parents and a long waiting list of children needing homes.

Clearly, the French and US political, legal and cultural contexts on the issues of queer parenting diverge. Yet gay men, lesbians, bisexuals and transgender people in both countries want to create families just like anyone else. To reach that goal, however, they must not only contend with the limitations or advantages of their race, class and gender, but also with these specific national circumstances that constrain or enable their capacity to get the services and information they need. This chapter examines one tool, online resources, that

Figure 8.1. Adoption recruiting poster featuring a same-sex interracial couple and child. Los Angeles, 2015. Photograph by the author.

queer people – and the people trying to reach, serve and cater to them – use to create the conditions necessary to have children. It focuses in particular on websites run by LGBT organizations, commercial ART and co-parenting matchmaking providers, as well as professional organizations that serve same-sex couples and queer people hoping to become parents. By comparing these sites across France and the United States, we gain insights into the ways in which the restrictions on ART in France and their liberalization in the United States shape online resources, and ultimately same-sex parenting more broadly, in both countries.

The internet is an important site of analysis because of its radical potential to disrupt norms, connect people who share common goals, and facilitate the exchange of goods and services even in the face of harsh legal restrictions and social disapproval. Indeed, since the early days of the internet, feminists, for example, seized on the internet's potential to shrink or even neutralize geography and borders. In general, they described the internet as a tool for disadvantaged groups (Mele 1999; Shade 2002) to create collectives, share ideas and build a community (Harcourt 1999; Friedman 2010). Similarly, gay men, lesbians, bisexuals, transgender people and other marginalized sexual and gender minorities have turned to the internet to create and explore their identities. These online communities, as reflected in webpages ranging from commercial dating sites to activist organizations and forums, sustain activism (Pullen and Cooper 2010) and help people develop a positive sense of self as they connect with others like them (Davis and Brewer 1997; Craig et al. 2015; Hunter 2015). Moreover, such resources are especially important for people who live in hostile or unsupportive environments. Their online connections allow them to resist and overcome the limitations of their circumstances. Inasmuch as ART is impossible for queer people in France, the internet similarly gives them the agency to transcend restrictive legislation.

Previous research describes how queer families on both sides of the Atlantic have mobilized the internet to harness the power of new reproductive technologies and provide each other with solidarity in a largely heteronormative world (Mamo 2007). These spaces help gay men and lesbians develop a sense of what it means to be fathers, mothers and families (Deomampo 2015). Yet, because of the administrative complexities surrounding gay parenting – either their bans in France or state-level variation in the US – these online communities are also driven by the legal circumstances in which couples find themselves (Kazyak and Woodell 2016).

Engaging in 'economies of online cooperation' (Kollock 1999), queer parents share advice with each other about how to find the services and products, such as surrogacy, *in vitro* fertilization and gametes, they need. Surrogacy for gay men in the United States (Stacey 2004, 2006; Dempsey 2013), and France in particular where the illegality of the practice renders their needs especially problematic, is a salient example of the utility of this internet solidarity.[2] Similarly, lesbian couples network with each other to discuss strategies for finding appropriate sperm banks – especially for French women who have no access to local ART centres (Van Hoof, Pennings, and de Sutter 2015) – and tips about whether to use anonymous or donor-release sperm, for example (Hunter 2015; Donovan and Wilson 2008; Descoutures 2010; Gross, Courduriès, and Federico 2014). In so doing, queer families have helped developed online 'commodity networks' to facilitate the sharing of biological material between each other or to connect commercial providers, such as fertility treatment centres, to potential queer clients (Pullen and Cooper 2010).[3] As described below, these networks are visible in the online resources available to queer people seeking to become parents today.

Online spaces for queer family building are also caught up in local material circumstances relating to both the commercialization of ART and the ties between businesses and LGBT activism more generally (Scammell 2000). Online resources for queer families in the United States, for example, reflect the broader intersection between the economy and new forms of access to parenthood (Radin 2001; Almeling 2011). On the one hand, beyond the ethical qualms some have with the commercialization of health and reproductive services, the liberal commercialization of tissues and surrogacy means that these services are costly and unaffordable to many people. On the other hand, the framing of ART as a product in the US – rather than as a state-controlled 'medical' procedure as it is in France – has been a formidable advantage in helping queer families grow, especially white middle-class ones (Chasin 2000). Same-sex couples' desire to have children has created a formidable niche market that American service providers nurture as they seek to cater to queer customers (Ginder and Byun 2015). This means that US companies specifically target an LGBT clientele in some of their marketing. At the same time, in an effort to appeal to the values of queer consumers, some companies espouse pro-gay policy stances, sponsor LGBT organizations and events, or use their economic influence to persuade policymakers on gay rights issues (Stambolis-Ruhstorfer 2015; Badgett 2003; Boyd 1997). Justified warnings about the neoliberal co-optation of queer mobilizations and the fraught economic and racial issues it generates notwithstanding (Duggan 2002; Twine 2015), activists and queer families alike have successfully used markets to help propel gay rights and families forward in the United States (Brown 2009). The liberal commercialization of ART and the 'corporatization' of gay rights are reflected in American online resources for queer families in the United States. Inversely, their absence is visible in the lack of certain resources, especially for-profit ART agencies, in France.

National Differences in ART Online Resources

Online resources for same-sex couples reflect the specific challenges people in each country face and the broader national trends in legal, political and economic circumstances across contexts described above. I find four major types of websites addressing the access needs of potential queer parents: (1) LGBT advocacy organizations; (2) commercial ART providers; (3) commercial matching services; and (4) professional organizations. Each contributes in specific ways to the ability of same-sex couples to have children. Each also varies according to national context. The types of services they offer, their level of commercialization, their commitment to activism and expanding the rights of queer families, and their relationship to queer people – either treating them as a target audience or growing organically out of LGBT initiatives – have characteristics specific to France and the United States.

Broadly speaking, unlike in the US, in France there are no local commercial providers of any services, but some international websites for surrogacy and donor sperm try to reach them. However, both LGBT websites and commercial providers in France feature matching services in which men and women of a variety of sexual orientations seek one another to create arranged non-medical donation and parental sharing. In the US, LGBT advocacy organizations and professional organizations, such as the American Society of Reproductive Medicine, are primarily geared to providing future parents with information and resources on how to navigate legal complexities that come from differences across states or how to find a suitable for-profit agency. LGBT organizations in France, however, help couples find ART services abroad and deal with the legal and medical challenges that arise from the lack of local legal access. Finally, unlike their American counterparts, French professional organizations remain largely silent on the issue. Table 8.1 and the following sections describe these characteristics in further detail.

Table 8.1. Online contributors to queer family ART access in France and the United States.

	Queer advocacy organizations		Commercial providers	
	France	US	France	US
Examples	adfh.net adheos.org apgl.fr	familyequality.org hrc.org lamdalegal.org menhavingbabies.org	No local providers cryosinternational.com	Many providers circlesurrogacy.com ctfertility.com fertility-docs.com pacrepro.com surrogaycenter.com
Services	Connecting families Legal advice Information Reviews/Ratings Connecting co-parents Helping ART access	Connecting families Legal advice Information Reviews/Ratings Financial assistance	Information Delivery and clinical ART Surrogacy services	
Commercialization	Non-profit Paid member services	Non-profit Paid member services Corporate sponsorship	For profit and Not-for-profit	
Activism	Core mission		None	Some
Queer family presence	Organic		Targeted	Organic and targeted

	Commercial meeting groups		**Professional organizations**	
	France	US	France	US
Examples	co-parents.fr co-parents.co	familybydesign.com modamily.com	academie-medecine.fr s-m-r.org	apps.americanbar.org apa.org asrm.org
Services	Connecting co-parents		None	Information
Commercialization	For profit		Not-for-profit	
Activism	None		None	Some
Queer family presence	Unspecified	Unspecified	Absent	Targeted

Queer Advocacy Organizations

Growing out of queer movements, LGBT advocacy organizations focusing on parenting push for legal and administrative reforms. They aim to help queer people have children and make their families more secure and safe in a context of anti-LGBT discrimination and heteronormative family law (Garnier 2012; Gross 2007; Stambolis-Ruhstorfer 2015). Activism is their primary goal. As a result, their policy agendas and demands are intimately tied to specific political circumstances in each country. Not surprisingly, French organizations, such as the Association des Parents et futurs parents Gays et Lesbiens (APGL) and the Association des Familles Homoparentales (ADFH), focus on pushing lawmakers to open ART access to same-sex couples and litigation in courts to secure the citizenship rights of children of same-sex couples conceived through surrogacy abroad.[4] Their US counterparts, such as the Family Equality Council, Lamda Legal or Men Having Babies, are more geared towards pushing to secure the legal recognition of same-sex families that already exist. Their websites describe and document these various activist activities.

Complimenting their advocacy work in the policy sphere, these organizations also provide services and information to their online communities that help same-sex couples navigate their local circumstances as they seek to become parents. In both countries, their websites give detailed legal analysis, contact information for allied lawyers and agencies, as well as ratings and recommendations about ART agencies, sperm banks and other service providers. These groups act as curators, ensuring that the organizations and agencies they recommend to their internet users are welcoming to queer clients.

Beyond these similarities, several key differences characterize advocacy organizations and their online presence in each country. In the United States, they offer a range of information and services about how to create local family groups and parenting clubs, reflecting the relatively large size and scope of American organizations, especially on the national level. They also share information about legal situations in order to help families navigate the legal complexities that come from state-level variations and inconsistencies. It appears that American advocacy organizations do not connect families in online forums for the purpose of finding potential co-parents or known donors to the degree that they do in France. Rather, American LGBT family advocacy organizations forward their users on to local fertility clinics and surrogacy agencies that cater to queer customers. In addition, unlike French organizations, US organizations benefit from corporate sponsorships and ties to businesses, which help support their activities.

In France, advocacy organizations are unable to point their members to French fertility clinics. Instead, they list advice and information about services in countries such as Spain, Belgium, the United States and elsewhere. This information addresses the specific needs of future parents who, because of legal restrictions in France, must travel abroad and navigate challenges in different languages, legal regimes and medical systems. Furthermore, some French LGBT advocacy organizations offer specific services for a membership fee. These include personal profiles and forums that allow people hoping to exchange gametes for at-home inseminations to find one another as well as couples and individuals seeking to establishing co-parenting arrangements.

I did not find evidence of American advocacy organizations setting up such matchmaking. This is likely due to the easier availability of both surrogacy and sperm banks in the US, which reduces demand for co-parenting and non-medical artificial insemination. French advocacy groups also use their websites to provide detailed instructions, reviews and explanations about fertility clinics and mail-order sperm delivery companies servicing France. To access these areas of the advocacy organization websites, potential parents must join the organization, pay a membership subscription and, in some cases, go through a verification process to verify their identities and trustworthiness. The heavily-laden political controversy around queer parenting in France – as well as disagreements between organizations about whether or not ART and surrogacy *should* be made legal – makes it particularly important for these groups to keep much of their information and services behind this private pay-wall.

Commercial ART Providers

Commercial ART providers, such as sperm banks, fertility clinics and surrogacy agencies, are also among the ways in which prospective queer parents find access to parenthood. As described above, many LGBT advocacy organizations provide links to and recommendations about these service providers. While generally providing the same services in both countries – including access to gametes and surrogates as well as many of the medical and legal amenities necessary for assisted procreation – French and American families face a stark contrast in online commercial options. Most fundamentally, in contrast to France, US providers are plentiful, based in a range of states, and some cater explicitly to queer families. It is difficult to estimate the number of these private for-profit clinics and agencies but it is evident that they are present across the country and range in size and scope. They have no doubt flourished from a combination of high demand and low regulation.

The websites of these US companies show a range of involvement and engagement with a queer clientele. On the lowest end of this spectrum, fertility clinics and surrogacy agencies will often have a section of their website that specifically addresses the needs, concerns and questions of gay, lesbian, bisexual and (sometimes) transgender future clients.[5] On the other end of the spectrum, some US fertility clinics not only cater to queer families; they emerge out of them and fully integrate the specific issues of LGBT families into their mission statements and marketing. For example, Pacific Reproductive Services, based in California, describes itself as a 'lesbian-owned sperm bank' that is a 'trusted resource for women planning alternative families' (Pacific Reproductive Services 2016). In addition to providing the largest number for identity-release donors, according to its website, the organization grew organically out of the lesbian family movement and accumulated knowledge and practices over time that are especially useful to these kinds of women.

In addition to their varying level of involvement with queer families, these for-profit providers also show a range of interest and willingness to engage in activism. Unlike advocacy organizations, these groups are not primarily geared towards changing public policy. Nevertheless, inasmuch as they have contributed to the growth of certain kinds of LGBT families – those with the means to access for-profit fertility services – they have changed the political and social landscape in the United States. Some have also engaged in a degree of advocacy in the direction of policymakers in order to facilitate the access of LGBT clients to their products. Expanding access also necessarily increases their client base. Most engaged, however, are the fertility clinics that grew out of the LGBT movement or were founded by queer people themselves. They have included activism and fighting for expanded rights and protections for non-heteronormative families in their range of activities.

In sharp contrast to the US, no commercial service providers exist within French borders. The alternative, state-run fertility clinics, are legally inaccessible to same-sex couples and single women and men. Not surprisingly, websites for these clinics make no mention of queer families or queer parenting. Thus, the only option available to these families and future parents is to seek commercial providers abroad. They often research these websites based on the recommendations of French queer family organizations. Capitalizing on tight French legislation, some international commercial providers market their services online directly to French queer families. This is the case for surrogacy organizations, including those in the United States, and sperm banks. A notable example of these sites is Cryos International, a Danish sperm bank that includes mail-order donor sperm, which they ship to countries such as France (Cryos 2018).

Commercial Meeting Groups

Same-sex couples hoping to become parents can also turn to non-medically assisted forms of procreation. This usually involves informally having children in co-parenting agreements with other people. Although technically beyond the scope of ART, it is important to mention the online resources that facilitate these kinds of arrangements because they provide a more accurate description of the realities queer families face on their paths to parenthood (see Martine Gross in this volume). Commercial matchmaking companies, which exist on both sides of the Atlantic and facilitate this process, operate much like dating services. They feature individual profiles that display pictures and explanations of what kinds of exchanges people are seeking. In the examples of websites in either country, such as Co-Parents.fr in France or Modamily.com in the US, people of all sexual orientations and situations can find future co-parents. Yet, unlike LGBT advocacy groups that also facilitate co-parenting – at least in France – these commercial matchmaking services operate for a profit and do not tailor their services to gays, lesbians, bisexuals or transgender people. Nevertheless, upon fee payment, LGBT clients of these websites can browse profiles that would allow them to find others willing to either provide them with sperm or, more rarely, carry a child. Of course, in all these situations, the companies warn customers that all legal and medical issues are their own responsibility.

Although there are few differences between French and American commercial meeting groups, my analysis of them suggests that French websites have a more visible presence of future queer parents. In particular, given French lesbians' lack of access to state-run fertility clinics, it makes sense that these women would turn to online offers in order to obtain access to informal donor sperm. This would also be the case for women seeking access to sperm in which the identity of the donor is known, an option that is forbidden in French clinics. The American matchmaking websites appear to be primarily aimed at heterosexual single people, particularly women, who do not want to use commercial ART agencies. They are generally seeking men willing to donate their sperm or co-parent without being in a romantic relationship.

Professional Organizations

Professional organizations complement the range of online resources that same-sex couples and other queer people can use on their path to parenthood. Although they do not engage in directly providing future parents with access to ART, I highlight them here because they serve an important role in guiding people in their decision-making about reproduction. Unlike people who do not seek ART in order to have children, queer families who do use such techniques may also seek guidance and advice that comes from medical, legal and scientific professionals and experts. Indeed, doctors, lawyers, psychologists, psychiatrists, and the professional organizations that represent them, are part of the web of people involved in facilitating – or hindering – queer people's ability to procreate.

As of 2016, French professional organizations that are mostly likely to directly address issues related to reproduction, such as the Académie Nationale de Médecine and the Société de Médecine de la Reproduction, include no mention of same-sex couples or indeed of LGBT people at all on their respective websites, www.academie-medecine.fr, and www.s-m-r.org. They discuss parenting and access to parenting according to the legal limits of French law and clinical practice. Judging from their websites, they do not conceive of or consider the possibility that non-heterosexual people want to have children through ART. The erasure of queer families from these professional organization websites highlights the steep barriers these families face when dealing with official French institutions. These websites mirror the timidity – or hostility – with which many French medical professionals speak about gay parenting in the French media and legislature (Stambolis-Ruhstorfer

2015). The invisibility of queer parenting from these groups is all the more apparent when contrasted with their American counterparts.

Indeed, as of 2016, a range of mainstream American professional organizations openly acknowledge, promote and aid LGBT people on their path to parenthood. From the American Society for Reproductive Medicine and the National Infertility Association to the American Academy of Assisted Reproductive Technology Attorneys and the American Bar Association, US professional websites specifically speak to the issues and needs of queer families on their respective websites, www.reproductivefacts.org, www.resolve.org, www.aaarta.org, and http://www.americanbar.org/groups/sexual_orientation. Complementing LGBT advocacy organizations, these groups provide legal or medical advice, guidance and counselling to future queer parents. Their willingness to openly address the issue of LGBT parenting not only reflects the relatively long-standing legality of same-sex couples' access to ART in the United States. It also suggests that these families enjoy a certain amount of institutional legitimacy, at least from a professional perspective, in the country. At the same time, that such professional services are necessary also emerges out of the complex financial and legal frameworks American people face as they seek fertility treatments.

Conclusion

The range of online resources French and American queer families use as they strive to have children through ART reflects the specific national circumstances they face in each country. The public French ART system that currently bars same-sex couples and single women and men from using fertility treatments and donor sperm while also fully banning surrogacy, drives LGBT people to international websites. Local French LGBT advocacy organizations help people organize to overcome these hurdles while pushing for change at home. Finally, for-profit matchmaking services fill the gap as they connect co-parents and facilitate the exchange of gametes and reproductive capacity. In a context of liberal commercial access to fertility treatments, donor gametes and surrogacy, American online resources are geared towards selling products and services to future queer parents. As a result, this population is visible and represented even in mainstream professional organizations and for-profit clinics. Furthermore, this model has also allowed LGBT people to develop their own self-designed clinics and services specifically geared towards queer parenting.

These divergences also have implications for the meaning and future of LGBT parenting more broadly. Although in general the French system is currently hostile to queer parenting, it also has the potential to create a much more inclusive system of access for queer families. Although the capitalistic, market logic of ART has helped to both create and normalize queer families in the United States, it has also reproduced inequality on the basis of class. Because ART in France is public, opening access to queer families could allow working-class and poor queer families to use these services. Such a change would ultimately be a greater advance in social justice because it would theoretically avoid the inequalities inherent in the American situation.

The commercialization of ART has been an undoubted boon to the growth and visibility of some – largely privileged – LGBT families in the United States. Coupled with the power of the internet to deploy resources that facilitate access and create communities devoted to queer parenting, access to ART seems easier for LGBT people there. Nevertheless, as demonstrated by the kinds of resources described in this chapter, French sexual and gender minorities also use the internet to successfully overcome the barriers of their national context to have children. We can expect that if the French government were to legalize access to ART for lesbians and single women and open surrogacy to all, the powerful organizational resources of the French bureaucracy could potentially create a system that is more open, equal and legible than that in the United States.

Michael Stambolis-Ruhstorfer is a sociologist and Assistant Professor of American Studies at the Université Bordeaux Montaigne. His research examines the intersection of law, culture and sexuality from a cross-national comparative perspective.

Notes

1. These critiques have come from lawmakers and public intellectuals on both the left and the right. See Borrillo 2015 for a discussion of these arguments and positions.
2. See also the chapters by Courduriès and Gross in this volume on the particular challenges and rewards gay couples face as they seek access to surrogacy across national borders.
3. Though it is not the focus of this chapter, it is also important to note that surrogate mothers, some of whom work for same-sex couples, also mobilize the internet to create community, develop collective identities as surrogates, share advice and support one another (Berend 2016). In so doing, their online communities are also linked to those of queer families.
4. Note that the APGL was founded over a decade and a half before the ADFH. These organizations diverge on some policy issues. For example, surrogacy, which also splits French feminists, tends to divide their memberships.
5. The multi-service fertility clinic/surrogacy agency, The Fertility Institutes (www.fertility-docs.com), is a good example of this type of LGBT engagement. For example, under the tab for surrogacy, it includes a section devoted to 'Gay Surrogacy'.

References

Almeling, R. 2011. *Sex Cells: The Medical Market for Eggs and Sperm*. Los Angeles: University of California Press.

Badgett, L.M.V. 2003. *Money, Myths, and Change: The Economic Lives of Lesbians and Gay Men*. Chicago: University of Chicago Press.

Berend, Z. 2016. '"We Are All Carrying Someone Else's Child!": Relatedness and Relationships in Third-Party Reproduction', *American Anthropologist* 118 (1): 24–36.

Borillo, D. 2015. 'Mariage pour tous et filiation pour certains: les résistances à l'égalité des droits pour les couples de même sexe', *Droit et cultures: Revue internationale interdisciplinaire* 69 (April): 179–220.

Boyd, D.N. 1997. 'Shopping for Rights: Gays, Lesbians, and Visibility Politics', *Denver University Law Review* 75: 1361.

Brief of the States of Indiana, Virginia, Alabama, Alaska, Arizona, Colorado, Georgia, Idaho, Kansas, Montana, Nebraska, North Dakota, Oklahoma, South Carolina, South Dakota, Texas, Utah, West Virginia and Wisconsin as *Amici Curiae* in Support of Petitioners, *Hollingsworth v. Perry*, 570 U.S. 12-144 (2013): 31–32.

Brown, G. 2009. 'Thinking beyond Homonormativity: Performative Explorations of Diverse Gay Economies', *Environment and Planning A* 41 (6): 1496–510.

Chasin, A. 2000. 'Interpenetrations: A Cultural Study of the Relationship between the Gay/Lesbian Niche Market and the Gay/Lesbian Political Movement', *Cultural Critique* 44: 145–68.

Craig, S.L., L. McInroy, L. McCready and R. Alaggia. 2015. 'Media: A Catalyst for Resilience in Lesbian, Gay, Bisexual, Transgender, and Queer Youth', *Journal of LGBT Youth* 12 (3): 254.

Cryos. 2018. 'Deliver and Terms'. *Cryos International.com*. https://dk.cryosinternational.com/donor-sperm/delivery-and-terms. Accessed 30 June 2019.

Davis, B.H., and J. Brewer. 1997. *Electronic Discourse: Linguistic Individuals in Virtual Space*. Albany: State University of New York Press.

Dempsey, D. 2013. 'Surrogacy, Gay Male Couples and the Significance of Biogenetic Paternity', *New Genetics and Society* 32 (1): 37–53.

Deomampo, D. 2015. 'Defining Parents, Making Citizens: Nationality and Citizenship in Transnational Surrogacy', *Medical Anthropology* 34 (3): 210–25.

Descoutures, V. 2010. *Les mères lesbiennes*. Paris: PUF.

Donovan, C., and A.R. Wilson. 2008. 'Imagination and Integrity: Decision-Making among Lesbian Couples to Use Medically Provided Donor Insemination', *Culture, Health & Sexuality* 10 (7): 649–65.

Duggan, L. 2002. 'The New Homonormativity: The Sexual Politics of Neoliberalism', in R. Castronovo and D. Nelson (eds), *Materializing Democracy: Toward a Revitalized Cultural Politics*. Durham, NC: Duke University Press, pp. 175–94.

Friedman, M. 2010. 'On Mommyblogging: Notes to a Future Feminist Historian', *Journal of Women's History* 22 (4): 197–208, 327.

Garnier, E. 2012. *L'homoparentalité en France: La bataille des nouvelles familles*. Paris: Thierry Marchaisse Editions.

Ginder, W., and S.-E. Byun. 2015. 'Past, Present, and Future of Gay and Lesbian Consumer Research: Critical Review of the Quest for the Queer Dollar', *Psychology & Marketing* 32 (8): 821–41.

Gross, M. 2007. 'Quand et comment l'homoparentalité est-elle devenue un objet "légitime" de recherche en sciences humaines et sociales?', *Socio-logos. Revue de l'association française de sociologie* 2 (March). http://socio-logos.revues.org/803. Accessed 30 June 2019.

Gross, M., J. Courduriès and A. Federico. 2014. 'Le recours à l'AMP dans les familles homoparentales: état des lieux: Résultats d'une enquête menée en 2012', *Socio-logos: Revue de l'association française de sociologie* 9 (February). http://socio-logos.revues.org/2870. Accessed 30 June 2019.

Harcourt, W. (ed.) 1999. *Women@Internet: Creating New Cultures in Cyberspace*. New York: Palgrave Macmillan.

Hunter, A. 2015. 'Lesbian Mommy Blogging in Canada: Documenting Subtle Homophobia in Canadian Society and Building Community Online', *Journal of Lesbian Studies* 19 (2): 212.

IFOP. 2012. 'Les Français et les droits des couples homosexuels'. Study 110950 IFOP for le *Journal du Dimanche*. Retrieved 4 February 2019 from https://www.ifop.com/wp-content/uploads/2018/03/2080-1-study_file.pdf.

Kazyak, E., and B. Woodell. 2016. 'Law and LGBQ-Parent Families', *Sexuality & Culture* 20 (3), https://digitalcommons.unl.edu/cgi/viewcontent.cgi?referer=https://www.google.com/&httpsredir=1&article=1292&context=sociologyfacpub Accessed 30 June 2019.

Kollock, P. 1999. 'The Economies of Online Cooperation', in M. Smith and P. Kollock (eds), *Communities in Cyberspace*. London: Routledge, pp. 220–39.

Kovacs, S. 2013. 'Une clinique de fertilité américaine recrute des clients à Paris', *Le Figaro.fr*, 4 April, sec. Société. http://www.lefigaro.fr/actualite-france/2013/04/08/01016-20130408ARTFIG00504-une-clinique-de-fertilite-americaine-recrute-des-clients-a-paris.php. Accessed 30 June 2019.

Mamo, L. 2007. *Queering Reproduction: Achieving Pregnancy in the Age of Technoscience*. Durham, NC: Duke University Press.

Mele, C. 1999. 'Cyberspace and Disadvantaged Communities: The Internet as a Tool for Collective Action', in M. Smith and P. Kollock (eds), *Communities in Cyberspace*. London: Routledge, pp. 220–39.

Pacific Reproductive Services. 'Why a Lesbian-Founded Bank is a Positive Choice for Any Woman'. *Pacific Reproductive Services.com*. Retrieved 30 April 2016 from https://www.pacrepro.com/index.php?main_page=why_prs.

Pullen, C., and M. Cooper (eds). 2010. *LGBT Identity and Online New Media*. London: Routledge.

Radin, M.J. 2001. *Contested Commodities*. Cambridge, MA: Harvard University Press.

Scammell, M. 2000. 'The Internet and Civic Engagement: The Age of the Citizen-Consumer', *Political Communication* 17 (4): 351–55.

Shade, L.R. 2002. *Gender and Community in the Social Construction of the Internet*. New York: Peter Lang.

Stacey, J. 2004. 'Cruising to Familyland: Gay Hypergamy and Rainbow Kinship'. *Current Sociology* 52 (2): 181–97.

Stacey, J. 2006. 'Gay Parenthood and the Decline of Paternity as We Knew It', *Sexualities* 9 (1): 27–55.

Stambolis-Ruhstorfer, M. 2015. 'The Culture of Knowledge: Constructing "Expertise" in Legal Debates on Marriage and Kinship for Same-Sex Couples in France and the United States', Ph.D. dissertation. Los Angeles: University of California Los Angeles.

Swanson, K.W. 2014. *Banking on the Body*. Cambridge, MA: Harvard University Press.

Swift, A. 2014. 'Most Americans Say Same-Sex Couples Entitled to Adopt'. *Gallup.com.* Retrieved 15 November 2015 from https://news.gallup.com/poll/170801/americans-say-sex-couples-entitled adopt.aspx?utm_source=marriage&utm_medium=search&utm_campaign=tiles.

Twine, F.W. 2015. *Outsourcing the Womb: Race, Class and Gestational Surrogacy in a Global Market.* London: Routledge.

Van Hoof, W., G. Pennings and P. de Sutter. 2015. 'Cross-Border Reproductive Care for Law Evasion: A Qualitative Study into the Experiences and Moral Perspectives of French Women Who Go to Belgium for Treatment with Donor Sperm', *Social Science & Medicine* 124: 391–97.

Part IV

Cross-Border Practices

Chapter 9

Single Men and Women Barred from Using ART in France

Dominique Mehl

In France, medically assisted reproduction is reserved for heterosexual couples who are presently alive and of childbearing age. This was determined by the bioethics laws, which were passed by the French Parliament in 1994 and reauthorized in 2011.

The birth of the first bioethics laws was fraught with controversy, as was their revision seventeen years later. The first 'test tube baby' was born in France in 1982. Over the course of the decade that followed, public debates, seminars and parliamentary hearings were held one after another. Six official reports – more or less convergent, more or less tolerant, more or less liberal, and more or less restrictive – punctuated this highly controversial period. Seven parliamentary meetings decided the fate of a bill that revealed differences not only between the right and the left, but also within each political camp, as questions concerning social mores didn't quite fit into the category of institutional policy. Initial discussions brought together a broad spectrum of French society: doctors, biologists, lawyers and politicians confronted each other and clashed.

Religious figures, psychoanalysts, anthropologists and sociologists also came to attest to various kinship patterns of other countries and cultures. The only ones absent from the debate were the patients of ART (assisted reproductive technology) centres, those who had been affected by infertility and had, somewhat blindly, sought medical help. However, during the revision of the bioethics laws, which came after several years of discussion, members of civil society started to become involved in the various debates and discussions. Since then, several associations have been created, and criticism of the French legal system has increased. Meanwhile, in most neighbouring European countries, liberal laws are increasingly being passed. In light of accumulated experience, as well as the steady increase of questions and criticism from society, one could imagine that significant changes in the present legislation would be inevitable, but such changes have yet to happen.

For twenty years, the same rules have governed access to ART in France, which can only be granted to couples who are medically diagnosed as infertile, that is to say, a man and a woman unable to procreate 'naturally'. As a result, same-sex couples and single men and women find themselves, by default, on the list of those who cannot seek reproductive aid. In the same vein, it is legally impossible for an infertile couple to seek and enlist the help of a third party in the reproductive process. The anonymity of sperm and egg donors, which is highly regulated, ensures the support of this traditional model of parenting. Meanwhile, surrogacy remains prohibited in France, and the controlling hand of the medical community remains invisible.

In 1994, all of these issues surrounding the definitions of parenthood, motherhood, fatherhood, filiation and family were discussed and debated, and the resulting consensus, which promoted the traditional family model, did not incite any discord or indignation. Some twenty years later, the legal situation has changed only slightly, though reproductive medicine has become the norm, and is considered both commonplace and accepted in contemporary representations. Those seeking reproductive aid have begun to join forces within different groups and associations, making their voices heard both on the public stage and behind the scenes in parliament. Two fierce debates rocked French society at the time of the 2011 revision: first, the debate in which children born of anonymous sperm donations argued for their right to know their origins, and second, that which explored the question of allowing surrogacy for couples in which the woman was infertile yet had a functioning uterus. Both propositions were rejected, and the renewed law remained virtually unchanged. Two years later, during the debate leading up to the passage of the 2013 *Mariage pour tous* ('Marriage for All') law, gay and lesbian couples began to demand their right to seek reproductive aid through ART. As their right to marry also granted them the right to adopt, they asked that women be provided access to artificial insemination with the help of a sperm donor. They also requested, though much more tentatively, that men obtain the right to have recourse to surrogacy.

This debate has been deferred time and time again. It has once again burst onto the scene following the French National Ethics Committee (CCNE) report calling for access to ART for single women and lesbian couples (26 June 2017; http://www.ccne-ethique.fr/fr/publications/avis-du-ccne-du-15-juin-2017-sur-les-demandes-societales-de-recours-lassistance#.WZL7Koppzq1). The next step is debate in parliament, and the subject risks once again becoming explosive.

Access to ART thus remains denied to both homosexuals and single men and women in France. In neighbouring countries, however, the legal status of reproductive medicine has changed, and requests that would be rejected in France are now being accepted elsewhere. Single women and lesbian couples alike now cross borders in order to circumvent the French laws, which to these women seem utterly obsolete.

This chapter will present the yet-unpublished results of a sociological survey of single mothers and future mothers who have received reproductive aid abroad. We will focus on 'solo' mothers, the term used by women who have voluntarily sought to have and raise a child without a partner.[1] To this end, solo motherhood is different from the sort of single parenthood that results from a divorce or separation during pregnancy, at birth, or later when the child is grown. Indeed, in the case of single parenthood, which is becoming more and more common, the child is wanted, and is initially conceived as part of the joint parental project of a couple. Following the dissolution of the parents' conjugal relationship, the child (or children) goes on to share his/her home with only one parent. In the case of 'solo' motherhood, however, the decision to create the child is made solely by the mother, and the child will be raised by her and her alone – not due to desertion on the part of the father, but because of the complete absence of a paternal element in the mother's plans to have and raise the child.

Social developments behind this growing phenomenon are no mystery. Across the board, women are increasingly joining the workforce, prolonging their studies and starting their careers later in life, all of which contribute to the rise in the average age at which women first become pregnant. The increase in marital breakdowns has also contributed to the rise of single parenthood. Solo motherhood falls within this general movement, but is also linked to a general increase in singlehood. While these objective factors are evidenced by social statistics, the subjective conditions of these lifestyle choices are largely unknown. This survey sheds some light on the motives, values and experiences of these women: deliberately single mothers in an era of individualism.

The Ticking of the Biological Clock

> Personally, I think it would be worse to not be able to have children than to have one by myself. (Lydia)

Lydia is forty years old. After three unsuccessful IVF treatments in Belgium, where she tried to get pregnant with her own eggs, she decided to seek a donation, requesting a double donation (both oocyte and sperm) in Spain. All solo mothers display the same kind of conviction; they cannot imagine a life without children, even if having a child means giving birth outside the norm, and accepting the isolation that comes with single motherhood.

> Since I was a teenager, I have always seen myself having kids. It's just been obvious. I never wondered if it was right for me or not – I simply could never imagine myself without children. (Rebecca)

Rebecca is forty-one years old. She is pregnant with twins after having received a double gamete donation in the Czech Republic. Like Rebecca, the other single mothers and future mothers we met during the study never doubted their desire to have children. More often than not, it had been there since childhood, and had not been re-examined or questioned over the years. For these women, this desire comes without excessive analysis, self-assessment or questioning. The child that they hope to have, that they seek abroad through long and complicated processes, is not the result of a hesitant project. For these women, the child is not the result of a sudden urge, an adult whim or a sudden awakening, but is on the contrary inevitable. The desire has always been there, and has grown over time, despite often unstable personal lives and relationships. That being said, while the desire is certainly there, having a child is easier said than done.

Single motherhood by choice usually occurs later in life. The average age of the women interviewed in the study was forty-two.

For reasons mainly connected to romantic issues, plans to have and raise a child had never come up in previous partnerships. At some point in their lives, generally in their early forties, the women interviewed became fixated on their childlessness, often to the point of obsession. Embarking on the path of single motherhood is a project that takes shape slowly, but deliberately. For some women, the decision to choose this extraordinary path was preceded by the failure of a previous parental project conceived within a couple. These women tried to convince their male partners to have and raise a child with them, but the men resisted, recanted or slipped away.

Rebecca, forty-one, tried to have a child with her spouse, but fertility was not in the cards for the couple. Rebecca had been suffering from ovarian failure since 2008, and together with her spouse underwent a number of medical procedures in the hope of eventually conceiving: numerous medical evaluations, ovarian stimulation and four IVF procedures, each ending in failure. According to the French doctors who cared for them, conceiving with Rebecca's gametes was impossible, and the couple was invited to consider using a donated egg. Rebecca was quickly on board, compelled by her desire to have a child, but her partner was reluctant. The more Rebecca insisted, the more he recoiled, unable to imagine having a child that would not share both of their genes. The child, he thought, would not really be hers. For him, pregnancy was not enough – it was the transmission of genes that provided the foundation for the relationship between parent and child. 'For him, it was impossible. He wouldn't have felt like a real father. I was confronted with two choices: either abandon my plans to have children, or leave my partner.' She chose the latter, deciding to follow through with her plans on her own – a choice that still pains her today. 'The decision to take on this project alone was easy. I wanted very badly to have children, and this was my last chance. There wouldn't be a father in the picture – oh well. The hardest part was leaving my spouse, because I still loved him.' She is currently expecting twins, conceived using a double donation, but has not completely cut off from her ex-partner.

This, however, is not the most common scenario. The decision to take on pregnancy and motherhood alone is usually made in the complete absence of a companion. Whether the woman embraces single life or finds herself in the wake of a failed relationship, the day comes when her childlessness starts to become painful. Indeed, the biological clock, which around the age of thirty-five begins to mercilessly impair a woman's fertility, condemns many women to single motherhood, which they pursue for fear of 'missing their chance'. Their fertility, its quality and decline (which around this time becomes increasingly apparent), encourages them to change their life plans. They substitute the 'first the couple, then the child' model with a 'first the child and then perhaps the spouse' approach, where the order in which kinship is usually formed (a husband who will become the father of children) is abandoned in favour of a less orthodox pattern (a child who may later find an adoptive father or stepfather in his or her mother's eventual companion). This reversal of the generally accepted sequence of kinship is not undertaken for the sake of challenging societal standards, but under the pressure of biological urgency. All of the women encountered in this study had resigned themselves, often reluctantly, to disturbing the traditional family model, and reversing the order of conjugality and kinship, because of the steady ticking of the biological clock.

The Absence of a Father

> A father is not mandatory, nor is a mother. There are very many separated couples with children who are raised by their mother, or sometimes by their father, and they are just fine. I admit that I would have preferred that my child have a father. At first, I saw myself with a family where 'Dad and Mom have children together', but, then again, everything boils down to education. If we give children everything we can, if we love them, if we explain things to them … if the child feels loved, I'm not sure he or she needs two parents. (Rebecca)

While Rebecca does not make it a point to defend or endorse her 'fatherless' plans, she is also not worried about the future that awaits her twins, for whom she left her partner.

This nuanced and ambivalent outlook is quite reflective of the attitudes of women who choose to pursue motherhood alone. They are confident in their decision, but at the same time feel regret. They do not brandish the banner of freedom and autonomy, nor do they champion the superiority of the single-parent model over that of the traditional two-parent model. Their failure to start a parental project within a couple, along with the mounting biological pressure that comes with their age, is what has led them to choose this perilous path.

Delphine was thirty-five years old when she began the lonely journey abroad to receive a sperm donation. She does not consider the alternative of solo motherhood as an ideal life choice, but she also refuses to believe that her atypical family's future will be jeopardized. She herself had been part of a stepfamily – her parents separated when she was twenty-one years old, a decision that came as a surprise to few, as the couple had been less than blissful. Both of her parents remarried. Her father left to settle in a distant country, and soon became detached and remote. Her mother remarried a man whom she considers her 'quasi-father', and whose children she calls her 'quasi-brothers'. 'My quasi-father is almost more important to me than my father', she explains. 'There are families where no one really knows who the father is. I, on the other hand, differentiate between my biological father, and the father whom I consider part of my family.' Her personal experience has therefore given her a relatively relaxed view of the risks solo motherhood implies.

> I'm not worried about remaining a solo mother. I'm able to disconnect my romantic relationships from my familial relationships. Before, I had always wanted a family where my bond with the father would not be lost in the chaos of family life – I wanted to have a love life and a family life at once. Now I separate these two facets of my life. For me, not having a father in the picture isn't a huge deal. Besides, maybe one day there will be a father, and I have enough people in my life that I'll always have some help. I'm not afraid to raise a child alone. (Delphine)

However, not all of the women we encountered treated solo motherhood with the same degree of relativism. Céline, who at the time of the survey was seeking reproductive aid in Spain at the age of forty-three, responded: 'I have very strong family values. The idea of having a child without a father completely goes against who I am. Before, I felt it would handicap the child. It was absolutely essential for me that my child have a family'. It was with great resistance that she slowly began to change her mind – again, because of her advancing age. 'I asked myself a lot of questions about the lack of a father. How would I explain it to the child? It was my greatest burden. As time went on, though, I got used to it. You rarely get to tick off all the boxes in life. I could learn to accept not having a father for my child.'

The decision to become a solo mother, made under the pressure of advancing time, is often all but steadfast. The women in the study had chiefly resigned themselves to this choice as a means to avoid being childless for the rest of their lives. As a result, this decision often turned out to be an obligation as well, one that was endorsed but also imposed. In general, the women we interviewed seemed to have changed their minds so that they would not to need to sustain an even more painful loss than that of their partner: the absence of becoming a mother.

Ambivalence seems to be the rule. Most of the women in this study carry out their plans unburdened by regret, yet still live with a certain degree of guilt. Thus, the decision to embark on the adventure of solo motherhood takes time to mature. It is always made due to a failure to have carried out a parental project as a couple. It takes shape not in opposition to the traditional family model but because of the absence of a spouse they would have nevertheless hoped to meet or keep. This absence is not lived openly in a positive fashion – far from it. While the journey is certainly deliberate, it will always be tinged with disappointment: the disappointment of not having been able to want, expect and welcome the child as part of a couple.

Indeed, the portrait of the solo mother at the dawn of the twenty-first century differs profoundly from that of the typical post-May 1968 feminist: a woman who claims her independence and is certain of her ability to live without men.

Chaotic Relationships

The image of the intentionally 'solo' mother perpetuated in women's magazines has always revolved around the figure of the 'wonder woman', who is dedicated first and foremost to her professional success, and delays pregnancy so that she can first be recognized in the public arena.

The results of our investigation completely contradict this stereotype. The women interviewed were highly educated, had stable jobs and had enjoyed comfortable professional integration for years. They were committed to their studies and work, but did not attempt to balance them with their private lives. Both could have been carried out simultaneously or earlier if their life conditions were more conducive to a family project. In other words, it is not their career ambitions that delayed their decision to try and get pregnant, but the ups and downs of their relationships.

All the stories we heard attested to the difficulty of modern relationships, and the fragility and volatility of the households around them. All kinds of contemporary marital difficulties were represented, and each journey ended with the mother starting a new single-parent household in the absence of a life partner.

The first case we studied was perhaps the simplest, but by no means the least painful: a life of successive romantic involvements, most of them long-term, but without cohabitation, reciprocal commitment or a shared life project. Céline has never lived with a partner. She has a busy job for which she travels often. 'This is not conducive to sentimental attachment', she admits. When she was thirty-nine, she met a man ten years her junior, with whom she fell deeply in love. However, the relationship proved to be tumultuous – they broke up, then got back together, then separated again. For three years, their relationship lurched back and forth, until they finally decided to end it. Today, she says, 'No more men for me. I've tried, but I absolutely don't see myself dating anymore. I didn't like the men who were attracted to me, and vice versa'. At forty-three, she travelled alone to Spain to receive a double donation.

The second case offers a prime example of the circumstances that arise from the fragility of couples in the era of the deinstitutionalization of marriage. *De facto* unions can be long-lasting, only to fall apart once love is no longer there, with no long-term life plan requiring partners to stay together. Rebecca is forty-one years old. She has had several successive spouses. She only had parental projects with the last two, one of which included a few attempts at IVF. Her partner resisted, however, and was not really willing to have a child. They were not on the same wavelength. 'I realized that I did not love him enough. I didn't want to raise a child alone, there had to be a man in my life. But with him, I felt that the feeling wasn't strong enough, so I left him.' At forty-one, she is expecting twins, but only after receiving a double donation in the Czech Republic.

Among the women who ended up choosing to give birth alone, some have gone on to start relationships that are more stable, but in which the child is unable to find a place for himself or herself, since the mother's new partner has already been married, and does not wish to cut ties with his existing family. Mélanie met one partner when she was twenty-five years old. He was married with two children, and was expecting a third.

> I had hoped to build a life with him, but the question of whether or not we could have a child was an obstacle. When he met me, he said he wanted to start a new life with me, but he never addressed whether or not we would have children. In reality, he would never

> have separated from his wife. So when it came to the child issue, there were always excuses. Never no, never yes. He knew that if he said no, I would leave, but he didn't want to commit to another child either. I pressured him for four or five years, but he always avoided the issue. I was the mistress. (Mélanie)

At forty-four, she moved on, and returned alone from the Czech Republic with two twins: a boy and a girl, nearly two years old today.

Thus, domestic fragility, largely responsible for the spread of divorce and separation in the modern era, is the primary breeding ground for a new kind of single parenthood, both chosen and feared.

Choosing Medically Assisted Procreation

The decision to enter into motherhood alone is complex, fraught with hesitation and marked by guilt. The means of achieving solo motherhood are hardly any easier. The choice of medically assisted reproduction is rarely the first choice.

What could be simpler than conceiving by natural means when, in theory, you are not infertile? In the absence of a stable companion, the father could be a friend who would not claim his parental status, or a partner, ensnared during a fleeting relationship. More recently, with the advent of the internet, another way of meeting potential mates has become more common: men can now offer their sperm over the internet. Women who wish to have a child can contact these men in real life, and then meet with them for insemination. A site entirely dedicated to 'co-parent' encounter was launched in 2008. Shortly before his death, Dominique Baudis, the French human rights defender at the time, requested that the site be monitored, and considered shutting it down entirely. These kinds of sites are seen by many as encouraging illegal practices, namely the exchange of gametes outside accredited medical institutions. Since then, the website only offers 'co-parent' matches for partners who both want to assume their parental roles. However, single aspiring mothers can always find other ways on the internet to recruit unknown donors who do not want to be a co-parent.

All candidates for single motherhood have considered the possibility of natural fertilization, either through a personal relationship or a rendezvous with a stranger initiated on the internet. Yet all of the women we met in the survey had given up on this idea. Lydia says:

> One night stands are the worst option. I don't know the guy I'm going out with on a given day, where he's from, whether he has any diseases ... it's out of the question. Also, if I knew the father, I would have to tell the child who he is. My biggest problem would be having to lie. I have to take responsibility for my choices from the start. What if the father wants to claim his rights as a parent? For me, this is out of the question. I was on the Co-Parents site, but had the same problem. I didn't know who I was dealing with. If the man wants custody, that's not OK with me. I might have been able to have a child with a friend, but I wasn't too convinced by the idea. I wouldn't be able to do it through deception, either, because I hate lying. (Lydia)

Adoption is another possibility. This option has the advantage of being perfectly legal, since French law now permits adoption by unmarried parties. The process is transparent, and subject to strict administrative control, both social and psychological. The spectre of an intended father does not hover over this kind of birth, as it is officially recognized as the result of an individual commitment.

Among the solo mothers we met, several have seriously considered adoption; some of them had started the process before turning to medicine, and several others had taken or were taking both approaches simultaneously. Yet solo adoption is even more complex and perilous than adoption by conventional couples. Testing and approval for adoption often takes the form of an actual entrance examination, and it is not uncommon to fail due to the lack of a male parental figure. Even when solo mothers are allowed to begin the adoption process, finding a child turns out to be much more complex than for an ordinary couple. Indeed, France reserves its adoptable children first and foremost for couples. Furthermore, opportunities to adopt a child from abroad are much more restricted for single men and women, because few countries accept these kinds of atypical applications.

Rebecca's testimony is emblematic of the reluctance met by those seeking adoption and reinforces their choice of medical assistance.

> I'd thought about adoption, but I was very hesitant. The children are older. They come with a lot of liabilities. They will ask questions about what happened to their birth parents. I didn't want to add this problem to what was already an unconventional approach. Plus, I knew that some adoptions fail. I was too afraid that it wouldn't go well. I also would have regretted not ever knowing what it's like to be pregnant. It's part of the female experience, like breastfeeding. For me it's an obvious choice. I understand women who choose not to

> breastfeed, but I have always wanted children and have always told myself that I would breastfeed. If I had never been able to experience pregnancy, it would have been an absence in my experience as a woman. (Rebecca)

Another issue is reluctance on the part of social workers and psychologists who oversee the approval process for single women. Often, these professionals fear the effects a fatherless household could have on the child. International offers are reduced significantly when the request for adoption comes from a single person. Candidates also fear a long, drawn-out process that will make them mothers late in life, especially when they already feel like they're running out of time. There are recurring anxieties about a child's past in their country of origin, and of the reasons for and consequences of the child's abandonment. There is the desire to welcome a newborn into their home, and above all to physically experience the child's birth. All these reasons combined often tip the scales in favour of medically assisted procreation, even though adoption is legally permitted.

The Cost of Procreative Migration

In France, assisted reproduction is restricted to heterosexual couples consisting of a man and woman who are alive and of childbearing age. As a result, single men and women have no right of access to ART centres. This rule is non-negotiable, as only authorized centres are able to exercise this kind of palliative medicine for infertility. Private doctors and clinics cannot circumvent this law. Therefore, the only way for single women to use these techniques is to turn to foreign countries where laws are more liberal. Spain is the primary country to which they resort, but many women also travel to Belgium, the Czech Republic and Greece.

This is how procreative migrations are born. Those who are denied access to ART in France (single men and women, gay couples, and women over the age of forty whom Social Security no longer covers [starting at forty-three]) cross borders to access the procedures that are forbidden at home: fertilization then implantation. Often, they can continue their treatment back in France, and even give birth in their home country, but the use of a donor, whether for sperm or perhaps even the embryo, can only occur abroad. These trips have been very pejoratively dubbed 'reproductive tourism'. In truth, these women visit the clinics, and not the monuments of the cities they visit, and only for a short time, a time largely devoted to the medical procedure. These women do not exile themselves, however; they return to their home countries for the pregnancy and birth. They migrate, staying just long enough to get medical help, and then return.

These procedures are gruelling, much more difficult than if they had taken place closer to home. As with any protocol, the road to medically assisted procreation is a long one, often filled with pitfalls and failures. Some women attempt to conceive using their own eggs, using a sperm donor for insemination. However, given their age when making such a decision so late in life, their ovulation is often already irregular, of poor quality or at its end. Consequently, they must use an egg donation in addition to sperm donation. All of the women we interviewed had or will have their child thanks to a double donation.

These women are perhaps more prepared than others to give up the idea of passing down their genes because of their maturity and the awareness of their unreliable fertility. However, the switch to gamete donation, both for these women and for those couples who can legally undergo the procedure in France, requires intense psychological work, and deep reflection on the roles of what is innate and what is acquired in the construction of a family. This change of scenario is not trivial. Their voyage becomes part of a complex psychological situation.

Choosing to cross borders conceals significant details. On the positive side, the gamble is almost always successful, because the donors in the countries that are most frequented by solo mothers are numerous and young. The donors' ovulation, stimulated by hormone treatments, works well both quantitatively and from the point of view of the quality of gametes. The embryos created outside French borders are much more likely to become babies and newborns than those created in France, where until recently donors are likely to already be parents, and therefore are much older and less fertile.

However, these positive and happy results come with a steep price, and in the most material sense of the word. Indeed, the financial cost of these operations is high. The clinics are private, and the patients must travel at their own expense. Only women with relatively high incomes can access this procedure. Most of the women we met had comfortable jobs, such as in middle management, but many of them were forced to dip into their savings or take out bank loans in order to meet these expenses. One of the women in the study had to give up after two attempts, unable to finance a successful procedure. Such an endeavour remains inaccessible to people of modest means. Medical discrimination is thus coupled with economic discrimination, all due to the ban that reigns in France.

But the price can be even steeper, depending on the results of the medical procedure. Indeed, as in all IVF protocols, several embryos are available for transfer. At the moment of implantation, it is possible to introduce one or two embryos, and doctors often advise their patients to choose the latter in order to increase the chances of success. The risk of becoming pregnant with twins, and thus returning home a single mother and raising not one child but two children, is the price, both psychological and familial, that many women are left with. These women are thus faced with a dilemma that is exceedingly difficult to resolve.

Some choose not to opt for double implantation and, in turn, run the risk of reducing their chance of getting pregnant. Others choose double implantation in order to avoid having to return and reinvest their time and money in yet another procedure. As single mothers, they especially fear the possibility of finding their family confined to a small cocoon: one child, under the influence of one parent. The idea of having a second child is often present from the moment they become involved in this adventure. Why not have two at once?

If these women were accepted in France, the financial cost would be bearable. Above all, the psychological cost would be greatly attenuated. A second embryo transfer in Paris does not represent the same effort and investment as one that requires a return to Barcelona. Hence, receiving only one embryo, and therefore avoiding the constraints of having two babies and raising two toddlers of the same age, appears to be a more comfortable alternative than that of feeling obligated to maximize one's chances.

Though prohibited from accessing surrogacy in France, single women who do not have a functioning uterus also find a way around the ban. The situation of voluntary single mothers in France is much like that of same-sex families before they became visible and claimed their place in the family panorama, and demanded legislative changes. For now, however, these solo experiences are only in their infancy, as their existence is little known, and their desire to be recognized still unspoken.

The Gap between Laws and Customs

Such is the paradox of the present situation: voluntary single motherhood is becoming more widespread as social mores change, and the ban on access to fertility clinics for single women has once again become a public issue (see aforementioned CCNE report). That being said, an organization that could advocate for these women has yet to emerge, and any exchange of experience and information remains confined to the private sphere. From time to time, such exchanges spill over onto the internet, but public expression or representation is still lacking. No social controversy over these women's struggles has come up so far in public debate. This emerging phenomenon is more or less hidden under a cloak of invisibility, though it might come out of the shadows if the new French government decides to follow through on the advice of the CCNE which, as mentioned, proclaimed itself in favour of allowing access to ART for lesbian couples and single women.

Thus far, when the situation was discussed in parliamentary arenas, it was lost in a sea of other demands, notably as a codicil to the mobilization of lesbian women who wish to gain access to reproductive medicine. When the fate of single women is touched upon, it is usually by extension of the demands of the LGBT community. Otherwise unheard in the public sphere, these women are treated not in regard to their own situation, but in terms of a cause initiated by lesbian women and their supporters, then extended to 'all women', their own situation only considered by default. What results is not an analysis of the relationship between singlehood and motherhood in light of a change in attitudes, but an extension of a demand for equality to a silent group. With this issue, as is frequent with problems regarding private and family life, practice precedes discussion, discussion precedes claims, claims recede public and political discussion, and discussion precedes legislative action. Aspiring single mothers find ways to achieve motherhood without, for the moment, being incorporated into a wider, collective social group. Just as women found methods of contraception before the pill was debated and legalized, and just as gay parenting was a social reality well before being placed on the parliamentary agenda, we can see that with solo motherhood, society is once again a few steps ahead of the law.

Dominique Mehl is a sociologist and Research Director at the national CNRS. She specializes in urban sociology, the sociology of the middle classes and social movements, the sociology of communication, and the sociology of the family in the realm of procreation, kinship/family ties and children born via ART. She has published extensively on all these areas and has frequently been consulted by the French government on them.

Note

1. Between 2013 and 2015, this author carried out qualitative surveys of 28 French women, all single and voluntary solo mothers. Among them, ten had accessed ART abroad (six in Spain, three in the Czech Republic, and one in Greece). Eight chose adopting a child abroad. This sample is certainly not fully representative of solo maternity, but is nonetheless emblematic of these types of situations and thought processes that lead these women to come to this decision.

References

Bologne, Jean-Claude. 2004. *Histoire du célibat et des célibataires*. Hachette Littératures.

De Gaulejac, Vincent, and Nicole Aubert. 1990. *Femmes au singulier ou la parenté solitaire*. Editions Klincksick.

Faure, Guillemette. 2008. *Un bébé toute seule*? Flammarion.

Kaufmann, Jean-Claude. 2009. *La femme seule et le prince charmant*. Nathan.

Lardellier, Pascal. 2009. *La guerre des mères: Parcours sensibles de mères célibataires*. Fayard.

Mehl, Dominique. 2011. *Les lois de l'enfantement*. Presses de Sciences Po.

Chapter 10

Cross-Border Reproductive Care for French Patients in Belgium

Guido Pennings

Since 2007, Belgium has had a law regulating medically assisted reproduction. This law works according to the default rule: what is not forbidden by law is allowed. It is also a very liberal law in the philosophical sense: it expresses the position that no categories of persons should be denied access to treatment. In fact, the only group that is excluded by law is women over the age of forty-seven. Moreover, every standard treatment of medically assisted reproduction is allowed. The only prohibitions concern non-medical sex selection, eugenic interventions and cloning (Pennings 2007). This permissive law, in combination with restrictive legislation or regulation in neighbouring countries, has made Belgium a popular destination for reproductive travellers. Legal diversity on the application of medically assisted reproduction is a condition for cross-border care.

There are many different reasons why people decide to look for treatment across the border. Empirical studies show that the main reasons for people looking for treatment elsewhere are law evasion and donor gamete shortage (Shenfield et al. 2010; Pennings 2004). Probably for this reason, cross-border reproductive care has drawn a lot of attention. Many consider it unacceptable that people avoid the law of their country by going abroad. Moreover, this is considered fundamentally unjust because only people with the necessary financial means can afford to go elsewhere. While this is largely true, the first question that should be asked is whether the law can withstand scrutiny. Not surprisingly, people tend to approve cross-border movements when they disapprove of the law, and vice versa. The phenomenon in general raises very difficult issues about the relationship between law, ethics and politics.

Belgium and Cross-Border Patients

The four top-ranked countries of patients coming to Belgium for fertility-related treatment are France (38 per cent), the Netherlands (29 per cent), Italy (12 per cent) and Germany (10 per cent) (Pennings et al. 2009). These are data for the period 2000 to 2007. Although there is no more recent survey, anecdotal evidence indicates that the number of patients from Italy has decreased. The changes in Law 40, amended by different Italian courts, have certainly contributed to that.

In most countries, it is very difficult to obtain reliable data on the number of incoming patients from abroad. For Belgium, some data can be found in the reports by the College of Physicians of Reproductive Medicine, the so-called Belgian Register for Assisted Procreation (BELRAP). In that data base, one does not distinguish between resident and non-resident patients, but patients with and without social security. Although there is a large overlap between 'non-resident' and 'without social security', there is certainly a bias since the category 'without social security' refers to patients who are not reimbursed for their cycle. Women older than forty-three and couples going for a seventh or higher IVF cycle are not reimbursed, regardless of their nationality. This fact has been confirmed in the BELRAP data: the proportion of patients without social security increases when the women are forty-three or older and when they have already undergone six cycles (Pennings et al. 2009). The number of foreign patients will therefore be lower than the number of patients without social security.

The general attitude of Belgian fertility clinics towards foreign patients is very welcoming. They do not make much of an effort to attract foreign patients (apart from offering an English website), but they have adopted several measures to lower the burden of treatment. The majority of the centres have interpreters on demand, offer informed consent forms in a number of languages, collaborate with the doctor in the country of origin of the patient and congregate appointments at the clinic to reduce the number of visits the patients have to make (Pennings et al. 2009).

Between 2005 and 2007, approximately 2,300 French women received some form of medically assisted reproductive treatment in Belgium (Pennings et al. 2009). However, that study only included so-called B-centres that have a permit to conduct IVF and other high-tech interventions. There are also seventeen A-centres that are allowed to perform inseminations, and some of them had their own sperm banks at the time of the study (they no longer do, as they have to be certified as tissue banks). The number of French women going for donor insemination is therefore likely to be considerably higher.

While we will focus on French patients in this chapter, we should emphasize that this is not a homogenous population (Rozée Gomez and de la Rochebrochard 2013). Those using donor sperm are mostly lesbian couples and single women. Those using oocyte donation are mostly heterosexual couples. Also, their motivation for travelling is largely different; while lesbian couples and single women do not have access to medically assisted reproduction in France, oocyte donation is allowed and practised in France. The reason these couples travel is due to other specifications (obligatory anonymity, strict reimbursement of proven expenses only, etc.) resulting in a small and largely insufficient donor pool. Legal restrictions may affect candidate users in different ways. Exclusion of groups with certain characteristics or prohibitions of certain treatments are direct limitations. Other legal clauses may have a similar effect but work indirectly.

Donor Sperm

Belgium had and still has a shortage of sperm donors. Almost all clinics are struggling to maintain a reasonable stock in order to be able to match donor and recipient on a limited number of phenotypic characteristics. Public advertisement for the recruitment of donors by the centres is prohibited by law. Some of them distribute flyers on campus, put up posters in the department and try to recruit through their website. Like in most other countries, nothing is done by the government. Contrary to general awareness campaigns for blood and organ donation, not a single campaign has ever been organized in Belgium to recruit gamete donors. The political parties are clearly not ready to take that step.

There are two important sources of information: a Belgian study looking at all patients entering Belgium from abroad (Pennings et al. 2009) and a European study looking at patients entering six European countries (Belgium, Czech Republic, Denmark, Slovenia, Spain and Switzerland) for fertility-related treatment (Shenfield et al. 2010). In the Belgian study, the overwhelming majority (73 per cent) of French patients went to Belgium for sperm donation (Pennings et al. 2009). In the European study, only 57 per cent of the French patients travelled for sperm donation (Shenfield et al. 2010). However, the Belgian study covered a much more extended time period and included sixteen out of eighteen IVF centres. In the European study, only eight centres participated. As a consequence, the data from the Belgian study are much more reliable and representative. Most French patients are single or lesbian couples who do not have access to medically assisted reproduction at home. At the moment, treatment in France is restricted to heterosexual couples in a stable relationship (previously the law required that the couple be married or cohabiting for at least two years; this is no longer the case) (Pennings 1997). Even after the adoption of the law of 2013 permitting same-sex marriage, lesbian couples are still excluded from medically assisted reproduction (Law no. 2013-04 of 17 May 2013). An important justification for this continued ban is the rule that assisted reproduction should remedy infertility that can be medically diagnosed.

Of the seventeen centres performing artificial insemination by donor, four use only imported sperm, eleven use both imported and centre-recruited donors, and just two use only centre-recruited donors. In all Belgian sperm banks taken together, Danish sperm was used in 63 per cent of the insemination cycles (Thijssen et al. 2014). However, very little happens in terms of awareness campaigns and so clinics take the easy way out: import from Denmark. Remarkably, Belgium seems to import exactly as much as it 'exports'. About 63 per cent of all sperm is used for foreign patients and 63 per cent is imported from Denmark. It could be argued, therefore, that the Belgian centres are self-sufficient if only Belgian patients are taken into consideration. Recently, due to a discussion in the Belgian Parliament regarding the control of the centres on the number of children per donor (according to the Belgian law, the limit per donor is six women), a number of Belgian centres have decided to serve foreign patients only with imported donor sperm. Since the centres cannot control how many children have been created outside the country with the sperm of a foreign donor, they argue that they can only respect this rule for Belgian donors. However, since there is no central register, even this cannot be guaranteed and respecting the rule relies almost entirely on the promise of the donor not to donate at more than one centre. Moreover, the centres argued that foreign patients should be counted in their country of residence, not in the country that treats them.

At present nobody questions the solution of the Belgian clinics. However, if there was ever to be a problem with the supply from abroad (for example if the Danish sperm banks are no longer able to supply the rest of Europe, or the Belgian authorities decide to limit the import), the question will be raised whether Belgian patients should have priority over foreign patients. This discussion has been conducted in the context of organ donation where shortage is much higher. It seems to be justifiable to introduce a quota for foreign patients, but an outright exclusion when the shortage increases is a lot more difficult to explain.

Donor Eggs

In 1998, 61 per cent of the oocyte donation cycles were performed for non-Belgian patients. In 1999, this percentage had gone up to 75 per cent (College of Physicians for Assisted Reproductive Therapy 2011–2015). After that year, we have to deduce the number of foreign patients from the number of patients without social security. From 2010 onwards, the number of IVF/ICSI cycles performed on patients without social security remained stable. However, for egg donation, the percentage of recipients without social security is much higher. Slightly more than 40 per cent of the donor eggs go to recipients without social security (see Table 10.1). Without further information, one cannot be certain about the composition of this specific group, but very likely most of these recipients are foreign patients. This is corroborated by the data from one Brussels clinic that showed that between 1990 and 2007, 39 per cent of the recipients of donor eggs were French women (Aballea, Burstin and Guedi 2011).

In the Belgian survey that included sixteen of the eighteen Belgian IVF centres, five centres explicitly asked foreign patients to bring their own donor (Pennings et al. 2009). However, the number of centres demanding this was most likely higher. In the questionnaire, the question was asked whether the centres had 'special' rules for foreign patients, and some centres may not have indicated this condition because they also asked Belgian patients to bring their own donor if they wanted to avoid long waiting lists.

In a recent study on oocyte donation in eleven European countries, only forty-seven of sixty-five donors resided in Belgium (Pennings et al. 2014). No other country had such a high percentage of non-resident donors. A closer look at this group revealed that fifteen of the eighteen foreign donors came from France, and that twelve of these fifteen were donating directly to a family member or friend. This particular phenomenon can be explained by the French rule of compulsory donor anonymity. Since they are not allowed to donate directly to a sister or friend in France, both donor and recipient go to Belgium. In another Belgian study on oocyte donation, this finding was also mentioned. About 25 per cent of the French patients at the Erasme Hospital wanted known donation and therefore chose to go to Belgium (Laruelle et al. 2011). Moreover, the presence of the other French patients could also be explained by different legal restrictions in France. The Erasme Hospital in Brussels found that two-thirds of the oocyte recipients in their clinic were from Europe, and within this group 41.5 per cent were from France (Laruelle et al. 2011). About one in four of these patients wanted anonymous donation, but they had no donor and bringing your own donor was mandatory in France. In the third group that opted for known-anonymous donation or cross-donation (the recipient brings a donor but the oocytes of that donor are used for another recipient and the donor of another recipient is used for them), some could not use their donor either because they were too old or because the donor was not a mother herself (Laruelle et al. 2011).

The main problem is the huge shortage of egg donors in France. Most couples go to Spain but some prefer Belgium, probably because of the common language and the geographic proximity. The Czech Republic and Greece follow just behind (Aballea, Burstin and Guedi 2011). It is estimated that between 1,800 and 3,600 French women go abroad for egg donation per year, which represents approximately 80–85 per cent of the total (Aballea, Burstin and Guedi 2011). Moreover, the number of treatments abroad is rising, as can be deduced from the number of requests for reimbursement for treatment abroad in the French social security system. In 2005, there were twenty-three requests (representing 54 per cent of the total) for reimbursement of treatment received in Belgium, while in 2009, there were eighty-eight requests (representing 13.5 per cent).

Table 10.1. Patients without social security treated in Belgium.

Year		Percentage	Number of cycles
2009	All ages and ranks Donor eggs	10.5 41.5	1,761 609
2010	All ages and ranks Donor eggs	15.8 43.6	2,747 619
2011	All ages and ranks Donor eggs	17.4 43.7	3,226 551
2012	All ages and ranks Donor eggs	16.5 41.3	3,021 479
2013	All ages and ranks Donor eggs	16.1 43	2,911 430

The main evolution in the last few years is the enormous increase in patients travelling to Spain. The abundance of donors there undoubtedly influences this shift.

For oocyte donation, the percentages from the studies also differ. The Belgian study indicates that about 11 per cent of the patients from France came to Belgium for oocyte donation (Pennings et al. 2009). However, in the European study, 20.6 per cent of French patients indicated that they wanted oocyte donation in Belgium (Shenfield et al. 2010). Again, however, I prefer the data from the Belgian study for qualitative reasons.

The Attitude of French Physicians

When patients plan to go abroad, they need to find information on the multiple aspects of the treatment: where will they be accepted? How much will it cost? What language do they speak? French lesbians travelling to Belgium for donor insemination usually rely on information they find on the internet or directly from friends who conceived in Belgium. In their search for information on where to go (which clinic, which country), they contacted their general practitioner or gynaecologist. However, no doctor provided information on that point, and neither did they agree to refer the patient to a clinic abroad. The reasons for this position are unclear. It may be that they did not want to be involved, or that they simply did not know. Even Belgian fertility specialists would not always know what the rules are in other Belgian centres. The information on the modalities in each centre is not centralized, so patients have to find out for themselves by contacting the centre. Many of them did indeed visit several centres to find out the specifics (insemination with or without hormonal stimulation, identifiable or anonymous donation, etc.).

This attitude towards referral is interesting in view of the letter written in 2012 by the Director General of Health in France, Dr Grall, in which he stated that doctors who provided information on foreign clinics and organizations that practised gamete donation in a way that deviates from the French law could go to prison for five years and be fined €75,000. Dr Grall mentioned Spain as a popular destination for egg donation (Grall 2012). In a second letter, dated 30 April 2013, Dr Grall stressed which elements were important in the French law: a heterosexual couple, alive, of age to procreate, anonymity of donor and recipient, altruistic motivation and finally screening of donors (Grall 2013).

The French government clearly believes that doctors who provide information about foreign clinics in a different jurisdiction, or who refer patients to clinics in other countries, are helping patients to evade the law. This is an important issue in itself: should doctors be allowed to help patients evade the law of their country? In which circumstances are doctors complicit in this 'crime'? Ironically, the French social security system partially reimburses patients who go abroad for egg donation. The same report indicates that 649 demands for reimbursement of treatment outside France were received, of which 76.6 per cent were from Spain, 13.5 per cent from Belgium, 3.5 per cent from Greece and 3.4 per cent from the Czech Republic (Aballea, Burstin and Guedi 2011). Reimbursement seems to be a much stronger form of participation in the wrongdoing than providing information, mainly because without it the treatment might not have taken place. Without the physician's information, there is still a relatively high chance that the patient will find his or her own way to a clinic abroad.

Three positions can be distinguished among these doctors: (1) they refused all help; (2) they agreed to follow up on the pregnancy but did not want to take part in treatment; and (3) they supported the couple completely and even worked the system for the patient. The majority (nine out of thirteen) adopted the latter position, which meant that the physician filled out the paperwork so that every part of the treatment performed in France would be reimbursed (Van Hoof, Pennings and de Sutter 2015). From the participating physicians in a French study, 61 per cent indicated that they directly participated in the treatment planned in a foreign country (Jouannet and Spira 2014). In general, French physicians were fairly open about helping patients obtain treatment abroad. The European study showed that 21 per cent of the French patients received no help at all from their local doctor, 37 per cent of the doctors prescribed drugs, 6 per cent did the cycle monitoring and 36 per cent prescribed drugs and monitored the cycle (Van Hoof and Pennings 2015). Compared to other countries in the study, French doctors were among the most supportive. Most patients clearly valued the support of their physician as this implied that there was someone close to home who knew about the situation, who could help and who could follow up on the pregnancy.

The Experience of French Lesbian Couples

In a qualitative study with eleven lesbian couples and two single women from France, we found that these women had several reasons for going to Belgium, and more specifically to Ghent University Hospital, rather than elsewhere (Van Hoof, Pennings and de Sutter 2015). First, they wanted to avoid a commercial setting because they had heard stories of women in Spanish clinics who were treated in an unfriendly manner, overstimulated and badly informed. They thought this was due to the commercial nature of the clinics. Second, they wanted the treatment to be as natural as possible, meaning without hormonal stimulation. Finally, the Ghent clinic had no waiting lists for donor insemination, so they could start treatment immediately. Apparently, the biggest difficulty for French patients going to Belgium was the waiting period (Rozée Gomez and de la Rochebrochard 2013). If this is correct (no information was available on this point from other centres), the absence of waiting lists would be an important element in the decision.

Many patients encountered a whole series of practical challenges and difficulties. The first concerned the lack of information to help them choose the 'right' centre. When they collected all the information and had selected a treatment centre, they had to organize their personal life to include the treatment. This means many trips to the centre for most of them (sometimes over quite some distance), as the delivery rate per Intra-uterine Insemination

(IUI) with donor sperm is below 10 per cent (College of Physicians of Reproductive Medicine 2013–2015). Most women in this study worked, which raised the difficulty of obtaining leave, frequently on short notice (Van Hoof, Pennings and de Sutter 2015). Sometimes, doctors were willing to prescribe them sick leave.

Their attitude towards their home country was, not surprisingly, negative. They felt discriminated against and ignored by their exclusion from treatment. The fact that many people in France were convinced that a lesbian couple could not raise a child especially hurt them (the interviews took place during the debate on the same-sex marriage law). Simultaneously, they believed that French society was ready for change. They also indicated that they felt well accepted in their daily life. According to the couples, only the politicians and the priests lagged behind. The only option they had in France was to look for a donor in their social network. However, this not only meant that they would forsake medical screening and legal protection, but most of all, it would imply the involvement of a third person in something they saw as essentially their own project. Still, this position can probably be explained by self-selection: those who feel this way are the ones who look for a solution abroad. In a study about requests for assisted reproduction by same-sex couples in France, 35 per cent of the physicians indicated that advice was solicited concerning natural reproduction, and 48 per cent reported requests for self-insemination (Jouannet and Spira 2014). The authors stated that in those cases the women must know the donor, but that is not necessarily so. An increasing number of women are ordering sperm via the internet for delivery to their private homes (Schou 2015). It seems very likely that they will ask their gynaecologist or general practitioner on how to proceed.

The discrimination mentioned above was felt most strongly in the absence of a legal status for the social mother. This lack of status showed that they were not a normal family; it drove home the discrimination of which they were the victims. The social mother could not collect the child from school, could not go abroad with the child unless she got special permission, and so on. They also worried about what would happen if the biological mother were to have an accident or die. The legal recognition of the social mother would legitimate the family and protect the rights of the social mother. This was considered important because they started the parental project with a focus on equality between the partners.

Cross-Border Reproductive Care: Something to Welcome or Avoid?

Cross-border travelling of patients inevitably raises the question of access. Many people seem to believe that in a European context, these matters should be regulated at a European level (Penasa 2012; Flatscher-Thöni and Voithofer 2015). However, the plea for European harmonization carries some risks. First, will the countries settle for the most restrictive, the most permissive, or a compromise law? It seems that one's position at least to a certain extent depends on whether one believes in the existence of European values. Present politics very much wants to convince us that there are European values and a common European culture. However, when one looks at the regulation of medically assisted reproduction and other related issues in the bioethical sphere (stem cell research, abortion, euthanasia, etc.) in the member states, it is hard to maintain this position. Second, personal and ethical matters fall officially outside the authority of the European institutions. In reality, we see more and more meddling of European legislation and regulation in these domains. Simultaneously, adverse reactions from European citizens are steadily increasing, showing greater opposition by citizens to the constant and ubiquitous interventions by Europe in their private lives. Until a few years ago, citizens mainly showed a lack of interest in European politics (as demonstrated by low turnout for the European elections). This apathy has now turned into a clearly hostile reaction. Many European members of parliament seem to believe that pushing through legislation, no matter what, would be the way out. However, if decisions by European institutions are no longer supported by the citizens in the member states, this attitude may backfire.

An important question in the evaluation of the phenomenon is whether France should change its policies, and if so, how. The matter of same-sex couples is a hot issue in France. It is understandable, given all the commotion, demonstrations and so on, that policymakers move slowly. As such, allowing same-sex marriage without allowing same-sex couples access to medically assisted reproduction is defendable and strategic. But this is only a matter of time: it is difficult to see how one can continue to defend this particular prohibition when these couples are allowed to marry and when the social mother or father is allowed to adopt the child of their partner. Moreover, the stream of lesbian couples receiving treatment elsewhere and starting a family in France is a reality. Prohibition does not change that and cannot stop it. Interestingly, if lesbian couples and single women were to be eligible for treatment at home, this would worsen the existing shortage of donor sperm. From that moment, the problems that present themselves in the context of egg donation would extend to sperm donation.

While cross-border movements of lesbians and single persons are due to a direct prohibition, the movements to obtain donor eggs offer an entirely different explanation. No easy solutions can be proposed there (Aballea, Burstin and Guedi 2011; Taboulet 2014). It is far too simplistic to say that the shortage is entirely or mainly due to the reimbursement policy in France. Admittedly, France is the only country among eleven countries in a recent study on oocyte donation that reimburses proven expenses (Pennings et al. 2014). The mean amount offered to compensate egg donors is somewhere around €900. Although there is a grey zone between reimbursement of expenses and payment, it is arguable that this amount should not be considered as payment. Nevertheless, the question of how a sum of money should be defined cannot be decided for Europe as a whole, since the differences between the countries in terms of wealth, unemployment and so on are large. Moreover, payment or generous compensation is no panacea. Other countries, like Belgium, offer a much higher and sometimes even generous sum and are still struggling to cover the demand. Obviously, developments on the demand side (such as the continuing rise of women's age at first pregnancy) also play a role here.

Non-commercialization of bodily material is seen as a fundamental ethical principle in many European countries. Nevertheless, the position of most countries, as expressed in their reimbursement policies, shows a willingness to take into account other ethical values besides altruism in the context of donation of bodily material. France, on the contrary, wants to hold onto altruism as the sole and primordial value. As a consequence, very few candidate donors present themselves and French citizens go abroad (Letur and Merlet 2012). If a country accepts oocyte donation, it indicates that the use of donor eggs creates a good (in terms of happy families). This good can be promoted by attracting more donors. A policy of 'encouraged altruism' would be a nice combination (Pennings 2015). This position implies that donors can be compensated in money or in kind above the pure compensation for expenses, and this extra sum can be used to motivate people to come forward.

Since non-commercialization is mainly connected to money, it might help to shift to vouchers for vacations, dinners or trips. Even if these vouchers have a precise monetary value, they still have a different meaning (why else are they so popular as gifts?).

Conclusion

The data show that French citizens cross the border to Belgium for at least three reasons: no access to treatment for single women and men and lesbian couples in France; obligatory anonymity of egg donation and thus the impossibility to donate directly to a sister or friend; and the long waiting lists for oocyte donation. The French government will have to take a stance on how it will react to this phenomenon. It seems that there are many internal cracks and contradictions in the French system that push in the direction of a more lenient position. As far as lesbian couples are concerned, the adoption of same-sex marriage is an important step towards acceptance of these couples for medically assisted reproduction. The fact that the French social security system is currently reimbursing egg donations abroad is another inconsistency that may lead to a less principled position on reimbursement. Both adaptations may need some time and more debate, but eventually France will also realize that no country is an island.

Guido Pennings is Professor of Ethics and Bioethics at Ghent University (Belgium), where he is also the director of the Bioethics Institute Ghent (BIG). He has published extensively on ethical problems associated with medically assisted reproduction and genetics.

References

Aballea, P., A. Burstin and J. Guedj. 2011. *Etat des lieux et perspectives du don d'ovocytes en France. Rapport tôme I.* Inspection Générale des Affairs Sociales (IGAS).

College of Physicians of Reproductive Medicine. 2011–2015. *IVF Report.* https://www.belrap.be/Documents/Reports/Global/BelrapSummaryReport2015.pdf. Accessed 1 July 2019.

College of Physicians of Reproductive Medicine. 2013–2015. *Non-IVF Report.* https://www.belrap.be/Documents/Reports/Global/FinalReport_NonIVF13_20151015.pdf. Accessed 1 July 2019.

Flatscher-Thoni, M., and C. Voithofer. 2015. 'Should Reproductive Medicine Be Harmonized within Europe?', *European Journal of Health Law* 22: 61–74.

Grall, J.-Y. 2012. *Lettre du 21* décembre *2012. Ministère des Affairs Sociales et de la Santé.* Paris: French Government. https://solidarites-sante.gouv.fr/fichiers/bo/2013/13-01/ste_20130001_0001_p000.pdf, p. 305. Accessed 1 July 2019.

Grall, J.-Y. 2013. *Lettre du 30 avril 2013. Ministère des Affairs Sociales et de la Santé.* Paris: French Government. https://www.fiv.fr/media/REPONSE-DGS-30_04_13.pdf. Accessed 1 July 2019.

Jouannet, P., and A. Spira. 2014. 'Demandes d'aide à la procréation formulées par les couples de même sexe auprès de médicins en France', *Revue d'Epidémiologie et de Santé Publique* 62: 268–72.

Laruelle, C., I. Place, I. Demeestere, Y. Englert and A. Delbaere. 2011. 'Anonymity and Secrecy Options of Recipient Couples and Donors, and Ethnic Origin Influence in Three Types of Oocyte Donation', *Human Reproduction* 26 (2): 382–90.

Letur, H., and F. Merlet. 2012. 'Situation législative et réglementaire du don d'ovocytes en France', *Gynecologie Obstétrique & Fertilité* 40: 28–31.

Penasa, S. 2012. 'Converging by Procedures: Assisted Reproductive Technology Regulation within the European Union', *Medical Law International* 12 (3–4): 300–27.

Pennings, G. 1997. 'Gamete Donation from Couple to Couple in the New French Law', *Medicine and Law* 16 (4): 795–804.

Pennings, G. 2004. 'Legal Harmonization and Reproductive Tourism in Europe', *Human Reproduction* 19 (12): 2689–94.

Pennings, G. 2007. 'Belgian Law on Medically Assisted Reproduction and the Disposition of Supernumerary Embryos and Gametes', *European Journal of Health Law* 14 (3): 251–60.

Pennings, G. 2015. 'Central Value of Altruism in the Recruitment of Gamete Donors', *Monash Bioethics Review* 33: 78–88.

Pennings, G., et al. 2009. 'Cross-Border Reproductive Care in Belgium', *Human Reproduction* 24 (12): 3108–18.

Pennings, G., et al. 2014. 'Socio-Demographic and Fertility Related Characteristics and Motivations of Oocyte Donors in Eleven European Countries', *Human Reproduction* 29 (5): 1076–89.

Rozée Gomez, V., and E. de la Rochebrochard. 2013. 'Cross-Border Reproductive Care among French Patients: Experiences in Greece, Spain and Belgium', *Human Reproduction* 28 (11): 3103–10.

Schou, O. 2015. 'Trends in Recipients' Choices Regarding Donor Information', Presentation at the conference *Donor Conception: An Unfamiliar Path to a Normal Family?* Bioethics Institute Ghent, 27–28 August.

Shenfield, F., et al., on behalf of the ESHRE Taskforce 'Cross-Border Reproductive Care'. 2010. 'Cross-Border Reproductive Care in Six European Countries', *Human Reproduction* 25 (6): 1361–68.

Taboulet, F. 2014. 'Don d'ovocytes et tourisme procréatif: comment sortir de l'impasse?', *Médicine & Droit* 2014: 40–45.

Thijssen, A., et al. 2014. 'Artificial Insemination with Donor Sperm (AID): Heterogeneity in Sperm Banking Facilities on a Single Country (Belgium)', *Facts, Views and Vision in Obstetrics and Gynaecology* 6 (2): 57–67.

Van Hoof, W., and G. Pennings. 2015. 'Risks and Challenges for Patients Crossing Borders for Infertility Treatment', in B. Parry, B. Greenhough, T. Brown and I. Dyck (eds), *Bodies across Borders: The Global Circulation of Body Parts, Medical Tourists and Professionals*. Farnham: Ashgate Publishing, pp. 115–29.

Van Hoof, W., G. Pennings and P. de Sutter. 2015. 'Cross-Border Reproductive Care for Law Evasion: A Qualitative Study into the Experiences and Moral Perspectives of French Women Who Go to Belgium for Treatment with Donor Sperm', *Social Science and Medicine* 124: 391–97.

Chapter 11

Is ART a 'National Issue'?

Marie Gaille

It has become common to describe the contemporary era as a globalized market of reproduction (Spar 2006; Dickenson 2008). Throughout international literature, this phenomenon has stirred up harsh moral and political criticism: assisted reproductive technologies should be placed outside of the market (Sandel 2012); women, and especially poor women from the South, should be protected against the exploitation of their reproductive capacities. The market is seen as everything but a neutral space and a vector of gender domination (Satz 1992). Related to this issue, feminist theory occasionally mingles with Marxism to name and shame such exploitation (Wright 2006; Coburn 2011; Cooper 2008; Lafontaine 2014).

As the previous chapters have demonstrated, the French and Belgian cases are participating in this shift towards a globalized market of assisted reproduction. They illustrate the development of numerous cross-border practices in various manners. These practices sometimes imply a financial transaction between two individuals, one individual and a firm, and in some cases intermediary agencies, be they state-regulated, legal and documented or not. This observation highlights the idea that access to reproductive technology is no longer a national issue, if ever it was in previous times.

Focusing on surrogate pregnancy, this chapter aims to answer the following questions: to what extent has this dimension been taken into account in academic and public discussions? And if it has, what arguments have been developed to understand and assess its implications?

As the debate on surrogate pregnancy takes various shapes within different national contexts, this chapter will examine the issue with a focus on the French debate without assuming it has a general scope. To concentrate on a single context gives us an opportunity to propose an in-depth assessment of how, in that specific context, surrogate pregnancy is approached using certain arguments, while others remain hidden in the background. On the basis of the French context, we may understand how the structure of one specific debate on surrogate pregnancy helps us, or not, to grasp the cross-border dimension and formulate its implications. To introduce this debate, which is both academic and public, I will refer to arguments developed in a series of publications aimed at providing an ethical framework to public discussion, namely reports from ethical committees or scientific societies, and philosophical essays written for a wide range of readers.

I will first describe the general features of the debate and the various arguments that are elaborated within. I will examine whether they give room to the cross-border dimension of surrogate pregnancy, and if so, to what extent. In a second part, I will analyse the consistency of the arguments that confront each other in this debate so as to assess their capacity to grasp the cross-border dimension and define its moral scope. Finally, in a third part, I will emphasize the main blind spots and argumentative flaws of the French debate concerning surrogate pregnancy and highlight how they are obstacles in elaborating a frame of thought capable of fully grasping the implications of cross-border practices.

The French Debate on Surrogate Pregnancy: A Thick Web of Moral and Divergent Arguments

In the early 1980s, two French associations advertised their role in connecting 'would-be parent' couples and women who would agree to carry a baby for them. At that time, surrogate pregnancy was not forbidden by law. It became so shortly after this initiative. Almost forty years later, surrogate pregnancy is still a hotly debated issue from a legal, political and moral standpoint in French society. It is considered by experts from various fields within and beyond the academic field – legal experts, psychologists, sociologists, philosophers, medical professionals – as well as by political public figures who take an interest in 'bioethical' matters. The arguments circulate from one 'arena of speech' to another (Dodier 2003).

On the specific topic of surrogate pregnancy, concerns about an authoritarian state that would control reproduction within its national borders (in order to 'enhance' the genetic quality of its population or to grow in number) have become obsolete. When these arguments are advanced, they describe a form of 'negative utopia', for example in André Gorz's writings (Gorz 1988). Rather, today the discussion focuses on the following moral and legal questions: is surrogate pregnancy morally legitimate? Should France make it legal? How to proceed in this direction? Finally, what should French society do with children who were born thanks to surrogate pregnancy? The latter question is crucial because these children are presently devoid of legal status in France, though some indirect legal solutions are presently explored to solve this issue (and that of their right to inheritance).

Though the legal discussion is indeed crucial, one major feature of the French debate on surrogate pregnancy is also its moral dimension. As the anthropologist Raymond Massé stresses, human actions do not have to be and are not always judged from a moral point of view (Massé 2015). However, this is indeed the case for surrogate pregnancy in the French context: ethical concerns are at the forefront. I will first devote my attention to this moral side of the debate, providing a conceptual description and critical analysis of the arguments at stake.

In the French case, the ethical assessment of surrogate pregnancy first attributes an important role to a type of argument known as a 'categorical imperative' as defined from a Kantian perspective – that is to say, laws that can never be broken. According to Kant, a categorical imperative is above every principle, norm, value and desire. No 'circumstance' justifies breaking it (Kant 1997). Rejecting the instrumentalization of human beings and human bodies is the first affirmation that is attributed to this status of categorical imperative. Various types of identified or supposed risks are emphasized to complete this argument: the physiological and psychic risks associated with pregnancy; and the specific psychic impact of surrogate pregnancy on the 'surrogate mother', her family and the child to be born, both in the short and long term. In order to satisfy their desire for a child, would-be parents who turn to surrogate pregnancy neglect the bonds between the child and the woman who agrees to carry the pregnancy for them. Criticism of surrogate pregnancy based on rejecting the instrumentalization of human beings and human bodies is particularly strong when it is associated with a definition of motherhood as a block entity, starting with conception, then pregnancy, delivery and raising a child (Agacinski 2009).

The idea of solidarity is also given significant importance in the French debate, consistent with its role in French health care policies at least since the end of the Second World War (ter Meulen 2017). In contrast to the first argument, it is usually formulated to legitimate surrogate pregnancy from a moral standpoint, at least in certain cases. The reasoning is as follows: in the name of solidarity for infertile women, society must help them achieve their desire for a child, even through surrogate pregnancy if necessary. In France, this argument is expressed only when infertility is due to the absence of a uterus, uterine cancer/dysfunction or oocyte shortage, that is, when a physiological reason explains the woman's infertility. In this case, it is held that surrogate pregnancy should be organized by public health policies in a medical setting. Though it does not itself use the word 'solidarity', *Accès à la parenté: Assistance médicale à la procréation et adoption*, the report proposed by the left-wing think tank Terra Nova, formulated such a perspective on surrogate pregnancy (Terra Nova 2010). It considered it an ethically legitimate practice when a medical diagnosis of infertility was established because of the absence of a uterus, uterine cancer/dysfunction or ovarian shortage. Another report, drafted by the French National Ethics Committee and published in the same year, also evoked the struggle against 'injustice' – understood here as the physiological incapacity to procreate and/or bear children – as one of the most significant arguments in favour of surrogate pregnancy (CCNE 2010). It stated that surrogate pregnancy could be viewed as 'the solution to a painful physical and psychic ordeal', and stressed the fact that physiological infertility was a particularly unfair fate. It advocated that women 'who have everything to be mothers' should access ART, in this case a medically assisted surrogate pregnancy. In 2014, the Academy of Medicine mentioned arguments of solidarity as well. In its report on surrogate pregnancy, the Academy emphasized the ordeal experienced by infertile couples, and considered that society could not remain indifferent to such an unfair situation, especially when taking into consideration the complexity of adoption and the absence of alternative options (Académie nationale de médecine 2014).

The late philosopher Ruwen Ogien (who passed away on 4 May 2017) formulated another type of argument that broadens and enriches the discussion about surrogate pregnancy. On the basis of J.S.

Mill's work (particularly *On Liberty*, 1859), Ogien approached the issue of surrogate pregnancy from both a moral and political standpoint. For him, the main criterion to distinguish between a good action and a bad one from a moral standpoint is, generally speaking, the presence/absence of harmfulness to others. If one does not harm others, nothing may justify that one be prevented from living in one's own way. Ogien also considered that individual liberty was the most important goal to be pursued by society. As a result, the relationship between the state and its citizens should be organized to safeguard individual liberty as long as no harm is done to others. This frame of thought led him to criticize French society's 'hypocrisy'. From Ogien's standpoint, individual liberty is threatened by present-day conservatism. In this context, philosophy's main and urgent mission is to formulate arguments that resist conservatism and promote libertarian ideals (Ogien 2013). He believed that philosophers must primarily demonstrate that 'morality' should not be the focus of many issues and that the law should not be grounded on 'moral values'. On the contrary, political, institutional and legal action must remain focused on the preservation and promotion of individual 'negative' liberty. Ogien thus put forward what he called a 'minimalist' conception of politics. This position integrated the idea of a 'private' space in which each individual should be entitled to do whatever she/he wants with her/his life.

This political theory has direct implications in the debate around surrogate pregnancy: in Ogien's view, reproduction, family life and end of life issues are such 'intimate' realms that the society or state should never intervene as long as the person does no harm to others (Ogien 2013). No valid objection exists to refuse same-sex marriage; access to reproductive technologies should be granted to everyone, heterosexual or homosexual couples and single persons alike. Finally, surrogate pregnancy should be considered as a legitimate way to have children from the moment the woman consents to carry the child for would-be parents. According to Ogien, cultural prejudices or dubious psychological speculations lead to skewed thinking about these issues (Ogien 2013).

Despite the perception of the French bioethics discussion as principle-driven and devoid of interest for 'real life' situations (Mehl 2008), one must recognize that the French debate makes room for an analysis of the social and economic characteristics of surrogate pregnancy and their moral scope. In addition to these three visions based on Kant's philosophy, the principle of solidarity and that of minimalist conception of morals and politics, it specifically considers the issue of exploiting human beings and human bodies. Indeed, there is a strong suspicion that would-be parents deliberately turn to impoverished women who consent to surrogate pregnancy because they have no other choice. From an ethical standpoint, this is deemed a disputable option, as economic inequalities, especially in a post-colonial context, seem to give a decisive advantage to would-be parents. The exploitation argument is grounded on the observation that some women consent to surrogate pregnancy for the sake of money in various countries around the world. The gender dimension emerges in this argument, but most of the time is viewed alongside the economic issue, rather than singled out as a specific element to be considered.

Though we know that some experiences of surrogate pregnancy are unrelated to profit, much fieldwork has highlighted the testimony of women on this matter. The link between social and economic inequalities and surrogate pregnancy is, in some cases, undeniable. In some instances, an entire 'life of work' would not have permitted a woman to earn the amount of money she could via a surrogate pregnancy (Rudrappa 2012). From this follows the idea that poor women would never have consented to surrogate pregnancy if they had been in better economic and social conditions. Consequently, surrogate pregnancy appears as a morally unacceptable action grounded in economic and social inequalities. This argument definitely leads one to take into account reproductive cross-border practices, and thus considering them from a moral standpoint entails a negative assessment of surrogate pregnancy. In addition, specific attention is paid to the growing role played by commercial intermediaries that organize surrogate pregnancies on an international scale (CCNE 2017).

Thus far, the various arguments that have been presented do not carry the same weight when ethically assessing surrogate pregnancy in the French debate. Kant's categorical imperative prevails, and is exclusively used to criticize surrogate pregnancy's immorality. It matches French legal principles on the matter: the legal definition of motherhood as being the woman who gives birth, the impossibility to transform a human body into a good, the principle of the inalienability of persons. The French legal system and Kant's categorical imperative mutually reinforce themselves in their rejection of surrogate pregnancy. Furthermore, in a social context in which the value of solidarity is prevalent and stands as the main basis for access to health care, the argument based on solidarity is acknowledged but less powerful than the first one. Finally, Ruwen Ogien's 'minimalist' conception of morality and the ideal of political liberty receives much less attention and, up to now, carries no weight when faced with the prevalence of Kant's conception. In addition, it appears as a weak argument when surrogate pregnancy is considered within the context of the exploitation of women's bodies.

Crossing Borders in Order to Have a Child: A Moral Issue?

The previous description of the French debate on surrogate pregnancy highlights the manner in which the issue of cross-border practices is approached. In this second part, I would like to examine the capacity of the arguments that confront each other so as to grasp the issue of cross-border practices from an ethical standpoint.

As we saw, Kant's imperative lies in the rejection of the instrumentalization of human beings and human bodies, and when applied to cross-border practices, it may appear as an ethically relevant one. However, one may question the value of this argument. First of all, surrogate pregnancy is considered as an act that is accomplished on the basis of consent. Therefore, it cannot be compared or assimilated to slavery. This is an important point, as J.S. Mill stressed the fact that the criticism of paternalism encounters its limits when a decision threatens the present and future autonomy of a person (Dworkin 1971). Nobody should be granted the right to consent to slavery. However, in principle, one cannot affirm that a consenting person loses her autonomy.

Second, if one follows Kant's formulation of the practical imperative, the description of surrogate pregnancy as a form of instrumentalization is not so obvious: 'So act that you use humanity, whether in your own person or in the person of any other, always at the same time as an end, never merely as a means' (Kant 1997: 429–430). *Never merely as a means*. Can we affirm that a consenting person is only used as a means? From a Kantian perspective, what may be said about a woman's decision to act as a surrogate mother? This woman does consent to carry a child she will subsequently not raise. Does she thus make of herself a mere means? Does she discard the 'end in itself' that she is for herself, for others and thus for 'humanity'? The answer to these questions is certainly not obvious; the reference to Kantian thought does not bring a clear contribution to the debate on the moral status of the consenting woman.

Do we therefore have strong ethical reasons to prevent a woman, despite her own consent, from carrying and delivering a child as a response to the desire for a child by an infertile couple (due to either sexual orientation or pathological infertility)? It has been argued that these reasons lie in the impact of surrogacy on the woman who is the surrogate, her family and the child to be born. This particular view was already discussed in the past by the American philosopher Bonnie Steinbock, when she defined the 'Baby M' case as a tragic illustration of a situation wherein, after birth, the surrogate mother does not want to be separated from the baby (Steinbock 1988). It is one of the main lines of argument of the Comité consultatif national d'éthique 2017 report. Today, the bonds that are created during pregnancy between the woman and the baby are still an important concern and are not fully resolved. The aforementioned Terra Nova report extensively covered this question, both to highlight it and to 'reassure' its readers that every baby has, in normal life conditions, the psychic capacity to 'transfer' this pre-natal bonding and relate to the persons who will raise her/him (2010). It also insisted on the feeling of accomplishment expressed by 'surrogate mothers', the moral value they may grant to their act, the altruistic dimension it conveys in relationship to 'the gift of life' for infertile couples (Terra Nova 2010). In addition, some recent American studies and fieldwork stress the fact that children born thanks to surrogate pregnancy are raised in families that maintain relationships with the 'surrogate mother'. They grow up like every child, with the same problems and issues as other children. They adjust to this type of 'extended' family and sometimes value the bond that links them to their 'surrogate mother' (Golombok et al. 2011; Javda et al. 2011; Merchant 2012). Finally, when asked if we have good ethical reasons to prevent a woman, despite her own consent, from becoming a 'surrogate mother', one must acknowledge that conclusive elements have not yet been gathered concerning the psychic impact of surrogate pregnancy that would allow us to conclude firmly on this matter. Steinbock stressed this point in 1988 and it is still relevant today. The argument of instrumentalization seems overall inconclusive. It is thus shaky to use it in order to grasp and discuss the cross-border dimension of surrogate pregnancy.

Let us now address the argument of the exploitation of poor women. This argument entails a negative moral vision of surrogate pregnancy as (at least some) women consent to it to attenuate their poverty. This argument seems to be a powerful one, as it questions both the consistency of the surrogate mother's consent and the morality of would-be parents. Indeed, in some way, it may be said that these would-be parents fulfil their desire for a child thanks to economic inequalities. In addition, some argue that the narrative based on consent is mere rhetoric, even when used by women of the South to justify their decision to themselves: it may be viewed as a smokescreen that dissimulates unequal post-colonial relationships that would otherwise be unbearable (Pande 2011).

However, this argument may be put to scrutiny as well. How is it legitimate to question the value of a person's choice because she is part of an underprivileged economic/social group? Even under such conditions, the capacity to choose remains. A limited-resource context leads to choices that one may describe according to the Aristotelian conception of mixed actions (Aristotle 2002). These choices are both voluntary and counter-voluntary, but they still remain choices. Some contemporary fieldwork confirms this interpretation. For example, the sociologist Sharmila Rudrappa explains that the women she interacted with in India, though extremely poor, could not be described only as 'victims' (Rudrappa 2012). Some of them opted for surrogate pregnancy, and in doing so earned a very significant amount of money and escaped from what they described as 'the hell of assembly line'. They also expressed attaining an improved symbolic position within their families. Both their husbands and their parents came to view them in a different manner and took into account their opinions concerning child education and family organization.

Rudrappa's fieldwork also provides an interesting insight into how these women experience 'surrogate motherhood' from an emotional standpoint. Some of them do not deny psychic and organizational difficulties. They have to submit to strict pregnancy supervision and accept a caesarean delivery. They are separated from their own family for nine months. Finally, they have to cope with possible feelings of bonding with the child to be born. All this considered, even though suspicion over an 'illusion of consent' may in some instances remain (O'Neill, Shanley and Young 2008), these women make the choice to become 'surrogate mothers', meaning that they comparatively assess the advantages/disadvantages of this option. The money they earn, the autonomy as well as the power it gives them, prevails over emotional, psychic and organizational difficulties (Rudrappa 2012).

It seemed in the first place that the French debate provided a place for the cross-border dimension of surrogate pregnancy.

However, closer examination made through further arguments reveals that this dimension is approached through rather inconclusive arguments.

Enlarging Our Frame of Thought to a Post-Westphalian Context beyond the French Debate

As it presently exists, the French debate suffers from a lack of knowledge about surrogate pregnancy practice. This is a common feature shared with other national contexts (van den Akker 2007; Mehl 2008; Petitfils and Munoz Sastre 2014; Dolezal 2015). Indeed, the prohibition of surrogate pregnancy probably makes the quest for knowledge even more difficult in France than in places where it is legally organized. The effect of such ignorance is worrisome: insults, fuzzy formulas and vague notions easily replace sharp and well-defined concepts based on facts.

Consequently, the French debate on surrogate pregnancy has its blind spots and argumentative flaws. In this section, I would like to highlight three of them and examine how they impact the understanding of the cross-border dimension of surrogate pregnancy and its ethical implications.

First of all, French moral reflection on surrogate pregnancy pays less attention to the financial aspect than other national debates. This may be related to the fact that legal prohibition of the commodification of the human body and its reproductive capacities is a widely agreed-upon, even consensual viewpoint in France; it is negatively assessed by almost everyone and often does not seem to require further discussion. Hence, French research and publications on surrogate pregnancy as a globalized capitalistic practice are still lacking, though recent academic events intend to rectify this situation.[1] Those who advocate for the legalization of surrogate pregnancy promote it as based on being a gift or being compensated. As a result, interest in legally organizing surrogate pregnancy based on financial profit is very low, and analyses must be 'imported' from other national contexts (Merchant 2012). The result of this in France is also that Sandel's questioning concerning the social, moral and civilizational impact of the market is never raised, though it should be considered crucial when observing the implications of surrogate pregnancy as a cross-border practice (Sandel 2012). Along the same line of thought – and probably due to the widely agreed-upon rejection of the commodification of the human body and reproductive capacities – contemporary French debate offers little room for an argumentation in terms of reproductive labour. The idea according to which women could work and earn money through surrogate pregnancy seems simply out of place and thus cannot be used as a tool for analysis, so controversial is it, to consider the globalized market of reproduction (Fraser 2008).

In addition, the French debate on surrogate pregnancy remains almost blind to those members of its population who cross borders to fulfil their desire for a child. In principle, surrogate pregnancy could be the 'solution' to have a child in various cases: that of heterosexual couples when the woman is infertile or cannot become and/or remain pregnant; that of male homosexual couples or a single man, who need egg donation and a womb, from the same woman or not; that of a heterosexual couple or of a single woman unwilling to experience pregnancy.

In France, most of the discussion deals with the first case. The aforementioned Terra Nova report tackles the issue of homosexual couples and highlights a disagreement between its two authors on this topic. Regarding homosexual couples, it advocates for a reform of access to reproductive medicine in an indeterminate future (Terra Nova 2010). The French psychoanalyst Geneviève Delaisi de Parseval, one of the report's authors, elaborated from the early 1980s on a psychoanalytic conception favourable to surrogate pregnancy for homosexual couples (Delaisi de Parseval 1983). Still, her point of view is far from being mainstream. Male homosexual couples and single women are mentioned in the Comité consultatif national d'éthique report of 2017, but the main focus of the argument remains heterosexual couples with an infertility problem.

As surrogate pregnancy is considered ethically legitimate (notably in the name of solidarity), it is approached as a form of reproductive medicine aiming at solving the problem of infertility. Most of the time, the medical standpoint, along with a conception of the missions and duties of physicians (not to answer a wish or a desire, but to cure a disease or solve a problem defined as pathological), prevails in the framing of the discussion. As a result, cross-border practices are most of the time set aside from the discussion.

Finally, the assessment of the cross-border dimension within the French debate could presently benefit from a global ethics perspective. In this line of thought, we may refer to the analysis of the 'complicity in injustice' developed by the philosopher Erik Malmqvist. According to him, it may not be correct to consider as exploitative a situation in which people are unequal as far as they all consent to the same mutually beneficial act. The idea of a 'mutually advantageous action' must be taken seriously (Wertheimer 1992). Surrogate pregnancy does fulfil the desire for a child on the part of infertile couples. In addition, it significantly improves a surrogate woman's fate from both an economic and social standpoint. In a way, if I desire a child very much but am infertile, it is even more generous for me to invest my money in a surrogate pregnancy than to buy a house by the sea (Malmqvist 2015). Surrogate pregnancy may not be a morally good act, but it is probably a lesser evil once global economic inequalities are considered. From a consequentialist perspective, surrogate pregnancy may thus be morally justified.

Nonetheless, complicity in injustice also has to be taken into account (Kutz 2000; Malmqvist 2013). This entails that a person performs a morally wrong act if she/he makes a decision that reinforces global inequalities, even though she/he is not initially responsible for them. As a consequence, would-be parents who turn to surrogate pregnancy not only take advantage of economic inequalities, they also encourage them. In this respect, neither mutual consent nor benefit for both parties may legitimate surrogate pregnancy:

> Once we recognize that exploitation coexists with complicity when it arises from injustice it becomes less puzzling to think that it can be worse to exploit the global poor than to neglect them, even when exploitation is voluntary and makes them better off ... The point for now is that irrespective of our views on neglect, exploitation can be seriously wrong – even in its mutually beneficial and voluntary form. (Malmqvist 2015)

Among arguments that are relevant when taking into account the cross-border dimension of surrogate pregnancy and assessing its moral scope, it seems that the 'complicity in injustice' argument is a convincing one. It would allow us to take into consideration, besides the financial dimension, other potential aspects of exploitation (such as the medical risk run by any pregnant woman). As we see, in Malmqvist's view, it does advocate taking a critical ethical stand against the practice of surrogate pregnancy, though it is probably possible to use it also as a criterion to discriminate between acceptable and unacceptable forms of surrogate pregnancy. The 'complicity in injustice' argument would overall allow us to consider the issue of our moral responsibility for each other on a worldwide scale (Tronto 2012). However, it is not yet considered in the French debate.

Conclusion

In essence, in order to grasp the transnational dimension of surrogate pregnancy and its moral scope, the thrust of this chapter lies in the conviction that the most difficult border to cross is one's frame of thought. I have used the French debate on surrogate pregnancy to illustrate this point. Though not totally blind to the cross-border dimension of surrogate pregnancy, the French debate only offers a partial view of this dimension. Present arguments *may be* refined, other available arguments *may be* introduced, blind spots *may be* identified, frame of thought *may be* enlarged and/or *should be*.

Other national and cultural frames of thought may be examined in the same manner, all the more so if we realize that the arguments described and analysed above are not specifically 'French' ones. They are indeed present in various national, linguistic and cultural contexts, even if their scope has varied from one place to another. For example, the *British Warnock Report* already discussed both the physiological and psychic impact of surrogate pregnancy, and the issue of commodification (Warnock and the Committee of Inquiry into Human Fertilisation and Embryology 1984); most of the arguments related to the French context reviewed here were already discussed in the early 1990s in the United States (Arneson 1992).

Overall, the international discussion on surrogate pregnancy needs to be based on more refined knowledge than the data presently available. This knowledge can only be accumulated in a transnational perspective as it has to pay attention to people who cross borders, to children who are born in one country to be raised in another, to the woman who consents to meet foreign citizens, be paid by them and bond with them in a unique way: that of giving birth to a child she then will not raise.

There are good reasons to think that the cross-border dimension of ART will be taken more and more into account, as suggested, in the case of surrogate pregnancy, by the growing place occupied by the discussion of women's profit and the role of commercial intermediaries in the public debate. In present times, the arrival of children on the national territory and the claim for their legal recognition, the public expression of experiences or requests for the legalization of surrogate pregnancy give greater visibility to this cross-border dimension of ART.

To deal with this dimension from a moral and political point of view will not be an easy task as economic situations vary greatly from one country to another, and legal frames differ. Besides, the consideration of the cross-border dimension more often than not leads to a morally negative assessment of surrogate pregnancy, a conclusion that cannot be extended to every practice of reproductive technologies. However, this negative assessment leaves the political and legal dimension of the matter utterly unresolved. And the answer to the following question remains open: does this assessment establish surrogate pregnancy's prohibition once and for all? Or should it rather be attributed a legal framework in order, precisely, to allow 'surrogate mothers' and would-be parents to come out of the 'shadows' and avoid the risks of the 'Wild West' of international reproductive markets?

Marie Gaille is a senior researcher in philosophy at the National Center for Scientific Research (CNRS, France). Her research focuses on the history and the meanings of the relationship between medicine, anthropology and philosophy, and in connection with this, on the relationship between health, disease/illness and one's environment. It also deals with the ethical foundations of medical decisions and of health systems, especially in the context of prenatal life, aging and the end of life.

Note

1. International Conference 'Women's and Mother's Labor: The Stakes of Surrogacy', Grenoble, 2017; Interdisciplinary Workshop – Philosophy-Law-Economy, 'The Limits of the Market: Commodification of Nature and Body', Paris, September 2018.

References

Académie nationale de médecine. 2014. *La gestation pour autrui au regard du mariage entree personnes de même sexe.* http://www.academie-medecine.fr/wp-content/uploads/2016/01/tap-pages-de-917-%C3%A0-950.pdf. Accessed 1 July 2019.

Agacinski, Sylviane. 2009. *Corps en miettes: Critique de la marchandisation du corps humain.* Paris: Flammarion.

Aristotle. 2002. *Nicomachean Ethics,* trans. C. Rowe, introduced by S. Broadie. Oxford: Oxford University Press.

Arneson, Richard J. 1992. 'Commodification and Commercial Surrogacy', *Philosophy & Public Affairs* 21 (2): 132–64.

Cadoret, Anne. 2002. *Des parents comme les autres? Homosexualité et parenté.* Paris: Odile Jacob.

Coburn, Elaine. 2011. 'Globalization and Women: A Marxist Feminist Introduction', in L. Biggs and S. Gringell (eds), *Gendered Intersections* (2nd ed.). Halifax, NS: Fernwood Press.

CCNE (Comité consultatif national d'éthique). 2010. *Problemes éthiques soulevés par la gestation pour autrui (gpa).* Avis 110. http://www.ccne-ethique.fr/fr/publications/problemes-ethiques-souleves-par-la-gestation-pour-autrui-gpa#.VxezpM4fmQs. Accessed 1 July 2019.

CCNE (Comité consultatif national d'éthique). 2017. *Avis du CCNE sur les demandes sociétales de recours à l'assistance médicale à la procreation.* Avis 126. http://www.ccne-ethique.fr/sites/default/files/publications/ccne_avis_ndeg126_amp_version-def.pdf. Accessed 1 July 2019.

Cooper, Melinda E. 2008. *Life as Surplus: Biotechnology and Capitalism in the Neoliberal Era.* Seattle: University of Washington Press.

Delaisi de Parseval, Geneviève. 1983. *Un enfant à tout prix.* Paris: Le Seuil.

Dickenson, Donna. 2008. *Body Shopping: The Economy Fuelled by Flesh and Blood.* Oxford: Oneworld Publications.

Dodier, Nicolas. 2003. *Leçons politiques de l'épidémie du sida.* Paris: EHESS, Cas de figure.

Dolezal, Luna. 2015. 'Considering Pregnancy in Commercial Surrogacy: A Response to Bronwyn Parry'. *Medical Humanities* 41: 38–39. doi:10.1136/medhum-2015-010694.

Dworkin, Gerald. 1971. 'Paternalism', in R.A. Wasserstrom (ed.), *Morality and the Law.* Belmont, CA: Wadsworth.

Fraser, Nancy. 2008. *Scales of Justice: Reimagining Political Space in a Globalizing World.* Malden, MA: Polity Press.

Gaille, Marie. 2011. *Le désir d'enfant: histoire intime, enjeu politique.* Paris: PUF.

Godelier, Maurice. 2010. *Les métamorphoses de la parenté.* Paris: Flammarion.

Golombok, Susan, Vasanti Javda, Lucy Blake, Jennifer Readings, Polly Casey and Alex Marks. 2011. 'Families Created through Surrogacy: Mother–Child Relationships and Children's Psychological Adjustment at Age 7', *Developmental Psychology* 47 (6): 1579–88.

Gorz, André. 1988. *Métamorphoses du travail: Critique de la raison économique.* Paris: Gallimard Folio essais.

Gross, Martine. 2014. *Parent ou Homo: faut-il choisir? Idées reçues sur l'homoparentalité.* Paris: Editions du Cavalier bleu.

Javda, Vasanti, Susan Golombok, Lucy Blake, Jennifer Readings and Polly Casey. 2011. 'Surrogacy Families Ten Years On: The Relationship with the Surrogate, Decisions over Disclosure and Children's Understanding of Their Surrogacy Origins', *Human Reproduction* 26 (suppl. 1): i260–71.

Kant, Emmanuel. 1997. *Groundwork of the Metaphysics of Morals* (1785), trans. M. Gregor, introduced by Ch. M. Korsgaard. Cambridge: Cambridge University Press.

Kutz, Christopher. 2000. *Complicity: Ethics and Law for a Collective Age*. Cambridge: Cambridge University Press.

Lafontaine, Céline. 2014. *Le corps-marché: La marchandisation de la vie humaine à l'ère de la bioéconomie*. Paris: Le Seuil.

Leroyer, Anne-Marie. 2011. *Droit de la famille*. Paris: PUF.

Malmqvist, Erik. 2013. 'Taking Advantage of Injustice', *Social Theory and Practice* 39 (4): 557–80.

Malmqvist, Erik. 2015. 'Transnational Commercial Surrogacy, Exploitation and the Non-Worseness Claim', Presentation at the international workshop organized by V. Bourseul and M. Gaille, 'Médecine procréative, différence sexuelle et égalité des sexes'. Paris: CNRS-Université Paris Diderot.

Massé, Raymond. 2015. *Anthropologie de la morale et de l'éthique*. Laval: Les Presses de l'Université de Laval.

Mehl, Dominique. 2008. *Enfants du don: Procréation médicalement assistée - parents et enfants témoignent*. Paris: Robert Laffont.

Merchant, Jennifer. 2012. 'Une gestation pour autrui "éthique" est possible', *Travail, genre et sociétés* 2 (28): 183–89. doi:10.3917/tgs.028.O18.

Ogien, Ruwen. 2013. *L'État nous rend-t-il meilleurs? Essai sur la liberté politique*. Paris: Gallimard.

O'Neill, Daniel I., Mary L. Shanley and Iris M. Young (eds). 2008. *Illusion of Consent: Engaging with Carole Pateman*. Penn State University Press.

Pande, Amrita. 2011. 'Transnational Commercial Surrogacy in India: Gifts for Global Sister?' *Reproductive Biomedicine Online* 23: 618–25.

Petitfils, Charlotte, and Maria Teresa Munoz Sastre. 2014. 'French Laypersons' Views on Surrogate Motherhood: An Exploratory Study', *Psicologica* 35: 693–702.

Robertson, John A. 1983. 'Surrogate Mother: Not So Novel After All'. *Hastings Center Report* 13 (5): 28–34.

Rudrappa, Sharmila. 2012. 'India's Reproductive Assembly Line'. *Contexts* 11 (2): 22–27.

Sandel, Michael. 2012. *What Money Can't Buy: The Moral Limits of Markets*. London: Penguin Books.

Satz, Debra. 1992. 'Markets in Women's Reproductive Labor', *Philosophy & Public Affairs* 21 (2): 107–31.

Spar, Debora L. 2006. *Baby Business: How Money, Science, and Politics Drive the Commerce of Conception*. Cambridge, MA: Harvard Business School Press.

Steinbock, Bonnie. 1988. 'Surrogate Motherhood as Prenatal Adoption', *Law, Medicine and Health Care* 16 (1–2): 44–50.

ter Meulen, Ruud. 2017. *Solidarity and Justice in Health and Social Care*. Cambridge: Cambridge University Press.

Terra Nova (Geneviève Delaisi de Parseval and Valérie Depadt-Sebag). 2010. *Accès à la parenté: Assistance médicale à la procréation et adoption*. http://tnova.fr/rapports/acces-a-la-parente-assistance-medicale-a-la-procreation-et-adoption. Accessed 1 July 2019.

Théry, Irène, and Anne-Marie Leroyer. 2014. *Filiation, origines, parentalité: le droit face aux nouvelles valeurs de responsabilité générationnelle*. Paris: Odile Jacob.

Tronto, Joan. 2012. 'Partiality Based on Relational Responsibilities: Another Approach to Global Ethics', *Ethics and Social Welfare* 6 (3): 303–16.

van den Akker, Olga B.A. 2007. 'Psychosocial Aspects of Surrogate Motherhood', *Human Reproduction Update* 13 (1): 53–62.

Warnock, Mary, and the Committee of Inquiry into Human Fertilisation and Embryology. 1984. *Report of the Committee of Inquiry into Human Fertilisation and Embryology*. London: Her Majesty's Stationery Office.

Wertheimer, Alan. 1992. 'Two Questions about Surrogacy and Exploitation', *Philosophy & Public Affairs* 21 (3): 211–39.

Wright, Melissa W. 2006. *Disposable Women and Other Myths of Global Capitalism*. London: Routledge.

Conclusion

Jennifer Merchant

This collective work has brought together a diverse group of scholars, all specialists in issues pertaining to ART. It provides an unprecedented comparison of public policy, law and social realities in two neighbouring countries: France and Belgium. Each chapter, in its own right, makes a significant contribution to the field of ART, kinship and cross-border practices in two countries that have never, to this day, been studied, analysed and compared. The interdisciplinary approach provides detailed and broad insight to an already existing knowledge of ethical and social issues surrounding ART. Indeed, sharing a border yet having such different approaches to donor conception, the status of the embryo, surrogacy practices and how same-sex families, especially in France, navigate in and around prohibitive law makes for productive and interesting case studies throughout the book.

France is at present in the midst of widespread national public[1] and political and parliamentary debates[2] concerning the future revision of its bioethics laws first enacted in 1994. A vote is said to be programmed anytime between the autumn of 2019–early 2020. Optimistic analysts say the revision will be voted on by January 2020. Moderate and pessimistic analysts say the forces against will prevent it from passing. Even in the most optimistic scenario, i.e. the revision of the laws voted by parliament, we then must await the official government decrees that allow the laws to be applied. This could take anywhere from six months to two years, as previous experience has shown.

A certain number of think tanks and advisory boards, among them the highly respected Comité consultatif national d'éthique (CCNE, France's national bioethics advisory board), now support access to ART for single women and lesbian couples.[3] However, relative to surrogacy for heterosexual couples or male couples, the CCNE has continued to express a firm negative stance against legalizing surrogacy in France, as has every single other report and/or advisory board statement.

Meanwhile, other august advisory boards and/or political institutions have issued decisions and reports that often call for maintaining the status quo, that is, access to ART only for heterosexual couples who present a medically diagnosed infertility/sterility affliction.[4] Every single report or advisory document has French Deputies and Senators rely on these reports and documents from both advisory boards and political institutions as well as on the hearings they hold, but it is almost impossible to predict what the new majority party, La République en Marche, incarnated by the French President Emmanuel Macron, will do. This majority presents a spectrum of Deputies and Senators that extends from very progressive members on social issues to strong economic liberals who nonetheless remain highly conservative on social issues. The political weight of the Conseil d'état is far greater than that of the CCNE, hence the outcome of the revision of France's bioethics laws remains completely unpredictable.

Hence, it is almost certain that cross-border practices undertaken by French citizens desiring a child will be pursued, and statistics demonstrate that their numbers rise year after year, Belgium being the first preferred destination followed by Spain, England, the United States and, for financially limited French citizens, Ukraine, the Czech Republic and Greece. This book, the first of its kind, explores and analyses the cases of Belgium and France. The contributors to this book now encourage all social science scholars to study cross-border practices between France and the aforementioned countries. Each would be a comparative case study bringing forth new unexplored material, and assist all scholars in better grasping the specificities of who, why and how French citizens engage in these practices and what their experiences are from one country to the next.

Jennifer Merchant is a professor of Anglo-American legal and political institutions at the Université de Paris II (Panthéon-Assas). She is a leading researcher in bioethical issues of comparative public policy with expertise in North American and European policy, and politics and regulation of medical technologies involving human reproduction. She is also an expert in French law and politics on embryo research and assisted reproductive technology.

Notes

1. The most well-known and respected annual public encounter is the *Forum européen de bioéthique* which was held in 2018 from 30 January to 4 February in Strasbourg. Videos of all presentations can be found at https://www.youtube.com/watch?v=KDLbN3jdf6o. Accessed 1 July 2019.
2. A compilation of hearings can be found at http://videos.assemblee-nationale.fr/video.6698088_5bbc684fc9fc3.revision-de-la-loi-relative-a-la-bioethique--auditions-diverses. Accessed 1 July 2019.
3. CCNE Report, 5 September 2018: https://www.ccne-ethique.fr/fr/publications/contribution-du-comite-consultatif-national-de-thique-la-revision-de-la-loi-de. Accessed 1 July 2019.
4. The 2018 Conseil d'état's decision can be found at https://www.conseil-etat.fr/ressources/etudes-publications/rapports-etudes/etudes/revision-de-la-loi-de-bioethique-quelles-options-pour-demain. Accessed 1 July 2019.

Index

www.ingramcontent.com/pod-product-compliance
Ingram Content Group UK Ltd.
Pitfield, Milton Keynes, MK11 3LW, UK
UKHW021837100926
8556IPUK00004B/397

9 781789 204315